RESPONDING
TO THE CULTURE OF
BULLYING &
DISRESPECT
SECOND EDITION

To my children, in hopes that they will keep their bubbling enthusiasm and passion for learning;
To all the beautiful people of all ages I have had the privilege of encountering in schools.

—*MNB*

Dedicated to my daughters and all my students.
May you delight in Life and walk in Peace.

—*MT*

RESPONDING
TO THE CULTURE OF
BULLYING & DISRESPECT
SECOND EDITION

NEW PERSPECTIVES ON COLLABORATION, COMPASSION, AND RESPONSIBILITY

MARIE-NATHALIE BEAUDOIN
MAUREEN TAYLOR

CORWIN
A SAGE Company

For information:

Corwin
A SAGE Company
2455 Teller Road
Thousand Oaks, California 91320
(800) 233-9936
Fax: (800) 417-2466
www.corwinpress.com

SAGE India Pvt. Ltd.
B 1/I 1 Mohan Cooperative
    Industrial Area
Mathura Road, New Delhi 110 044
India

SAGE Ltd.
1 Oliver's Yard
55 City Road
London EC1Y 1SP
United Kingdom

SAGE Asia-Pacific Pte. Ltd.
33 Pekin Street #02-01
Far East Square
Singapore 048763

Printed in the United States of America.

Library of Congress Cataloging-in-Publication Data

Beaudoin, Marie-Nathalie.
Responding to the culture of bullying and disrespect: New perspectives on collaboration, compassion, and responsibility/Marie-Nathalie Beaudoin, Maureen Taylor.
    p. cm.
Includes bibliographical references and index.
Rev. ed. of: Breaking the culture of bullying and disrespect, c2004.
ISBN 978-1-4129-6853-9 (cloth)
ISBN 978-1-4129-6854-6 (pbk.)

  1. Bullying in schools—United States—Prevention. 2. School discipline—United States. 3. Education, Elementary--United States. I. Taylor, Maureen, 1967- II. Beaudoin, Marie-Nathalie Breaking the culture of bullying and disrespect. III. Title.

LB3013.32.B434 2009
371.5'8—dc22   2008055933

This book is printed on acid-free paper.

11 12 13 14 15 10 9 8 7 6 5 4 3 2

Acquisitions Editor:	Jessica Allan
Editorial Assistant:	Joanna Coelho
Production Editor:	Eric Garner
Copy Editor:	Gretchen Treadwell
Typesetter:	C&M Digitals (P) Ltd.
Proofreader:	Susan Schon
Indexer:	Jean Casalegno

Contents

PART II: APPLICATIONS AND EXAMPLES: SUCCESS STORIES OF OVERCOMING BULLYING AND DISRESPECT

Foreword

Honey Berg

We are constantly reminded of the ongoing bullying issues in the news. Statistics show that bullying is a common experience for many children and adolescents. Surveys indicate that as many as half of all children are bullied at some time during their school years, and at least 10 percent are bullied on a regular basis. It is imperative that educational leaders understand how to deal with this problem on a school campus and find ways to change the culture that is causing it to exist.

Unfortunately, the current emphasis on improving test scores, sometimes misguidedly, diminishes the attention paid to fostering a positive school climate. Many studies reinforce the idea that students in schools with a positive school climate have higher achievement levels. In this second edition of their book, Marie-Nathalie Beaudoin and Maureen Taylor combine their broad experience, training, and knowledge to provide educators with a realistic approach that can have a profoundly positive effect on the students in their schools. Their easy-to-implement strategies, real-life examples, and alignment with current brain research on how children learn provide educators with a clear, practical approach that can have a deeply significant impact on behavior and, thus, student achievement.

In addition, the authors present educators with the opportunity to reflect on their personal philosophies about discipline and, thereby, gain a deeper understanding of how to support their students. This new version of the book addresses the powerful role of the adults in reducing bullying behaviors. Instead of looking for "programs" to address the bullying issues schools are faced with, the authors suggest looking at the school climate—the way we interact with students, and our own behavior. All too often, teachers and administrators react to students' misbehavior with punitive measures. However, punitive discipline can be embarrassing, demeaning, humiliating, and, generally, have only a short-term effect on a child's behavior. In reality, as the authors point out, it can also model the bullying behaviors that we are trying to eliminate. In the last chapter of the book, real-life scenarios are outlined with reflections from teachers who are committed to creating respectful relationships. Powerful questions, designed to assist teachers in understanding the thinking that was used to support student success, provide an opportunity for teachers to look at their own response to these scenarios. The book outlines the tools that will support educators in learning how to respond in ways that support students in altering their behavior, thus reinforcing their understanding of the effects of their behavior and helping them create more appropriate responses.

As an educator with over thirty years of experience, including fourteen years as a site principal, and four years at the central office, I have had firsthand experience with a majority of the issues addressed in this book. I have seen well-intentioned educators—through lack of knowledge rather than lack of desire—inadvertently reinforce negative behaviors and cause problems to escalate rather than be eliminated. Strategies that can make a significant difference in the way we deal with our challenging students are sorely needed. *Responding to the Culture of Bullying and Disrespect* is an essential resource for educators. It is enlightening, empowering, and practical, as well as a necessary resource to support site staff in creating positive school climates and new realities for students who have traditionally been labeled as "troublemakers, bullies . . . " I believe this book can change the culture of a school.

Acknowledgments

We would like to express our gratitude to everyone—educators, students, and families—who have kindly participated in our research and enriched our own perspectives and ideas. We hope that some of the integrated philosophies and suggestions in this book will be equally meaningful and useful in all of your journeys.

At this point with this second edition, we have visited too many schools in the United States and abroad to thank each school individually for its contribution.

We would still like to acknowledge the staff from the following schools, who have taken the time to thoughtfully answer our initial lengthy surveys: Anderson School, Baker School, Country Lane School, Easterbrook School, Moreland Discovery School, and Rogers Middle School.

Heartfelt acknowledgment is continually sent to those teachers from other schools across California who opened their doors to us: Sequoia Baioni, Maria Diaz-Albertini, Melissa Freeberg, Mariah Howe, Cathy Klein, Karen Lam, Kayla Meadows, Peter Murdock, Mary Robson, Sara Saldana, Chris Telles, the staff at Christa McAuliffe, Stuart Williams, Washington Open, and the staff at Cedarwood Sudbury School.

Interviews, conversations, and e-mail communication with the following educators were also invaluable in that they provided a rich forum for personal stories and for in-depth accounts of their experiences in the education system. Given that some of these interviews were lengthy, we continue to be eternally thankful for these individuals' trust, honesty, and generosity of time despite their busy schedules: Les Adelson, Sandra Anders, Patty Aquino, Carolyn Barrett, Linda Boucher, Ann Dubois, Honey Berg, Martha Cirata, Nancy Cisler, Denise Clay, Carin Contreras, Harry Davis, Mindy Dirks, Ann Douminian, Bob Geddes, Lori King, Maria Hansen-Kivijarvi, Tom Kennedy, Mary Anne Landis, Rick Ito, Sue Healy, Joe Joaquin, Dale Jones, Debbie Judge, Barbara Lateer, Michele Mandarino, Bill Menkin, Alison Moser, Cleo Osborn, Joe Pacheco, Diane Paul, Beverly Prinz, Herb Quon, Jim Richie, Lorie Rizzo, Joann Rosatelli, Kathleen Ryan, Louise Santos, Maria Simon, Bitsey Stark, Gary Stebbins, Stephany Tyson, Tiffany White, and Jenny Wishnac.

We are also indebted to the gracious individuals who have provided wisdom, support, and a variety of ideas during the length of this project: Mary Layne Adams, Lilith Anderton, Ana Batista, Rikki Bloom, Leisha Boek, Poppy Brodoski, Kristi Busch, Nicola Call, Pam Cayton, Fritz Dern, Erin Devinchenzi, Marc Dhoore, Erin Dunivin, Ron Estes, Diana Fagundes, David Fissel, the Gitlin girls, Georgia Gorton, Miles Gordon, Ann Hayashi, Michiyo Kamoto, Amanda Katz, Joyce McClure, Heidi Meade, Caetano Miele, Diane Moore, Dora Ramirez, Christine Pavan, Julie Rogers, Todd Phoenix, Krista Poston, Michelle Potter, Annie Prozan, Dora Ramirez, Laura Rewerts, Mari Rodin, Linda Rough, Amity Sandage, Tamera Schmidt, Kristine Schmieding, Sherry Stack, Tara Stanbridge, Eduardo Villapando, Judy Volta, May Walters, Veronica Wetterstrom, and Anne Woida.

We have thoroughly enjoyed our individual interviews and group discussions with students. Many of these young people have contributed very articulate observations, words of wisdom, and anecdotes that are food for thought for adults. Special thanks go to Adam, Al, Alex, Alison, Aly, David, Denea, Eugene, Gabriel, Jacksen, J. Henri, Kate, Lainey, Larry, Laura, Leonel, Lori, Meg, Megan B., Meika, Melissa, Quentin, Roberto, Rostislav, Santee, Trang, and Yasha. We would like to particularly acknowledge the 180 students at Moreland Discovery School and Rogers Middle School who shared their expressive thoughts with us in classroom discussions.

We wish to also thank the numerous other principals, teachers, and students who contributed to this project and yet wish to remain anonymous.

Our gratefulness goes daily to those creative, inspiring folks from Bay Area Family Therapy Training Associates who have kindly reviewed and edited the manuscript for narrative congruency: Jeff Zimmerman, PhD, and Sonja Bogumill, PhD.

We are indebted to principal Cleo Osborn, who introduced us to one another as kindred spirits and provided unconditional support to the creation and exploration of these ideas.

Many thanks to Sarah Serafimidis for her assistance in procuring the "Train Story," one of our favorite stories of all times, and Deborah Simon for allowing us to use her creative "Bubble Trouble" story.

We would like to underscore the fabulous work of Jessica Allan, Megan Bedell, Joanna Coelho, Gretchen Treadwell, and Eric Garner from Corwin, for their assistance as we collaborated on this project. Rachel Livsey and Melanie Birdsall are well within our grateful memory for their support on our first edition of this book.

Finally, we offer eternal thanks to . . .

Our generous and kind families, Amelia, Brian, David, Emilie, Frederic, Jack, Jeff, Judy, Maggie, Marlene, Marc, Meikael, Mireille, Paul, Michele, and Jean. Thank you, Paul, for your patient, loving, time-consuming, never-ending support with computer issues and complex drawings.

Our dearest Francine-Esther, who gently and patiently provided nourishment, treats, teas, babysitting, suggestions, endless editing, and constant encouragement in our lives as authors.

PUBLISHER'S ACKNOWLEDGMENTS

Corwin gratefully acknowledges the contributions of the following reviewers:

Elizabeth Barrett, NBCT
Civics Teacher
Clark County Schools
Winchester, KY

Jeanne Marie Benoit
Seventh Grade Social Studies
   and Language Arts Teacher
Putnam Middle School
Putnam, CT

Carol Cox
Elementary Counselor
Floyd County Schools
Floyd, VA

Virginia Miller, LPC, LMFT, NCC
Counselor
Jessieville Middle School
Jessieville, AR

Joyce Stout, PsyD
School Counselor
Redondo Beach Unified School
   District
Redondo Beach, CA

Cookie Winburn
Instructional Coach
Richland School District Two
Columbia, SC

About the Authors

Marie-Nathalie Beaudoin, PhD, is the training director at Bay Area Family Therapy Training Associates (BAFTTA) where she supervises postmaster and postdoctoral counseling work in several schools in Silicon Valley, California. Marie-Nathalie has devoted much of her career to working with young people and their families in private practice, teaching tolerance projects, and improving staff-youth relationships in public schools. She also teaches cross-cultural awareness, family therapies, adolescent therapies, and group dynamics at John F. Kennedy University. Marie-Nathalie has presented in numerous international conferences and has published a number of professional articles about her work with youth. Her publication credits include *Creating a Positive School Culture* with Maureen Taylor (2004), a book of experiential activities titled *Working with Groups to Enhance Relationships* (1998), and the Portuguese version of this book.

Maureen Taylor is a parent, educator, and author. Her teaching experience ranges from preschool through the sixth-grade level, including being an environmental educator. She is the coauthor of *Creating a Positive School Culture*, a collaboration with Marie-Nathalie Beaudoin. Maureen is currently working in administration at a school in Northern California.

Introduction

John was a twelve-year-old boy living with his intact middle-class family in Los Angeles. He was relatively close to his parents and was an only child. John had always been an A student and a model citizen. In fact, John was very mature for his age and had already developed very strong values. Life was going relatively well for John until fifth grade. Even though he attended a reputable school and had very good friends, he started being regularly teased and harassed by a small group of five boys.

As John grew upset about these incidents, he and his family shared their concerns with the principal. The principal was unsure how to address the situation because most of the incidents were not witnessed by supervising adults. John's parents, like most parents, were also wondering if this was unfortunately part of the usual experience of school. The teasing and harassing continued to escalate; John's mood, relationship with teachers, and grades started to deteriorate. One day, as John tripped and fell playing basketball, one of the boys stomped John's hand, pretending to do it inadvertently. John screamed in pain, went to the nurse's office, and complained to the authorities. Because it was believed to be an accident, no actions were taken. John's fingers were sprained.

The next day, he didn't want to go to school. Not too sure what to believe, John's parents required that he go. The five boys spent the day taunting John and "accidentally" hitting his fingers whenever they could. John cleverly switched the cast to his other hand hoping to protect himself, but this wasn't enough. After school, the five boys pinned him down on the ground and rolled over his hand with a skateboard.

Is this an unusual story? Not at all. Sadly, many principals, teachers, parents, and therapists working with young people regularly hear bullying or teasing stories comparable to this. Most adults wonder what should be done to stop this endemic problem of aggression, harassment, and disrespect in schools. Ever since the Columbine shooting, our society has been trying to point the finger at a culprit. Educators feel that they have to be suspicious of any student that seems different, and they have increased their surveillance of the young people under their care. Parents are questioned as to whether they are suitable caretakers. The media have raised countless questions of accountability. Should the perpetrators be more seriously punished? Should school officials be held responsible? Where were the teachers?

Unfortunately, educators are an easy target for the media, who are seldom aware of educators' actual challenges with an ever-increasing curriculum, never-ending responsibilities, and little support. In addition, when problems become rampant in schools, educators end up spending a tremendous amount of time and energy addressing these problems instead of focusing on academia, their initial goal. Trapped between public expectations, institutional pressures, and disrespect with students, educators can burn out quickly and become exasperated or resentful with a profession they initially entered with enthusiasm.

As a result, in recent years, school personnel have been seeking consultation with our narrative therapy community to find efficient ways to help transform a disrespectful classroom or to work individually with a student. Narrative therapy, considered the cutting edge in systemic approaches, has been a relevant theoretical framework to understand and address school-related problems. It has been received with much enthusiasm internationally for its respectful, effective, and transforming effect on people's lives and broader communities. Students, in particular, have been very receptive to this approach as it is honoring of the person he or she prefers to be and it involves them actively in the process of taking a fresh, empowering perspective on their struggles.

Our intention in this book is to render narrative therapy practices and perspectives available to educators. We want to make the rich and powerful ideas embedded in this complex theory accessible to every school staff. With this in mind, the book is written in a practical, clear, and creative way. Tutorials, exercises, common questions and answers, transcripts of interviews, illustrations, cartoons, dialogues between the authors and students, and numerous examples are used to keep the readers engaged with the material. This work is the result of many years of successful collaboration between a narrative therapist and a dedicated elementary school teacher. By combining therapeutic knowledge with day-to-day educational experience, the text provides a rich and comprehensive approach to a vast array of school-related problems.

This book is not intended as an introduction to narrative therapy but rather as the application of narrative and social constructionist ideas to the field of education. For this reason, narrative concepts are only covered in their relevance to teachers and principals, and the clinical practices associated with the ideas are not thoroughly examined. The interested reader can easily find further information on the subject in the many excellent narrative therapy books readily available (Bird, 2000; Freedman & Combs, 1996; Freeman, Epston, & Lobovits, 1997; Madsen, 1999; White, 1997; White & Epston, 1990; White & Morgan, 2006; Winslade & Monk, 1999, 2000; Zimmerman & Dickerson, 1996). A glossary of the more technical words appears in Resource A in an attempt to assist readers' comprehension.

Given that bullying and disrespect happen repeatedly across the country and in a variety of schools, we believe that it does not make sense to focus on the isolated act of each individual involved or on a singled-out factor. We propose a much broader approach that does not blame either culture alone or individuals (whether they are the perpetrators, parents, or educators). In other words, this approach takes into account the interaction of many larger contributing factors and examines how they are experienced in the unique context of students' lives. Once understood in such a way, problems of disrespect and bullying can be transcended to promote choice, possibilities, and preferences.

In this second edition, we have not only added three chapters but we have also, throughout the book, made more explicit how the material is applicable to various grade levels. In our day-to-day work, these concepts are used with people of all ages, from preschoolers to high schoolers to adults. The difference lies mainly in the language used and an attentiveness to different realms of experience.

Part I of this book explores the general context of disrespect, bullying, and chronic behavior problems. This provides a theoretical foundation out of which new perspectives and solutions will emerge. Through stories and experiential exercises, we examine the contextual factors that inadvertently support disrespect and bullying, starting with the general culture, school environment, and educators' assumptions. Specifically, Chapter 1 briefly introduces the different cultural beliefs (discourses) that generally shape people's lives. A legend illustrates how these beliefs limit access to solutions and indirectly encourage disrespect and bullying. This second edition has additional insights into the limitations of the thought process that is generated in these troublesome situations. Chapter 2 examines some effects of these cultural beliefs on schools as institutions and their implications for students struggling with disrespect and bullying. In this edition we have added some and deleted other sections to make these ideas clearer and more applicable. Our intention in writing this chapter is to foster a greater understanding of people's struggles and experiences in schools. Chapter 3 explores the different assumptions that may cloud educators' minds as they are handling problems with disrespect and bullying. Although challenging, this section sets the stage for fresh perspectives and new ways of dealing with problems. In this second edition we have added reference to existing literature and additional common teacher questions. We have also added a classic and inspiring true story that reminds us all that compassion goes much further than aggression.

Chapter 4 introduces innovative practices that empower students to reflect on, articulate, and change their ways of being in the unique context of their lives. These practices are informed by a narrative therapy metaphor and offer simple yet effective ways for principals, teachers, parents, and counselors to promote respect. Chapter 5 integrates all of the material discussed earlier into a complete view of the actions that must be taken to effectively reduce the occurrence of disrespect and bullying. Chapter 6 discusses detailed ways of ensuring that changes will last and will be owned in a meaningful way by students. In this second edition we have added the transcript of a conversation with a seventeen-year-old young man who was struggling with hatred and ideas of violence.

Part II of the book consists of lively and creative examples of this work in action. It begins with Chapter 7, where students' experiences of school are made visible through transcripts of interviews and class discussions. Chapter 8 then offers concrete ideas on how to promote collaboration, respect, and appreciation throughout schools. We invite adults to move away from telling students what to do or not do and to reduce the ever-increasing temptation to externally control students. Respect cannot be imposed by force. Respect, tolerance, and appreciation grow much more effectively when young people are invited into an environment that manifests such philosophy and that empowers them personally to make better decisions despite the struggles of their lives. These ideas come from extensive research conducted with more than 230 educators in Northern California, who kindly shared with us ways they have found to foster a successful school climate. In this new edition, we have added strategies and stories from teachers committed to collaborative relationships with their students in spite of the mainstream pressures for control and evaluation.

Chapter 9 describes a fun and dynamic program to invite entire classrooms into respect, tolerance, and appreciation. This program is presented as detailed, week-by-week, antibullying activities that have been implemented successfully in a large number of schools in the Silicon Valley in California. In this edition, we explain how this program can be lengthened or shortened to better address the unique needs of each particular class. We have also added specific examples of its application in high schools where this program would be based more on meaningful conversations rather than creative exercises. In Chapter 10, we share a case example of work done one-on-one with a student having an established bullying reputation. Chapter 11 is a new addition to this second edition. It makes visible what happens in the brains of young people as they struggle with anger and disrespect. It also presents how educators can understand and use brain research to foster change in young people who have a history of conflict with their teachers. Through an example, we illustrate how a young person's brain-wiring can be repatterned through a consistent, trusting, and caring relationship with an educator.

Part III of the book is entirely new to this second edition and focuses on preventing problems in the first place. In Chapter 12, we discuss aspects of school experiences that need to be *decreased* to reduce the buildup of negative emotions associated with disrespect and bullying, as well as other experiences that need to be *increased* to maximize the likelihood that students will experience themselves and others positively. It is argued that the components of a culture of respect, tolerance, and care are constituted by a careful attention to beliefs, people, and their relationships. A story, discussions, and an exercise provide a clear vision for the synergetic partnership that can be created between proactive educators and "response-able" youth. We present strategies to assist educators in remaining connected to their values and preferred ways of being in spite of the challenges of the day. We also discuss the process by which young people become response-able, meaning not only responsible but also capable of handling many situations in a constructive de-escalating manner.

Chapter 13 then goes on to highlight prevention success stories, both of individual educators making peace-promoting choices and a public school which stands out as having a very low rate of problems with bullying and disrespect. The individual success stories are presented with the unfolding of the situations, making visible the thinking of the educator, the temptation to engage in high-intervention responses, the anchors to compassion/perspective, and the final constructive choice with its positive impact on both the student and the school culture. The successful public school is first introduced with a description of what it minimizes and maximizes in its school culture as well as some of its special programs. This description is followed by interviews with the principal, a veteran teacher, a few students, and a poignant account from a parent.

Finally, the book concludes with a series of resources such as a glossary; a summary table of strategies; an essay on cultural discourses; an example of a staff exercise to cultivate collaboration, appreciation, and tolerance; and a problem-solving question list.

The material in this book may be uncomfortable, at times provocative and counterintuitive. We believe that this flavor is part of its biggest value as it would not be useful if we simply replicated other manuscripts that promote the redundant cultural standards. We have striven to gently ask important and serious questions, while honoring the responses and attitudes each reader ultimately chooses to believe in. We hope that every reader will be inspired by at least one of the dilemmas exposed and will finish the book energized to explore new possibilities with colleagues and young people. Above all, we hope that you enjoy reading this book as much as we have rejoiced in the researching and writing of its pages.

You may be wondering how the story ended. What happened to John? After all, he was a "good" kid and the victim of a horrible assault. Aside from extensive physical pain, he had to transfer to a new school. He couldn't and wouldn't go back to his regular school, especially since the five boys were not even suspended (the incident happened off school grounds). He, the victim, had to endure switching schools in midyear, losing his friends, and starting with new teachers who were at a different place in the curriculum. His procrastination and inability to concentrate on homework started to cause conflicts with his parents and teachers. As he was becoming at risk of being expelled from his new school, John was referred for therapy because of suicidal thoughts and . . . violent fantasies about his previous school.

And the cycle goes on, where victimized students become perpetrators, perpetrators become victimized, and disrespect creeps from student–student relationships to student–teacher relationships and then to teacher–student interactions. Given everyone's good intentions and efforts and the large number of programs and books on the subject, why is bullying still pervasive in our schools? To answer this question, let's explore the big picture and powerful ways of responding to the culture of bullying and disrespect.

Part I
Laying Foundations

1

How Problems Develop

A Frog Story and a Shift in Perspective

One sunny morning, a big frog decided to swallow all the water of the earth. It sat there proud, full. It looked like a mountain of water, blue and green, its skin almost transparent under the tension. It could not move; it was too heavy. So it just sat there, staring at all the animals and humans gathered in front of it. "What are we going to do?!" cried all the living beings. "We will all die if it does not give back the rivers, brooks, and oceans." For three days, they prayed and begged the frog to let go of the waters. But the frog would not move. The children were crying, the elderly suffering, and the desert sand could be seen creeping closer to the horizon. Something had to be done.

—Translated and adapted from Gougaud (2000)

Reflection Questions

- What would you do? How would you get the frog to open its mouth and free the waters? Write your ideas.
- Can you think of five or six solutions? If so, write them down.
- Where do your solutions come from? Which life experiences might have inspired these solutions? Have you been exposed to similar methods of solving other problems? Explain.

LESSONS FROM THIS STORY

Behaviors and Intentions

Most people—even mental health professionals and educators in bullying prevention workshops—would poke, hit, or shoot the frog. This simply shows that, despite our best intentions and our most genuine stance against aggression, our solutions may be remarkably incongruent with our values. There is a false belief in Western cultures that people's behaviors, particularly youth's misbehaviors, are a reflection of "bad intentions." This oversimplification of the complexity of factors affecting human behavior is quite saddening in that it leaves educators taking drastic measures to control students instead of building on what is generally already there: young people's desire to please, be loved, and avoid trouble. Many young people who engage in disrespectful or bullying interactions feel rather stuck in, and resentful about, their unhappy lives. Given a chance to share their hopes and dreams, their values and preferences, many would actually prefer to be appreciated and stay out of trouble. These intentions are clearly not reflected in the school behaviors most visible to the staff. We will come back to this idea in subsequent chapters, as well as how to help young people articulate and live in ways more congruent with their intentions and preferences.

The Observer's Versus the Actor's Seat

So far you were simply a reader, an observer of the challenges in the story. You are not (hopefully!) starving, sleep-deprived, or in danger. Usually, from a place of comfort and perspective, your mind generates the most solutions. If only a few solutions to this problem came to your mind, you can only assume that even fewer ideas would be generated under duress. This is often what happens to students, especially the younger ones. In the quiet space of an office, they so badly want to stay out of trouble and yet, in the midst of an upsetting interaction, they wind up reacting in the only way that comes to their mind and body: disrespect or bullying. The actor's seat is much more demanding than the observer's from which many ideas can be generated intellectually.

Quantity and Quality of Solutions Generated

Why do we struggle to find a list of various solutions to this story? Both the quality (type of) and quantity (total number) of solutions we generate are shaped by our life experience and, in particular, the context and culture that surrounds us. Cultures can shape the options that are available to you, as well as render other options impossible. You simply cannot imagine a solution outside of the social *discourses* (see Glossary) that have shaped your life, unless those solutions are somehow exposed.

For example, most workshop participants in the United States think of individual actions in response to this story's problem. This is not the case when this story is presented in more collectivist countries where people are culturally trained to consult with elders and include the community in their decision. People from the South Pacific Islands, where this story is told, came up with a remarkable ending:

> The animals and the humans caucused to find a solution. One of them finally proposed to organize a feast, where everyone could try to make the frog laugh. So they each, one by one, tried their silliest grimaces, their funniest dances, and their most creative jumps. The frog, although obviously interested, would simply not move. Finally, a little snake, who had been rather quiet throughout this journey, started to twist and turn in all directions, as if tickled by an imaginary being. The frog first hiccupped, tried to regain his composure, and eventually, unable to control his giggles, laughed all the waters out of his gigantic mouth, replenishing the earth and the living beings of their oceans, brooks, and rivers.

Triggering laughter in an opponent is just one of many possible options in solving the problem. It is a solution that is more readily thought of in certain cultures. This is not to say that in this story laughter was the ideal solution. There are many ways of solving the problem in the story: the frog can be tickled, massaged, introduced to an appealing partner, presented a juicy fly, made to be too hot, etc. Solutions do not necessarily have a value in and of themselves. As mentioned above, what really matters is access to a variety of solutions and the possibility to choose one that is congruent with personal values and intentions. Aggression comes to most North Americans' minds as not simply one solution but as the only solution, even if aggression is incongruent with their values. This example illustrates the limiting power of culture and context in the process of generating solutions. Such a narrowing and impoverishment of possibilities affects everyone, everywhere, in all spheres of life, and it becomes particularly evident in contexts such as schools, where the social pressure to follow certain norms is particularly strong.

For example, a teacher brings her students to an assembly. One of the students talks excitedly to his peers. Several thoughts go through the teacher's mind:

- "He's enjoying this performance so much. It makes me happy to see that."
- "I wonder if he's going to get out of hand; maybe I should calm him down now."
- "What will my colleagues and principal think if I don't do anything?"
- "What if all the students start thinking they can do that, too?"

These thoughts only happen in cultures and education models where teachers are expected to keep control of a large number of students and are evaluated for their performance. This teacher would not, for instance, have the following thoughts:

- "He is possessed by an evil spirit today."
- "He is shaming his whole family in public."
- "When he realizes that he is upsetting the community, he will be so embarrassed."
- "I hope that the eldest in the class will soon tell him to be more quiet."

These thoughts would not fit in the dominant North American culture but would fit in other countries with different social structures. The cultural context of one's life shapes the options that come to mind in a challenging situation.

USEFUL OPTIONS ARE ALSO ELIMINATED

Once an individual thinks of a series of options to deal with a problematic situation, can that person simply choose his or her favorite option? Unfortunately, no. The person's thoughts will typically, once again, be subjected to a cultural filter of what is acceptable in a specific context given specific protagonists. If solutions are visualized as keys to solve problems, then the impact of culture is to limit the number of keys that an individual has access to in a given situation (see Figure 1.1).

Figure 1.1   Culture limits access to a wide range of solutions.
              (Keys represent solutions to problems.)

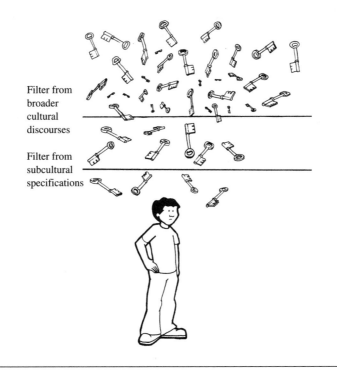

Let us consider an example of a student who regularly engages in bullying behaviors. Since this example is a classic scenario found in various grade levels, we will not specify the age. Antonio was bigger and stronger than most other students his age. Antonio did not hesitate to punch or push other students when a game was not evolving as he wanted. He intimidated most students, including those from upper grades, because he was more physically fit than anyone else and was a brown belt in karate. By the time Antonio was referred to counseling, he was getting sent to the office almost daily and was suspended from school regularly. Everyone had talked to him, created special disciplinary plans, invited him to reflect on consequences, consulted with his parents, and tried a variety of behavioral modification programs, all to no avail. Most people could think of numerous options other than aggression and would share them with him. The following are some of the options suggested to Antonio:

- Choose to simply let go of the little annoyances and not react to everything.
- Express the frustration in other ways.
- Explain and talk about your frustration, instead of hitting.
- Give others a chance—you just can't be the winner all the time.
- Ask your teacher for help when you have a conflict with other students, instead of trying to solve it yourself.
- Realize that sometimes nobody's at fault, and the situation is just frustrating; frustration is a normal part of life.
- When a situation feels unfair, trust that your teacher, principal, and counselor will support you; you have to give them a chance to help you.

Although these options seemed perfectly reasonable to many, none of them were reasonable to Antonio—none of them fit with his life experience and the beliefs he was taught. Like many students who engage in bullying, Antonio would, without even thinking about it, eliminate these options because of the cultural training he received. As shown in Figure 1.2, his cultural training created powerful blocks that rendered each of the previous options very unappealing.

DOES EVERYONE HAVE THE SAME CONTEXTUAL BLOCKS?

Contextual blocks come from people's experiences with a broader set of cultural specifications. By *specifications* we mean the specific "shoulds" that members of a culture generally ascribe to. For instance, in Western countries there is a belief that young people should learn to think for themselves

Figure 1.2 Cultural training creates powerful blocks that render many options unrealistic.

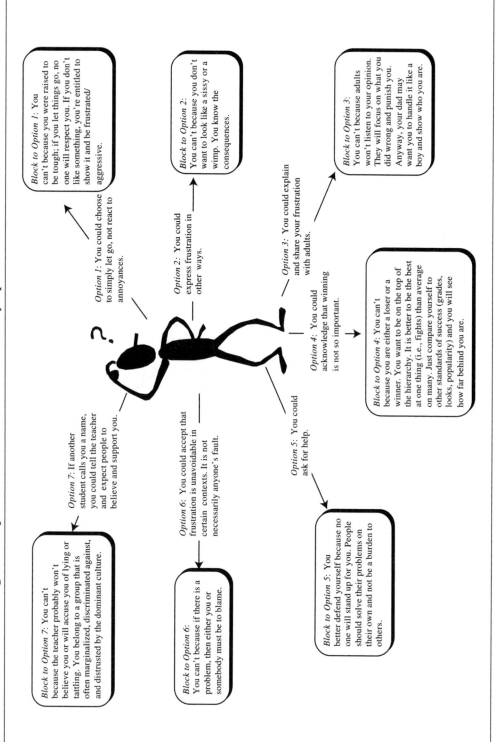

Block to Option 1: You can't because you were raised to be tough; if you let things go, no one will respect you. If you don't like something, you're entitled to show it and be frustrated/aggressive.

Option 1: You could choose to simply let go, not react to annoyances.

Block to Option 2: You can't because you don't want to look like a sissy or a wimp. You know the consequences.

Option 2: You could express frustration in other ways.

Option 3: You could explain and share your frustration with adults.

Block to Option 3: You can't because adults won't listen to your opinion. They will focus on what you did wrong and punish you. Anyway, your dad may want you to handle it like a boy and show who you are.

Option 7: If another student calls you a name, you could tell the teacher and expect people to believe and support you.

Block to Option 7: You can't because the teacher probably won't believe you or will accuse you of lying or tattling. You belong to a group that is often marginalized, discriminated against, and distrusted by the dominant culture.

Option 6: You could accept that frustration is unavoidable in certain contexts. It is not necessarily anyone's fault.

Option 5: You could ask for help.

Option 4: You could acknowledge that winning is not so important.

Block to Option 4: You can't because you are either a loser or a winner. You want to be on the top of the hierarchy. It is better to be the best at one thing (i.e., fights) than average on many. Just compare yourself to other standards of success (grades, looks, popularity) and you will see how far behind you are.

Block to Option 6: You can't because if there is a problem, then either you or somebody must be to blame.

Block to Option 5: You better defend yourself because no one will stand up for you. People should solve their problems on their own and not be a burden to others.

or to be independent. These shoulds are specifications that result from a broader cultural discourse of individualism, where individuals are expected to function autonomously.

These shoulds (i.e., specifications) are not bad in and of themselves but can have negative effects in certain contexts, and they certainly limit options. A culture's particular set of shoulds has a significant impact on the types of problems that develop. For instance, anorexia can only develop in a culture that values thinness; stealing can only develop in a context of unequal distribution of resources or of valuing material possessions, or both; domestic violence mostly happens in cultures where men have more power than women; bullying happens mostly in cultures where boys have to show that they are tough; teenagers only rebel against adults in cultures where they are given little power as youngsters.

As such, Antonio, or even his family, did not invent the contextual blocks described previously. Blocks generally come from the broader culture. Families and communities play a role in emphasizing—or not emphasizing—certain discourses as well as adding certain particularities to existing beliefs, but they do not create them in a vacuum. In the case of Antonio, as with many other students perpetrating bullying, the blocks came from patriarchy, capitalism, individualism, racism, and adultism. The following list includes some underlying cultural discourses of cultural blocks:

- Patriarchal cultures generally invite boys to be tough and physical (Ashton-Jones, Olson, & Perry, 2000; Katz, 1999; Kimmel & Messner, 1998; Kivel, 2002; Pollack, 1999).
- Capitalistic cultures emphasize the importance of being a winner, being right, and being on top of the hierarchy (Dewey, 1989; Huntemann, 2000; Jhally, 1998; Katz, 1999).
- Individualistic cultures promote a focus on one's own needs, desires, and rights, often at the expense of the community; most important, causality also becomes located in individuals as opposed to context (Dewey, 1999; Gergen, 1991).
- Cultures with issues of racism are associated with problems of distrust between races in such a way that relationships become polarized between power and disempowerment (Hall, 1997; Hooks, 1996; Kivel, 2002; Robins, Lindsey, Lindsey, & Terrell, 2002).
- Cultures with adultist beliefs often inadvertently minimize young people's rights and knowledge by assuming that age determines a person's competency. Adultist practices unfortunately create a situation where adults are entitled to yell disrespectfully at youngsters and are unfairly given more credibility and responsibilities than young people in almost all spheres of life (Zimmerman, 2001). Adultism is about misuse of power and does not refer to the normal responsibilities of adults in relation to young people.

Table 1.1 summarizes common effects of these discourses.

Table 1.1

Patriarchy	Individualism	Capitalism
Effects on Girls/Women • Focus on others' needs • Sacrifice • Please, be gentle • Look good, even if it is uncomfortable or unhealthy • Be a good caregiver • Express emotions *Effects on Boys/Men* • Be tough/strong • Be independent • Look unaffected • Be uncomfortable with affection and closeness • Focus on being the best at something • Disconnect from fear, pain, care, etc. • Be interested in sports • Act as protector	• Focus on personal needs and rights • Attain personal success • Emphasize privacy • Strive to own what they need (e.g., lawn mower, car) • Understand problems and successes as being located inside individuals • Be minimally connected with families, relatives, and ancestors	• Focus on success as defined by financial or material ownership • Function in an environment of comparison, competition, and evaluation of performances • Dichotomize people as winners or losers • Create hierarchies (standards) • Allow exploitation of resources with little regard for environmental implications • Emphasize future gains over present time • Value doing over being
	Adultism	*Racism, Homophobia, Sexism*
	• Hold the following beliefs: Adults are entitled to yell, but kids are not. Kids are rarely given power to make decisions. Kids are rarely given a voice or asked for their opinions. Teens rebel and don't know what they think or want since they are always told to listen.	• Create a false belief of entitlement and superiority of one group over another; develop an intolerance of differences • Make invisible the values and richness of diversity • Create self-hate, self-doubt in oppressed groups • Struggle for power, which might include violence • Suffer fear, isolation, distrust • Hold narrow, stereotyped beliefs

Of course, not everyone is affected by all these specifications, and the intensity of each experience depends on race, class, gender, socioeconomic status, ethnic identity, and so on. All of these discourses interact in such a way that they can create a cage around a person's sense of options (see Figure 1.3). Specifically, each of these discourses can rigidly structure people's experiences and reduce the space for individuals to be at their best.

As mentioned earlier, most educators try to assist students in thinking of other options. Unfortunately, the more serious the student's struggles, the less efficient this method is. In our experience, for change to

Figure 1.3   All of these discourses interact in such a way to limit a person's options.

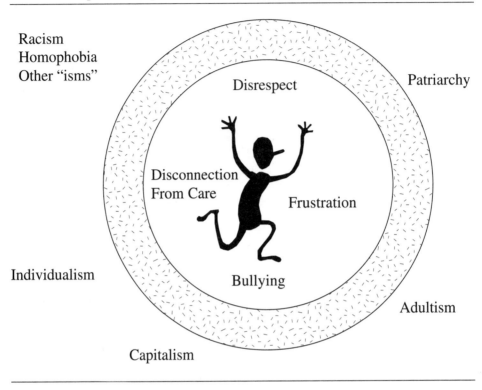

happen—for students to move away from disrespect and bullying—both options and contextual blocks need to be explored in a way that is relevant to students' lives. Let us first explore in more depth some of the contextual blocks in school that may specifically contribute to problems of disrespect and bullying.

NOTE

For the interested reader, a more extensive discussion of certain discourses can be found in Resource C. We believe the "-isms" are the most fundamental contributors to the problems of disrespect and bullying. However, given the complexity of these theoretical concepts, we chose to describe them further in the resource section. We encourage readers to familiarize themselves with the application of this material and then plunge further into the depths of these critical ideas. Ultimately, it takes a lot of courage to honestly explore the profound influence that discourses have on our lives and on the lives of young people. We may not always be pleased with what we discover and may feel unsettled by the sudden visibility and insidiousness of these discourses.

2

Are Problems of Disrespect Inadvertently Supported?

How do contextual blocks manifest in school? While most people are aware that we live in a capitalistic, individualistic, patriarchal culture that is often intolerant of differences (narrow standards of normality, little acceptance of different race, sexual orientation, etc.), many do not realize the implication of these broad discourses in their day-to-day lives. Generally speaking, institutions in these cultures become structured by themes such as competition, rules, achievements, evaluation, reward and punishment, and hierarchies of power. Nothing is wrong per se with cultures functioning under these structures (discourses) or the structures themselves; it is their extreme, constant, and rigid application that can lead to negative effects. Indeed, while some people may function well within nuances of those structures, many feel contrived and experience these structures as contextual blocks (or pressures), which limit options and identities. In particular, some of these blocks may contribute to disrespect and bullying because students struggling with these problems generally get an extra dose of teaching practices, such as rules, evaluations, and pressure to improve. These students can also react with resentment in competitive activities, which often bring the worst out of them.

In this chapter, we discuss the particular ways in which some of these contextual blocks take form in the public school system and the effects they have on young people's sense of options. In particular, we focus on five contextual blocks that inadvertently exacerbate the problems of disrespect and bullying: competition, comparison, rules, an overemphasis on achievement, and evaluation.

Our intention is to reveal the implications associated with these taken-for-granted practices that affect the educational climate of the classroom and people's experience in schools. Many of the ideas discussed may seem somewhat controversial to our gentle readers, and we certainly have no intention of throwing the baby out with the bathwater, so to speak. By questioning these topics, we do not mean to offend or outcast anyone who feels comfortable with the system. However, we can only distinguish the new and different ideas in this book from traditional practices once we have clearly articulated and examined these practices in terms of their implications. Our aim is to raise questions so that educators can reflect on the assumptions that exist, explore situations with a fresh viewpoint, and make choices based on their own preferences, styles, and experiences. We are also aware that educators may have limited power to change some of these practices; at the same time, however, understanding their influence on students' behavior, in itself, can in many instances contribute significantly to progress. In other words, educators with a flexible mindset about the relative appropriateness of these educational practices will be able to adapt them to bring the best out of their students in various educational environments.

COMPETITION

In North America and in many capitalistic countries, competition seems to be the glue that binds school activities. It is used as the ultimate motivator to seduce young people into performance, especially in elementary and middle schools. A significant amount of teachers' comments throughout the day are competitive—without teachers ever being aware of the hidden implications. For example, teachers commonly make the following competitive statements:

> *"The first one to clean up gets to help me with snack."*
>
> *"Stand up when you finish this math problem."*
>
> *"The first person to be in line quiet and orderly will get to be the light monitor."*
>
> *"Which students can be first to get out their homework folder?"*
>
> *"Let's see which students can get to their seats and sit quietly. You'll go to break first."*

If elementary and middle school teachers were to pay attention to their speech for a mere half hour in a classroom, they would be astonished at the number of competitive statements they utter.

Implications of Competition

Competition can be an easy way of building enthusiasm in an otherwise tiresome activity. It is inexpensive, readily available, and quick. While competition has a druglike way of creating a high during activities, it also has serious implications. For one, only one person wins and numerous others are left disappointed or frustrated. Competition can also promote a mentality that fosters the following consequences:

- Students focus on themselves rather than the community.
- Students feel the end justifies the means.
- Sharing and cooperating with others become less attractive options.
- Conflicts and put-downs are more likely.
- Disinterest in and boredom with less intense, noncompetitive activities grows.
- Students' sense of self is driven by winning status or material gain rather than preferences, values, and intrinsic motivation/satisfaction.
- Criticism and evaluation of themselves and others infiltrate students' experiences.
- Disconnection colors interaction with others, who are perceived as competitors.

For students who struggle with disrespect and bullying, competition provides an invitation for problems. The unavoidable stress and frustration of seeing others as opponents can be overly stimulating. Typically, students who have problems question their self-worth as a person, and the competition becomes either a context to prove that there is self-worth (which means a lot is at stake) or is another opportunity to confirm to themselves that they are "losers" or inadequate.

> *We are discouraged from asking why the children have been set against each other in a race for artificially scarce rewards. Or what the long-term effects of that practice may be on their attitudes about themselves or each other or the task itself.*
>
> —Alfie Kohn (1999)

Competition as the Sole Motivator

Competition is most harmful when it is the main motivator used throughout the day. Because of its implications, competition is used in only some educational systems, or it is used sporadically in certain events. A principal shared with us his reflections on the topic:

> *You can look at the cultural ties to competition. You can look at certain cultures where competition is not the honored thing. I saw a study done where white and Hispanic kids were given the same game to play. The game involved a checkerboard with pieces that moved forward. The object was to get across the board to the other side. For every chip you were able to get across to the other side, you got a prize. The white kids, as they started moving, would go and block the path of the other kid to the point where they were all stalemate. Nobody got a prize. The Hispanic kids were moving out of the way of each other to let each other pass, and they both got prizes. They thought, "I don't have to beat you. I don't have to stop you." Culture has a lot to do with competition, and in our culture, competition is big; the guy with the most money wins.*

Although this quote explains the difference of behavior by a visible factor (race), it is likely that the actual variable is young people's constant involvement in competitive environments.

Many classroom experiences are far more educational and enriching to our young people when facilitated in a noncompetitive way. Examples of these are discussed further in Part II of this book. In the meantime, however, we would like to invite you to reflect on your personal experiences of competition.

Reflection Questions

- How many times per day do you promote competition in your classroom?
- Are you concerned by the long-term and deeper effects of competition on your students?
- Do you think it's possible in the United States to create a context where students can experience as much enthusiasm from a shared process of collaboration as they would in competition?

COMPARISON

Similarly to competition, comparison is constantly used to motivate students. While comparison of one's own performance in improving on a subject is fine if not overly used, comparison of one's performance to that of others can have many unhelpful effects. Take, for example, the following statements commonly used at all grade levels: "You are eighth graders; you should be better at this than sixth graders." Or to high school seniors: "You're behaving like a freshman." These statements do not accomplish anything in terms of motivating students to do better. They mainly create put-downs of the lower grade students, which may seem insignificant in and of itself, but still contribute to a culture of bullying and disrespecting younger grades.

Implications of Comparison

Frequent use of comparison contributes to the following behaviors:

- It creates a context where self-confidence is increased by the put-down of another instead of by acknowledging and trusting one's own value (e. g., "I'm better than you."). This also leaves young people vulnerable to a self-worth roller coaster that is dependent on others' flaws.
- It creates a context where youth are set against each other as opposed to collaborating. (I can run faster than you.)
- Adults may fall into overly imagining and comparing the young person to what they could be instead of appreciating who they are now. It can contribute to the feeling of "never being good enough."

Reflection Questions

- What is your intention when you use comparison? When is it helpful and when is it not?
- How often do you see comparison verbalized by students?
- What percentage of the time is this comparison socially productive?

RULES

Sometimes in a fast-paced, pressured environment, we end up relying on rules to simplify our lives. And, in many situations, rules *can* simplify our lives. For many young people, rules provide a reliable structure and a sense of safety. However, the more stress educators experience, the more tempting it is to follow the letter of, or increase, the rules. In that process, the initial intentions behind the creation of rules are often lost and long forgotten.

In light of the relativity of right and wrong, you can always find a context in which a completely logical rule does not make sense. This can be the case when dealing with students who are affected by a wide range of experiences, such as mental health issues, cultural and class differences, and abuse, and also when dealing with those who are struggling with disrespect and bullying.

Students who struggle in the educational system are generally unhappy. Because of the long hours spent in school and the destabilizing effect of unhappiness, these people become very preoccupied and rebellious. This process usually involves a significant amount of questioning about their own self-worth and about the situations that are causing pain in their lives. The more students dwell on questioning their self-worth, the more they may question the situation and the rules that get them into trouble. As a result, these students typically stand out more than others and will sometimes force adults to question rules in a way that is uncomfortable and hard to justify. In an attempt to survive, these students question things as a way to cope with the system.

Once a rule is found irrelevant or illogical, it becomes very difficult to adhere and subject oneself to it without frustration. Frustration exists because either one is following the rule and is forced to disconnect from one's values or one cannot follow the rule and is facing punishment.

The ultimate irony is that young people who challenge the rules are often subjected to more rules as adults attempt to contain their behaviors. In the end, some students feel boxed in and suffocate in rules that structure every action. Let us clarify that our point is not that rules should be eliminated but rather that an extreme amount of rules and their rigid application invite student problems. Here is a sample of a new set of rules that was created by a discipline committee in an attempt to reduce the large amount of bullying, disrespect, and chronic problems that were plaguing an elementary public school. Note, the people writing this list had good intentions and were really hoping to address the needs of their students and promote academic success. They wanted to make their school a safer place for all students.

The following behaviors were considered infractions that were automatically punished:

- throwing grass or sticks
- contact during sports or play fighting
- not stopping and kneeling immediately when the whistle was blown
- blocking access to cafeteria or rooms
- running in the no running zone
- playing in line
- using the restroom after the whistle was blown
- playing in the bathrooms

Infractions during recess were followed by an immediate benching and a loss of the next recess. Infractions during lunch were punished by an immediate dismissal to the time out room. Students were given three minutes to get to the time out room after which they were assigned another time out.

Our discussion with the students allowed us to make visible a large number of unhelpful effects of these rules. Surprisingly, all students, whether they had problems or not, felt that these rules were extreme which left them feeling generally nervous and unable to fully enjoy recess. The inability to fully relax contributed to an inability to fully pay attention later on during the long academic lectures in classrooms. The general stress also contributed to a general intolerance of each other's behaviors and, ironically, more student conflicts.

The teachers that secretly felt that this set of rules were unrealistic did not follow through consistently which not only divided the staff but also students' perception of both the rules and the teachers. The teachers who believed in the rules felt exhausted monitoring such a large list of infractions, were burning out by the sheer number of conflicts with students that filled their days, and were starting to overlook certain infractions.

So, while the adults' intentions were to make the school safer for all and increase academic success, their actual effect was just the opposite; it made all students nervous and unable to focus on learning.

Overall, educational systems with a large number of externally determined rules implemented in various ways by different people have more disrespect and rebellion than systems where rules are meaningful and internalized as personal values. Rules that are more internalized are cocreated in a democratic way and are much less oppressive in quantity and quality. Students are personally more committed to these types of rules as they were involved in articulating some of them and can simply accept the limited others. We discuss these types of rules in Part II of this book.

Reflection Questions

- Have rules ever gotten you to do something against your better judgment?
- Does relying on rules always simplify our lives?
- Have you experienced times when a rule created more problems instead of solving them?
- Given the relativity of all things, how do you decide if using a rule will be helpful, likely to have more negative effects, or would simply be a waste of time? In other words, when do you decide to follow the spirit of the law versus the more rigid letter of the law?

ACHIEVEMENT AT ALL COST

The current educational system pressures teachers and students to work for concrete, visible results, such as test scores. In this process, quantity, as determined by the curriculum, is often favored at the cost of quality. As illustrated in the following quotes, many educators have shared with us their grief at the necessity to remove experiments, discoveries, and art projects to accommodate the ever-increasing curriculum.

My greatest regret, which goes against my very best judgment as a teacher, is that I have been forced to drop most scientific exploration in my classroom. These types of activities involving discovery and experimentation are just so time consuming. It's unfortunate and sad, and I see it happening in classes throughout my district.

—Sandra Anders

What they require of a kindergartner these days is quite different from what they used to require. You teach more, teach sooner, and teach faster. Really, it doesn't matter if the child is not emotionally ready to do it.

—Bob Geddes

The state has required that the introduction of algebra be done at an earlier time than ever before. To my knowledge, it is now not even developmentally appropriate for a significant number of children. I don't understand what the hurry is.

—Stephanie Tyson

Capitalism and the Academic Treadmill

It is at times as if people are on an academic treadmill. Why are concrete and superficial outcome scores replacing the journey of deeper and integrated learning? Why do scores become the goal, rather than just the measure?

In many ways, this reminds us of the trend that has evolved in capitalistic cultures, where, for instance, expressions of love have been replaced with material gifts: Clever marketing strategies have successfully influenced people to perceive a diamond or roses as the most powerful expression of love, rather than people's honest and more simple gestures of love. Brides-to-be often talk more about the diamond ring than they do the person they are marrying. The concrete representations (e.g., grades, scores, roses, diamonds) of the deeper and more important experiences (i.e., learning, love, commitment) have become mistaken for the items of significance (see Resource C for more on capitalism).

Similarly, the visible, quantifiable measure of a test score has become more important than invisible yet profound interactions or discoveries. In this process, the current education system has increasingly treated students as products (represented by scores) that can always be improved, as discussed by the famous South American writer Paulo Freire (1970/2000).

The stress and pressure to work all the time is particularly evident with the issue of homework. Students have many demands on their time. Adults want young people to be well-rounded, with varied interests, which are not necessarily met at school. We want families to be close. We want young people to exercise and enjoy sports. Yet, we give large amounts of homework that take many hours to complete. These hours escalate as students grow and develop and peak in high school. In certain districts, the total amount of time a student spends in school and on homework totals more than the time required in an adult's full-time job. As students get older, they often question the necessity of homework and its relevance to their lives. Students become frustrated, sensing they are wasting their time with meaningless, repetitive workbooks while missing interesting life opportunities.

Granted, it is true that one can always learn more. But *how* young people learn, *what,* with *whom,* and at *what pace* can be equally or more important than the raw quantity of material ingested. In the name of this excessive curriculum, many teachers (who also feel trapped in this system) end up teaching the required curriculum against their better judgment and taking actions that increase the likelihood of marginalizing, alienating, and disconnecting students. In so doing, teachers become more vulnerable to engaging in disrespectful interactions that inadvertently feed students' resentment or express criticism to students' parents. As a result, parents then also become harsher with their child and increase the pressure at home to perform.

While some amount of pressure to succeed can increase young people's performance, too much pressure leads to the exact opposite as illustrated in Figure 2.1. Moreover, the exact amount of pressure that will generate the best performance varies for each student. A student who has encountered harsh punishments at home or at school for underperforming may react negatively to pressure far quicker (Curve A) than a student who has always felt successful, supported, and has self-confidence (Curve C). The student who has experienced harsh punishment can quickly fall into a neurological reaction of fear of punishment (flight or fight), which triggers the cerebral production that biologically blocks the ability to process deeper cognitive function. This was the case for example of a second grader who was sentenced to do one hundred squats every time her teacher called her father to complain about her inability to concentrate on assignments. The teacher's intention was to help the child and collaborate with the family. Little did she know that she was inadvertently

Figure 2.1   A small amount of pressure can increase performance, but a large amount has the opposite effect.

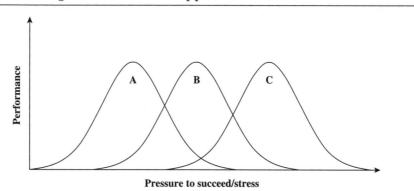

contributing to the problem. The culture of this little girl was very strict about family privacy and speaking badly about fathers. It took a lot of time building trust with the BAFTTA[1] advocate to share this experience.

This bell curve relationship between pressure and performance also happens when students just progressively become discouraged, overwhelmed, behind, or exhausted by the amount of material to ingest and the subsequent conflicts. These students, more than others, will experience frustration and resist pressures to be curriculum gobblers, sometimes through disrespect or comments mistaken for disrespect. The following story from an assertive teenage girl illustrates the point:

> I got in trouble today because our teacher said we were now going to take the last hour of the day to have fun . . . and as we were getting all excited she gave us the choice between two "fun" math exercises. Nobody dared to say anything, so I raised my hand and said, "Well, if the goal is really to have fun, can we play a game instead?" And the teacher got all mad at me.

The pressure to ingest excessive amounts of meaningless material squashes learning and curiosity, which are natural in all young people. As one principal from an underprivileged school mentioned, "It's so sad to see that by age 6, many students hate school." Boredom, disconnection, and frustration then creep into school relationships and invite disrespectful interactions, even though initially everyone is trying to do their best.

Finally, when it is time to have fun and move around, some students just go crazy and become excessive in their expression of freedom for having been constrained to sit and perform for so long.

EVALUATION

Evaluation is so embedded in our culture that it is often not questioned. Evaluation is assumed to be an effective method to promote quality and improvement. In the education system, superintendents evaluate principals who evaluate teachers who evaluate students, all based on a set of preestablished variables. While feedback, rather than evaluation, provides a powerful opportunity to improve, how it is *interpreted* and the *way* it is done has a significant impact on whether it will facilitate improvement or simply generate discouragement and frustration.

Evaluations are often interpreted and mistaken for truths about people's knowledge, abilities, and potential, when in reality they represent only a narrow snapshot of a performance situated in a certain context, time, and relationship. At their worst, evaluations sometimes only give us a glimpse of the worst of an individual and may not even represent the most common performance. This can be the case with principals' evaluation of teachers (discussed at greater length in our second book, *Creating a Positive School Culture,* Beaudoin & Taylor, 2004) or with psychological assessment. From a developmental and biological model, and given how much young people grow and change, it is surprising that we are so quick to label them with lifelong diagnostics. Moreover, when teachers evaluate students negatively they harm not only the student by pigeon holing the performance but also themselves by pigeon holing their own minds and limiting their own creative thinking.

The way evaluations are conducted will shape how young people experience the process. Important variables to consider are its meaning (does that mean I'm inadequate?), its frequency (the total number of adults commenting negatively on the issue, including teachers, parents, extended family, etc.), and its extent (sheer amount of personal aspect evaluated), as will be discussed below.

Evaluation at Every Step

Students are evaluated in a large number of ways. Evaluation, at the students' level, can be even more detrimental because students lack the power and the life experience to limit the devastating impact of negative feedback. Students who struggle with bullying and disrespect, in particular, may end up feeling like they are evaluated on every possible aspect of their being. Because of the troubles in their lives, these students are under the microscope of educators.

The following Table 2.1 shows the many facets on which students are scrutinized. Our intention in making these facets visible is to foster a greater understanding of students' frustration, resentment, and powerlessness in schools.

Table 2.1   Students are evaluated in a large number of ways.

Students Are Evaluated on How They . . .

Learn	Talk	Write
Hold a pencil	Read	Play
Behave	Relate	Walk
Run	Sing	Eat
Drink	Sit	Dress
Listen	Express themselves	

Students Are Evaluated on Their . . .

Cleanliness	Posture	Performance
Personality	Friendships	Athletic abilities
Musical abilities	Artistic abilities	Attentiveness
Class work	Homework	Organization of desk/backpack
Responsibility	Promptness	Attendance
Preparedness	Stamina	Penmanship
Level of participation	Feelings	Nutritious value of
Leadership abilities	Patience	snacks/lunch
Problem-solving ability	Parents	Communication style
		Choice of seating partners

The Results of Constant Evaluation

In many cases, the end result of intense scrutiny is students feeling as if they can never do anything right and they can never be good enough. It is not unusual for students who develop a problem reputation to feel like the little guy illustrated in Figure 2.2. When students feel as if they are under constant scrutiny, they end up discouraged, which either exasperates their anger or alienates them. They lose confidence, perform worse, become intolerant, impatient, and are less likely to concentrate. Consequently, the likelihood that they will bully their classmates and disrespect the adults at school increases.

Figure 2.2   Students feel evaluated on everything.

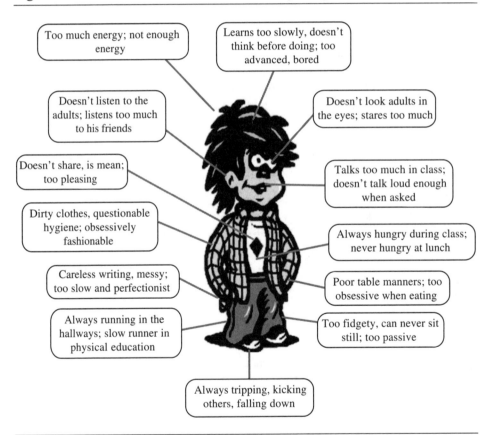

Reflection Questions

- What is the difference in your ways of being and in your performance when someone is evaluating you? Specifically, what is better and what is worse?

- How do you know if an evaluation reflects the actual potential of someone or if it reflects the context?
- How do you decide whether you comment on the student's poorest versus best performance?

Given the number of items in Figure 2.2, it becomes obvious that although some students may have the good fortune of fitting into this narrow and specific mold, many others may not. And for those who don't fulfill all the specifications, the experience of trying to accommodate themselves into school can be completely overwhelming. This is the case for many minority students whose cultures dictate standards other than those imposed by school. These students may struggle with the standards required by the dominant, white, middle-class culture of educators. Indeed, most adults would also be disrespectful if they were subjected to—and powerless against—such pressure, criticism, and scrutiny. With these points in mind, we invite readers to consider a few questions.

In sum, the broader culture limits the quality and quantity of options that students experience in their lives, and certain structural aspects of school, such as evaluation, rules, competition, and overemphasis on achievement can inadvertently exacerbate problems. Does this happen to educators too? In the next chapter, we explore how educators, like everyone else, are significantly affected by cultural ideas that guide their choices and sense of options.

NOTE

1. The BAFTTA advocate is a postmasters or postdoctoral intern in psychology who provides counseling and consultations in schools and is supervised by the first author.

3

Unraveling Assumptions

Educators' Roles and Students' Behaviors

Culture is like water; it constitutes every cell of our being. It is insipid, invisible, intangible, and yet everything soaks in it.

Educators, in general, typically go into their profession because of their love for learning, their compassionate nature, and their commitment to educating young people. They are dedicated and sacrifice much of their time and life, while, unfortunately, being undervalued and underpaid.

In fact, most educators spend a great deal of time figuring out the right thing to do for students, particularly for students who struggle. Given the limited amount of time teachers have and the large number of students in their care, they often become vulnerable to cultural myths and taken-for-granted assumptions.

THE EFFECT OF MYTHS AND ASSUMPTIONS

It is important to examine these myths and assumptions because they affect teachers' actions and decisions. To assist in unraveling the implications of common assumptions, we provide an example of a typical student interaction. This example is an analysis of the general process that unfolds during student conflicts in school, along with its invisible cultural underpinnings. To facilitate the explanation of this process, we ask that you imagine your reaction to the scene shown in Figure 3.1.

Figure 3.1   You witness this situation on the playground. What do you do?

A common response from educators is to immediately walk to the scene, discipline the student who pushed, and assist the victim. Sometimes educators will also ask for explanations in an attempt to understand what happened. If the educator has the assumption, however, that one of the students always gets in trouble, the educator will be more likely to blame the student for the incident, regardless of whether or not this student is the pushed or the pusher. Typically, both students are upset, and the one feeling accused will try to offer an explanation in defense of his or her actions. This explanation often includes blaming others. This is particularly true when the accused feels unheard, is uncertain of the outcome, and fears punishment. The accused may be tempted to lie; however, it is important to remember that lying reflects not so much one's values as one's sense of powerlessness in a given situation. (Adults who fear important consequences to their lives also tend to misrepresent their experiences.) In the end, the educator is expected to make a judgment about the truth and about who is right and who is wrong—with the possibility of a disciplinary action as a consequence.

This common process is based on several taken-for-granted assumptions:

1. Problems are caused by individuals who are believed to have a significant control over their lives.

2. Someone is in the right and someone is in the wrong.

3. There is a truth that can be retrieved somehow, if everyone would relate the exact course of events.

4. Adults need to get involved to solve student conflicts.

5. A punishment is necessary to teach students that these behaviors are unacceptable.

These five assumptions reflect cultural views (discourses) and warrant further analysis (see Figure 3.2).

Figure 3.2   The broader culture impacts the school climate, which in turn affects educators and their assumptions.

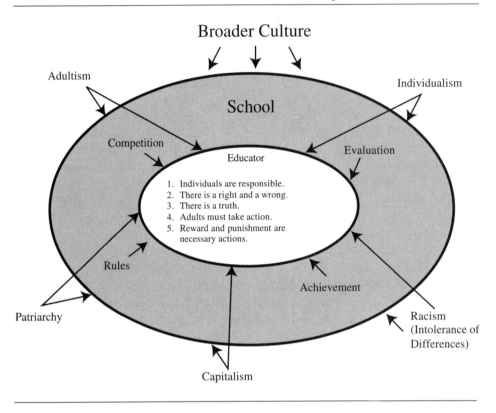

We now explore, deconstruct, and unravel each assumption. This section may be unsettling and uncomfortable as it may tug on the carpet under your feet. However, this examination will expose new and inspiring territories.

Assumption 1: Problems Are Caused by Individuals

Exploration

Consider the following questions: What if problems are not caused by individuals? What if students actually have limited control over their behaviors? Because these assumptions are not present in all countries of the world, we must consider a possible contextual source such as individualism. Individualistic cultures view the individual as the ultimate unit of analysis. Conflict is believed to arise when individuals' needs, goals, desires, and interests are perceived as conflicting. When adults witness the scene in Figure 3.1, they likely automatically ascribe bad intentions as motivating the boy who is pushing. This perspective is not necessarily erroneous, but it is important to be aware that what was witnessed was only a very brief snapshot of a whole sequence of events and interactions, taking place in a broader context at a specific time. In other words, can one really make an accurate judgment of this scene without knowing on a metalevel *who* actually held power in this scene (either through race, class, popularity, threats, etc.), *what* the broader cultural issue was (proving who's tougher, gaining material reward), *why* this happened in the context of school, *where* power struggles are happening (e.g., competition for the teacher's acknowledgment, retaliation for class humiliation), and *when* the issues are arising (during major projects or before a holiday the young person dreads because of family issues).

These factors ultimately have a much more powerful impact on the situation than the isolated individual. In other words, when a student makes a statement or engages in a behavior, individualism sways educators to think that it is the student's choice. A more relational narrative view will acknowledge that this choice was not created in a vacuum, but rather it comes from conversations with his parents, uncles, aunts, grandparents, and friends; TV shows and movies; and life experience in a community. We have at times worked with boys who desperately tried to fulfill their fathers' wish that they be the toughest one in school and show everyone what they were capable of. Disrespect and bullying, then, simply became a superficial performance of an invisible yet much deeper set of complex influences and meanings. Contextual analysis moves the conflict away from the individual in such a way that he or she simply becomes a protagonist, perhaps an important one, but still one in a much larger context of life.

It is important to realize that what appears to the observer as an individual's choice is often not experienced by the individual as a choice. In fact, students in those situations may experience a great deal of frustration and simply react with the only method that comes to mind. From this perspective, then, the reaction is not even a choice per se because choice involves a selection from a variety of options. This is very similar to people's reactions to the frog story discussed in Chapter 1. The only option that might have come to your mind may have been one of aggression, even though it may be against your values. Although there are many solutions to this story, your mind, taken by surprise and shaped by the context of life experiences, may have conceived only one reaction. This does not mean that protagonists in problem situations do not have some responsibility and control over their behaviors, but rather that acknowledging the role and impact of context may render more responsible and effective actions possible. Young people with issues of disrespect and bullying need assistance that will create for them experiences of options so that they actually can make different choices. By experiences of options, we do not mean adults telling them about options but rather young people being invited into a deeper process of self-exploration in which they connect with more personal and profound sense of possibilities. (Practices to foster responsibility, control, and a sense of options, while taking into consideration the broader context, are discussed in many of the subsequent chapters of this book.)

Teacher Question

I already consider the context, but I focus mostly on the student who is pushing. Regardless of the contributing factors, we just can't have people pushing at school. What should I do?

Response

It is unlikely that addressing the behavior of pushing in isolation will be effective. It may promote additional frustration and resentment that will increase the likelihood of additional disrespect and bullying. Also, you may think that you are already addressing the context, but in reality you are probably only extracting historical information that supports your story of an isolated individual. For example, if the victim has no known history of problems, you may be more likely to ignore the context and simply discipline the pusher. If the victim has a short history of problems, both students may be given a punishment in hopes of preventing future incidents. If the victim has a known history of problems, then the victim may actually be blamed for the pushing. All of these conclusions draw more information from problem stories about students than from the actual scene that just took place. (Chapter 6 discusses problem stories further.) In addition, how do you determine what was more hurtful: the physical pushing, which may not leave a single scratch on the recipient and will be forgotten the next day, or the invisible hurtful words that preceded the pushing and which may torture the student's heart for weeks or months? In light of these complex nuances, the observer's quick conclusion is often unfair and biased against students who struggle. The only way to be fair is to be aware of your thinking, move away from problem stories, understand context, and address the situation in a way that is less blaming of individuals in a vacuum (see Chapters 4 and 5 for more on problem stories and strategies).

Summary of This Alternative Perspective

There are multiple factors that contribute to someone's engagement in behaviors of disrespect and bullying. Students are not the problems; experiencing a lack of options (because of contextual blocks) is the problem.

Assumption 2: Someone Is Right, and Someone Is Wrong

Exploration

Consider this: What if no one is really right and no one is really wrong? Traditional beliefs, which can promote judging others on a narrow set of acceptable views or behaviors, often form the concepts of right and wrong. This is sometimes seen historically as an effect of religious movements that have regulated people's lives for centuries and dictated simplified notions of what is right versus what is wrong. It is also connected with racism, ethnocentrism, and intolerance of differences because individuals are always tempted to perceive their ideas as the right way and others' as the wrong way. A more recent postmodern view invites us to notice that right and wrong are highly dependent on context and cannot be unilaterally generalized. For instance, in many people's minds, it is generally wrong to kill, but killing is okay in a war; it is wrong to steal, but understandable if a parent has a sick and starving child; it is wrong to start a fight, but it's okay to fight in self-defense; it is wrong to lie, but heroes who defeat enemies with clever misrepresentations are glorified.

A close examination of right and wrong can always find a context where the wrong makes complete sense. Right or wrong, then, simply becomes a matter of quick judgments that often simplify a situation and overlook the multiple perspectives and experiences that justified the behavior. People always have a reason for what they do; to them at that particular moment in time and place, it seems like a good and valid reason. To them, it seems like the right or only option, and, from a narrative approach, this experience is the important piece to understand.

Teacher Question

Shouldn't students be told what's right and what's wrong?

Response

It is our belief that an inflexible distinction between right and wrong does not clearly exist and that it cannot be simply imposed on young people by outside observers. Such imposition risks being completely outside young people's experience—irrelevant to their lives and alienating them further from school. Some students who bully may have learned to fight for survival in their neighborhood, and they certainly feel that it is right to defend themselves. We do believe, however, in the usefulness of assisting these young people in noticing the multiple effects of their behaviors, creating a space of reflection for them, and determining their preferred ways of being in relation to others.

Summary of This Alternative Perspective

People always have a reason for what they do.

The situation described in this section is a good example of the potential irrelevance of qualifying the young boy's pushing behavior as wrong. It was just a snapshot view from which it is impossible to extract the boy's reason for pushing. If the educator had a chance to see the situation earlier (see Figure 3.3), he or she might have perceived the perpetrator and victim roles reversed. Basically, the educator would arrive at a conclusion that is the opposite of what was assumed. Yet is this really the truth?

Assumption 3: There Is a Truth That Can Be Retrieved

Exploration

What if truth did not really exist? What if it was impossible to separate an objective reality from the biased and subjective perspective of the human mind? The very idea that truths exist has been heavily discounted in the last few decades. Scientists in most fields of research have begun to realize that knowledge is always biased by the perspective and context of the seeker. We can only strive for objectivity and neutrality by being aware

Figure 3.3   A broader perspective of the situation reveals a relational
context that was invisible in the initial snapshot view and
reverses the ascription of blame.

of the factors that may ultimately color our judgment. A historical review
unveils that many beliefs that were once taken for objective truth (shape of
the earth, arsenic to treat tuberculosis, etc.) were sooner or later found to
be erroneous. Our generation is certainly not immune to this process,
despite our advanced technology.

Teacher Question

All that history is fine and well, but if I get two conflicting accounts of
the same event, someone's got to be lying. What do I do?

Response

It is difficult and tricky for a third party to clearly distinguish a lie from
a different perspective, and we question the actual usefulness and necessity
of this distinction. The risk of further alienating students by questioning
their credibility may have more disadvantages than simply getting a biased
description of the incident. Moreover, in the narrative approach, people's
accounts of events are taken as representations of their experiences or of the
context, or both. Lying, then, can simply become a "true" representation of
the student's experience of terror at being punished. In other words,
conflicting accounts of events on the playground are believed to simply
reflect each student's perspective or experience of the situation. Similarly,
adult couples who have a conflict will often share radically different
accounts of the issue to their respective friends. This difference, therefore,
is expected and normalized. In fact, in this approach, if two students give
identical accounts of a conflict, we could view this agreement not as truth
about the situation but as both protagonists possibly agreeing simply to
avoid punishment. Based on the context, it could also be viewed as an
exercise of power: Which one of the protagonists would have the power (or
status) to dictate his view? Which one of the protagonists has threatened

retaliation after school? Which one of the protagonists can humiliate or isolate the other from his peers? Those of us working from a counseling perspective are very familiar with young people's stories around misrepresentations of events that can take place in disciplinary conversations with principals. Factors such as reputation, ability to articulate the situation, calmness or confidence, peer pressure, and fear, to name only a few, may often bias what is then recorded on paper as a truth.

If educators acknowledge that no actual truth, but rather only each student's perspective and subjective experience of the situation, can be found, a very different type of conversation follows. Students then feel heard and respected in their experience, they may not try to prove or defend anything, and a context is created where understanding and problem solving can emerge. Such meetings allow the educator to obtain an even broader perspective of the events, which in reality may not be as serious as initially thought or may be more easily solvable by students themselves (see Figure 3.4).

Figure 3.4   An even broader perspective of the situation may reveal that it was less serious than initially anticipated. The young man was initially perceived as a perpetrator; as a victim, he is now seen as a helper.

Summary of This Alternative Perspective

Truth cannot be retrieved, yet a multiplicity of perspectives can be considered.

Assumption 4: Adults Need to Get Involved to Solve Student Conflicts

Exploration

What if adults did not need to get involved all the time to solve student conflicts? What if students were empowered to solve many issues on their own? A common assumption is that adults need to be present to solve young people's conflicts. This is often based on the assumption that young people need to be controlled or contained and that they do not have the knowledge necessary to function independently. In this context, young people usually do not learn to solve conflicts on their own, which then does justify a need for adult mediation. A repetitive and complementary pattern of relationships is usually established between students and educators, where one group fights and the other reconciles. Neither students nor adults necessarily know any other way of dealing with the situation. Many schools have opted for problem-solving programs and the training of peer mediators, thus taking a step in creating a more favorable school climate (Cheshire & Lewis, 2000). Problem-solving training teaches people to compromise following a set of techniques; the punishment-fear factor is reduced, if not eliminated. This can certainly be useful, but the general cultural context of adult–student relationship throughout the day remains unaddressed.

From a historical perspective, it is again interesting to realize that the concepts of childhood and adolescence have been very recently developed in the Western hemisphere; that is, at the beginning of the twentieth century (White, 2000). In Renaissance Europe, and in certain countries still today (India, Peru, Thailand, etc.), young people typically treated by Westerners as dependent or immature youngsters get married, have children, and contribute to their communities as worthy workers. This is not to say that we support child labor or child marriage but simply that we question the sometimes extreme perception in North America of young people as incapable. What is it that guides an educator's decision to intervene in a child's play or interaction? We believe that it is an important question, as ultimately there is a lot of evidence that young people in many situations (not all, obviously) can be trusted to solve conflicts and create resolutions without outside help.

Teacher Question

My students are having a hard time lately. They are arguing a lot. Does this mean that I should just let them hash it out without guidance?

Response

The concepts we are discussing here have profound implications on students' and educators' views of themselves, of others, and of the world. Traditional cultural beliefs have been ingrained for many years and can take some time to be unlearned. Educators interested in using these concepts should keep in mind that change will happen gradually. The first step may simply be intervening with the least amount of authority possible and empowering students to think about the situations differently. This is discussed further under adultism in Chapter 7 and in the Resources, and a classroom example of this process is described in Chapter 8.

Summary of This Alternative Perspective

If adults could use power in a situation, does that mean they should? Young people can learn to solve conflicts on their own and be responsible in their interactions.

Assumption 5: Punishment Is an Effective Way to Teach Students That the Behavior Is Unacceptable

Exploration

What if punishment increased the problem as opposed to reducing it? The behaviorist movement in the 1970s popularized rewards and punishments. While it was originally designed to train animals, it was quickly adapted to alter human behaviors, young people in particular. Behaviorism was a product of the cultural movement of the time, which, along with the Industrial Revolution and the development of capitalism, focused on productivity, efficiency, and quick methods of controlling behaviors. By the end of the twentieth century, an increasing number of researchers had shown that behaviorism and, in particular, rewards and punishments assumed a simplified, ineffective, and reductionist view of humans. During our writing of this book, we heard a perfect example of these limitations on the radio:

> In an effort to build public safety, police officers were rewarding children seen wearing bicycle helmets by giving them coupons for free ice cream. The local police station has recently halted their program, however, after officers noticed long lines of children riding back and forth in front of the station with helmets on.
>
> —Source unknown

The human mind is simply too complex and sophisticated to change genuinely under these strictly behavior-focused programs. Despite the large amount of evidence regarding their limited effectiveness, rewards and punishment have remained pillars in the educational system. Given that teachers are expected to impart a large curriculum, be responsible for and control young people's every behavior, it is not surprising to see a large number of educators using this seemingly quick method of management.

Rewards and punishments may offer some advantages when they are small or when they help young people connect with their own internal motivation. Otherwise, when used extensively, as listed in the following table, they mostly promote compliance and fear, and they have questionable long-term effects on self-directedness. Rewards and punishments promote change through external motivation, which is often associated with little internal motivation and accountability (for readers interested in exploring the issue of rewards and punishments further, see Kohn, 1996, 1999).

Effect of Traditional Practices of Authority, Such as Rewards and Punishments

---

- Students may change because of a fear of adults or a desire to please them.
- Students' internal motivation decreases.
- Surveillance is often necessary.
- Relapse is common, especially when students are left alone.
- Frustration and resentment may grow with added punishment, which generally increases the likelihood of engaging in problem behaviors.
- The consequence itself—and not the lesson being learned—may dominate students' minds.
- Students become increasingly upset, resentful, and alienated by their relationship with educators, which they often experience as disrespectful or humiliating.
- Students remain unclear and inarticulate about their personal reasons and options for being different.

Teacher Question

Shouldn't students have consequences when they misbehave?

Response

Punishment is clearly distinct from the process of implementing consequences. We do believe that everyone, adult and youth, should face the responsibilities of having engaged in a destructive or hurtful action. The process of punishing, however, is usually a very hierarchical and unidirectional process where an unpleasant decision is imposed on young people. Implementing consequences involves two considerations: (1) It is typically a more democratic process embedded in discussions of intentions and effects as well as an awareness of the implications on others and the community. The consequence is not loaded with anger and resentment. (2) It implies conversations with the young person as to what kind of consequences makes sense given the issue and what might assist him or her in learning from or reflecting on the situation. In that sense, the most helpful consequences are those that have a connection to the problem that occurred (natural consequences) or those that follow logically from the problem event (logical consequences) (Belvel & Jordan, 2003; Dreikurs & Grey, 1970). In sum, many situations warrant a consequence, not to make the child suffer, but rather to create an opportunity for learning. This learning potential is dependent on the manner of communication and the logic of the consequence.

Teacher Question

If a student misbehaves continually, doesn't she deserve to be yelled at?

Response

If more than 50 percent of your interactions with a student are conflictual, you are inadvertently contributing to the problem. Research shows that young people's behavior can only improve once a safe and satisfying relationship is established with the educator (Belvel & Jordan, 2003). Moreover, childhood is a process of learning and making mistakes. Yelling clouds messages (Smith, 2004). Students ruminate on the interaction and are overwhelmed by their emotions, rather than considering the event. It also has the effect of reducing connection between the adult and the child.

Teacher Question

What about rewards? Shouldn't I be able to reward those who try hard and follow the rules?

Response

Reward is also a hierarchical process where one group systematically has the power to grant the reward, while the other group in lesser power is the recipient. This inadvertently forces young people to spend valuable time on the quest to please others rather than on the simple act of being a self-disciplined person. Maureen once witnessed countless students collecting trash in exchange for a school reward. Did these young people integrate the environmental value embedded in the action enough to continue doing this on their own? Probably not. In this situation, cleaning up specifically for the reward actually reduced the likelihood that students would own the value. A discussion of the importance of the gesture followed by the activity, simply for the sake of contributing to an improvement of the community environment, would have had a greater educational impact.

Teacher Question

Maybe rewards are not in fashion anymore but I have to say, I've seen them work.

Response

It is true that students' responses to reward may vary. Some students may improve with teachers' disciplinary actions, some students continue to struggle and some get worse. Why do some improve and some get worse? What is the difference between these two groups?

Research shows that students who have a stable home environment, feel loved by their families, and have developed a sense of themselves as capable, worthy human beings may respond to consequences and challenges with motivation. These students understand their struggles as a mistake or a bad habit and feel capable of changing. They have had experiences at being successful and at overcoming difficulties. They have a sense of being worthy and lovable which sustains them through the unavoidable conflicts with adults. These students may make an effort to win the reward and please the adult but the learning is more likely to be very superficial if any.

Students who have had a difficult life, whether burdened by poverty, domestic violence, child abuse, gangs, losses, alcoholism, and so on, have a different relationship with motivation. These students develop resilience, which is an ability to tolerate hardship and conflicts. They become immune to hearing anger; they must. While their sense of self-worth may be more fragile and their tolerance for frustration may be lower, their threshold to take action and be motivated to do something is different. They are used to feeling that they can't do anything about their suffering. They are used to resenting silently and stuffing their anger until they blow up, like many of the adults around them. They may mismanage anger and fall into hatred of themselves and others. These students do not respond well to consequences. Most disciplinary actions will simply push these students over the edge, worsening any problem they harbor. The only thing that can really help these students is relationships—relationships that provide support, kindness, and appreciation; relationships that provide examples of both tolerance of mistakes and limits.

Marie-Nathalie spoke with numerous teachers and principals who felt discouraged because a problem behavior would come back after a behavioral program terminated. In elementary school, a typical example of such practice is telling a student that for every day he or she interacts in a respectful manner, one letter of the word *respect* will get written on a chart or a good color card will go in the day's chart. When a certain amount on the chart is completed, the student is granted a previously agreed-on reward. In middle and high school, these programs often have to do with limiting or increasing students' freedom around preferred activities or schoolwork. These practices may work with students who initially do well or who are slightly slipping. They do not work with students struggling with personal problems and facing contextual blocks because the real issues remain unaddressed. For those particular students (who are, ironically, the most common target of these programs), these experiences often just reinforce the problem by adding an additional sense of failure, inadequacy, and incompetency, and they strain further the important teacher–student relationship. Indeed, when problem behaviors do not respond or return after a brief improvement, teachers are tempted to assume that the student is unwilling or uncaring, which often leads to an increase in punishment, frustration, and mutual dislike.

Summary of This Alternative Perspective

Punishment and reward can sometimes be useful, but often they actually contribute to problems instead of fostering change. Although consequences are important, there are other ways of assisting students to reflect on their behaviors.

Congratulations! You have successfully walked through the deconstruction of five challenging assumptions. It is important to remember that students who engage in bullying and disrespect usually struggle with accumulated frustration that is magnified by interactions colored by these assumptions. Remember also that these assumptions really come from the interaction of several cultural and institutional (school) pressures.

COMMON SCHOOL QUESTIONS: NEW WAYS OF THINKING

"Why Do Students Choose to Bully? Aren't They Tired of Being in Trouble All the Time?"

This is a common and very important question. Why would anyone choose to engage in bullying? In adults' minds, bullying, especially in elementary school, causes only trouble, discipline, marginalization, and exclusion. To understand the response to this question, we must first look at how we choose to have certain problems. For example, when was the last time you actually chose to have a conflict with your intimate partner? Or the last time you decided that you wanted to have a conflict with a family member? This may be hard to remember. Some of you may not remember any problems that you chose to have. Most people do not choose to have problems. Rather, given a choice, most adults and students (even those who bully regularly) would rather be popular, successful, and appreciated. If you do remember a problem you feel like you chose to have, think about it again. Often, the perceived choice of problem behavior is more the result of feeling you had no other options. If there had been other options that you found relevant and realistic, you probably would not have engaged in the problem behavior.

Young people who engage in bullying are generally unhappy and have even less of an experience of choice as their lives are dominated by resentment and anger. It is hard to measure the possible invisible self-hatred and inadequacy that they have (Thompson, Cohen, & O'Neill-Grace 2002). These students are also believed to experience an unstable sense of "self-esteem" (Baumeister, Bushman, & Campbell, 2000; Perez, Vohs, & Joiner, 2005) and poor experiences with their parents (Garrett, 2003).

When you think about it, these students may bully child A, but as a result they can end up being somewhat bullied themselves too by adult A (yard duty), B (teacher), C (principal), and D (their parents). For an adult it would be equivalent to having a conflict with a coworker, then having your employer be angry at you because of the situation, then your employer's boss, and then arriving home from work and finding that your partner is also angry at you because of the incident. You would never experience a break from the negativity. The likelihood that you would wake up refreshed, energized, and full of positive energy the next day would be fairly small. The lives of young people who bully are saturated with conflicts and negative interactions in all arenas of life.

"Every Time I Think This Student Understands the Problem and Will Change, He Goes Right Back to Bullying. What Can I Do?"

Consider this description from a teacher: "This student is unbelievable. You talk to him about his disrespectful behavior, he gives you the impression that he feels terribly guilty and will not do it anymore, and within ten minutes of being back on the playground, he's done it again. He has to be the best manipulator I've ever met."

This is an absolutely frustrating scenario that many teachers and principals experience on a regular basis. It leaves adults resentful, distrustful, and exasperated. Moreover, the sense of growing power-lessness from not knowing what to do to assist this child or maintain safety at school often leads the teacher or principal to make increasingly harsher disciplinary decisions in a desperate attempt to stop the disrespect. This action, most of the time, is to no avail for three reasons:

1. Increasingly punishing a student on a regular basis usually increases his or her level of frustration and resentment. The student progressively becomes like a walking bomb of negative feelings and will explode more readily at any slight annoyance. This in turn will typically lead to more punishment, frustration, and, of course, more problem behaviors. Educators and the student become intertwined in a problem-saturated vicious cycle, where more of the same reactions happen. The educators' initial intention of reducing the behavior through punishment inadvertently supported the problem.

2. The second reason this scenario is common is that many adults assume that young people have total control of their problem behaviors. Many parents and educators ask, "Why doesn't the student just stop this?" This is an interesting question, given that most adults recognize that they do not have control over their own personal problem behaviors. How many times, for instance, have you promised yourself to eat less sugar, salt, or fat? How many times have you tried to change your sleeping habits? How many times have you decided to be more patient with some-one and then did not follow through? If adults with all their knowledge, experiences, and resources have difficulty changing a problem behavior from one minute to the next, how can we expect young people to do so? Young people, just like adults, need support, time, processing, and space to make mistakes in their journey toward change.

3. The third reason this scenario is common is that most educators focus on major punishments for a misbehavior and minor acknowledgments for the intentions and the successes of the student. As we were finishing the write-up of this second edition of the book, one of Marie-Nathalie's interns shared the following story: "On Monday, Aiden, first grader, was told he could not go on the field trip to the Discovery Museum because he had bitten Nick when he was frustrated. Today, the day before his field trip, at recess, Nick broke Aiden's favorite pencil. His teacher and the intern saw Aiden become absolutely furious, red and ready to explode but he clenched his little fists and his mouth and did not attempt to hurt Nick back. The intern wondered if the field trip would be given back given that the success was significant. It wasn't, the teacher said "good job" a few times and that was the end of it. She didn't even call the parents to share the

success while the problem incident was shared with a number of witnesses. Was giving back the field trip a solution? Not necessarily either, it could have created an external roller coaster of giving and taking. The solution was to not have punished so severely in the first place, allowing the student more opportunities to learn, to be happy, and enjoy peers on field trips.

Finally, the educator's perception of the student's guilt and his or her commitment to not do it again is usually genuine. Most students don't want to be in trouble and upset adults. Unfortunately, however, simply having the intention to avoid a problem is often insufficient for actual change. Good intentions are certainly very important in the process of change, but students also need to be empowered to change. Adults assist students by helping them articulate the sequence of problem development, their successes, and the procedures they can use to handle things differently.

"Don't These Students Have the Intention of Hurting Someone?"

Many teachers are familiar with a description such as this one: "Now, this is truly a mean boy. He actually wants and likes to hurt others. I saw him with my very own eyes pick up the ball and throw it as hard as he could in Shelly's face. You could tell that he had the intention to hurt her."

Witnessing a student hurt another is very upsetting. Not only does the harm seem so unnecessary, but it also can seem like an act of defiance to the momentarily powerless adult. Unfortunately, whether you want it or not, most people in the throes of anger have ideas of hurting others, verbally if not physically. Angry interactions are always ugly to watch. Have you ever imagined what it would be like to see a videotape of yourself in your last heated argument with a close relative? Think about that argument honestly for a moment. Are you satisfied with how you handled it? Horrified? What would an observer say about you if they witnessed that interaction? Do you feel that this interaction is representative of who you really are as a person? Many would respond that this interaction is a snapshot of their worst attitude. In other words, it does not fit with the person they actually see themselves as, or their preferred identity. Anger is often experienced as taking over and getting people to do or say things they would rather not do or say if they had a chance to think about it.

Of course, even if many do not behave in the most admirable way when angry, it does not mean that such gestures should be excused or that the responsibility should be waived. Quite the contrary, perpetrators of aggression must be held accountable for their actions. Yet, this can be done in several ways that are all guided by the assumptions we hold about the perpetrator. A multiplicity of assumptions can be used to understand such behaviors. If you assume the perpetrator is a bad person or likes to intentionally hurt, then you will want to discipline and hurt back through punishment. The goal behind this theory is to inflict a form of pain on the perpetrator so that he or she understands and remembers what the experience is like. Unfortunately, this theory does not acknowledge that many perpetrators are already in pain because of a life situation and that additional pain may simply increase the problem. If you are able to understand that the student is probably overtaken by anger—and that there is a whole other side to the student—then there is suddenly more space for compassion, interest, and understanding. There is also space to assume that, like everyone, this student must have a preferred self and some special talents that may be invisible in a context saturated by problems, trouble, and frustration. Your actions, as an adult who must set limits and invite this young person to be responsible, will be different. Think back to your own experience as a young person.

"What Do I Do About a Student Who Gets Mad and Disrespectful Over Trivial Things? Everything Becomes a Big Deal for No Reason."

Everyone knows that familiar feeling of being very busy and having to deal with a person who seems to dwell constantly on little details.

It becomes increasingly harder to be patient and understanding. Yet, there is always a reason why people react the way they do. If the issue is repeated, then it is even more important to understand the experience of that young person and what makes the issue important. An issue's importance is always very relative to a person's life—it all depends on the person's priorities and experiences. For adults, a good example of important issues involves spending money, where each individual has his or her own priorities, which are often judged by others as being unreasonable, especially if there are financial struggles.

"Bob's Parents Keep Telling Me That I'm His Favorite Teacher Ever. I Just Can't Believe This. If He Likes Me, Why Doesn't He Listen to What I Say?"

Unfortunately, liking someone may not have the power to free a student from the influences of certain problems or enable the student to accomplish complex activities. For example, many couples would not struggle as much if the quality of their relationship depended only on their attachment to one another. Yet as adults working hard at helping students, this distinction can easily be confused by the myth that young people have total control of their problems.

"I've Been Trying Hard to Help This Student Be Respectful, With No Progress. I Guess She Simply Does Not Want to Do Her Part. Am I Wasting My Energy?"

Most people typically see themselves as caring and as having good intentions in relationships. In school, educators work extremely hard, and many go well beyond their assigned duties to assist a child. After reading books and consulting with psychologists, nurses, and principals, educators may be at a loss as to what can be done to assist a student. After one has done what seems like everything, it may then become tempting to think that the problem remains because the student is not trying or does not want to change.

In most Western, individualistic cultures, problems are usually believed to be associated with someone's bad intention. As a result, when a problem happens, the tendency is to automatically assume that the other person wanted this or contributed in some willful ways to the problem. In reality, most people feel very stuck in and overtaken by problems. In a situation like this, educators may consider changing their approach. Simply asking the struggling students more questions about the effects of the externalized problem, what the problem gets students to do that they don't like to do, exploring why students struggling with the problem may hate it, and assisting in the process of noticing and articulating moments where the problem was absent may be most useful.

"What About the Student Who Has a Perfect Life and Perfect Grades, but Is Still Disrespectful to Teachers? What's a Good Reason for That?"

Each student has his or her own personal reason for engaging in these behaviors, and, as with adults, the reason is not always clearly articulated, even to the student. Marie-Nathalie was once referred an eighth grader who baffled his teachers and principals by only getting in trouble for his voracious defense of other students who were in trouble with the school. Everyone was puzzled about his sudden verbal attacks toward the adult disciplining any student in the school. This young man would get in serious trouble, and no one understood why he would commit self-sabotage. Both parties thought the other was wrong. Adults (and possibly some students) thought he was wrong for intervening in such a way in issues that were not his, and he thought adults were wrong for punishing students. This young man saw himself as an activist in the world and was particularly upset by the way adults treated students at his school. Narrative conversations with this young man assisted him in keeping a broader contextual understanding of situations affecting educators, connected him further with his values, and empowered him to address issues of fairness in ways that were more congruent with his values and more appropriate and successful for all involved. In the end, the reading of the train story by Terry Dobson, as follows, completely transformed his way of being an activist in the world.

If educators try to move away from these assumptions, how then, can they fulfill their responsibilities of maintaining safety and fostering learning? Is it really possible to be efficient while remaining aware of cultural blocks and assumptions?

A Kind Word Turneth Away Wrath

THE TRAIN CLANKED and rattled through the suburbs of Tokyo on a drowsy spring afternoon. Our car was comparatively empty—a few housewives with their kids in tow, some old folks going shopping. I gazed absently at the drab houses and dusty hedgerows.

At one station the doors opened, and suddenly the afternoon quiet was shattered by a man bellowing violent, incomprehensible curses. The man staggered into our car. He wore laborer's clothing, and he was big, drunk, and dirty. Screaming, he swung at a woman holding a baby. The blow sent her spinning into the laps of an elderly couple. It was a miracle that she was unharmed.

Terrified, the couple jumped up and scrambled toward the other end of the car. The laborer aimed a kick at the retreating back of the old woman but missed as she scuttled to safety. This so enraged the drunk that he grabbed the metal pole in the center of the car and tried to wrench it out of its stanchion. I could see that one of his hands was cut and bleeding. The train lurched ahead, the passengers frozen with fear. I stood up.

I was young then, some twenty years ago, and in pretty good shape. I'd been putting in a solid eight hours of aikido training nearly every day for the past three years. I like to throw and grapple. I thought I was tough. Trouble was, my martial skill was untested in actual combat. As students of aikido, we were not allowed to fight.

"Aikido," my teacher had said again and again, "is the art of reconciliation. Whoever has the mind to fight has broken his connection with the universe. If you try to dominate people, you are already defeated. We study how to resolve conflict, not how to start it."

I listened to his words. I tried hard. I even went so far as to cross the street to avoid the *chimpira*, the pinball punks who lounged around the train stations. My forbearance exalted me. I felt both tough and holy. In my heart, however, I wanted an absolutely legitimate opportunity whereby I might save the innocent by destroying the guilty.

This is it! I said to myself, getting to my feet. *People are in danger and if I don't do something fast, they will probably get hurt.*

Seeing me stand up, the drunk recognized a chance to focus his rage. "Aha!" he roared. "A foreigner! You need a lesson in Japanese manners!"

I held on lightly to the commuter strap overhead and gave him a slow look of disgust and dismissal. I planned to take this turkey apart, but he had to make the first move. I wanted him mad, so I pursed my lips and blew him an insolent kiss.

"All right!" he hollered. "You're gonna get a lesson." He gathered himself for a rush at me.

A split second before he could move, someone shouted "Hey!" It was earsplitting. I remember the strangely joyous, lilting quality of it—as though you and a friend had been searching diligently for something, and he suddenly stumbled upon it. "Hey!"

I wheeled to my left; the drunk spun to his right. We both stared down at a little old Japanese man. He must have been well into his seventies, this tiny gentleman, sitting there immaculate in his kimono. He took no notice of me, but beamed delightedly at the laborer, as though he had a most important, most welcome secret to share.

"C'mere," the old man said in an easy vernacular, beckoning to the drunk. "C'mere and talk with me." He waved his hand lightly.

The big man followed, as if on a string. He planted his feet belligerently in front of the old gentleman, and roared above the clacking wheels, "Why should I talk to you?" The drunk now had his back to me. If his elbow moved so much as a millimeter, I'd drop him in his socks.

The old man continued to beam at the laborer.

"What'cha been drinkin'?" he asked, his eyes sparkling with interest. "I been drinkin' sake," the laborer bellowed back, "and it's none of your business!" Flecks of spittle spattered the old man.

"Ok, that's wonderful," the old man said, "absolutely wonderful! You see, I love sake too. Every night, me and my wife (she's seventy-six, you know), we warm up a little bottle of sake and take it out into the garden, and we sit on an old wooden bench. We watch the sun go down, and we look to see how our persimmon tree is doing. My great-grandfather planted that tree, and we worry about whether it will recover from those ice storms we had last winter.

"Our tree had done better than I expected, though especially when you consider the poor quality of the soil. It is gratifying to watch when we take our sake and go out to enjoy the evening—even when it rains!" He looked up at the laborer, eyes twinkling.

As he struggled to follow the old man's conversation, the drunk's face began to soften. His fists slowly unclenched. "Yeah," he said. "I love persimmons too . . ." His voice trailed off.

"Yes," said the old man, smiling, "and I'm sure you have a wonderful wife."

"No," replied the laborer. "My wife died." Very gently, swaying with the motion of the train, the big man began to sob. "I don't got no *wife*, I don't got no *home*, I don't got no *job*. I am so *ashamed* of myself." Tears rolled down his cheeks; a spasm of despair rippled through his body.

Now it was my turn. Standing there in well-scrubbed youthful innocence, my make-this-world-safe-for-democracy righteousness, I suddenly felt dirtier than he was. Then the train arrived at my stop. As the doors opened, I heard the old man cluck sympathetically. "My, my," he said, "that is a difficult predicament, indeed. Sit down here and tell me about it." I turned my head for one last look. The laborer was sprawled on the seat, his head in the old man's lap. The old man was softly stroking the filthy, matted hair. As the train pulled away, I sat down on a bench. What I had wanted to do with muscle had been accomplished with kind words. I had just seen aikido tried in combat, and the essence of it was love. I would have to practice the art with an entirely different spirit. It would be a long time before I could speak about the resolution of conflict.

—Terry Dobson (1985)

SOURCE: Essay by Terry Dobson anthologized in *Aikido and the New Warrior*, edited by Richard Strozzi Heckler, published by North Atlantic Books, copyright © 1985 by Richard Strozzi Heckler. Reprinted by permission of publisher.

4

Responding Effectively to Problems

Obviously, you cannot change the broader culture. To a certain extent, you can have a local effect in the subculture of your school. With the understanding that cultural blocks and assumptions can pressure everyone into nonpreferred ways of being, you will relate to young people very differently. Specifically, you will develop a fresh attitude while in the midst of conflict and be able to externalize problems.

A FRESH ATTITUDE

With a contextual understanding, a shift happens in your perception. You are then in a position to acknowledge the following points:

- People would not choose to have problems if they were given a choice. Adults and young people alike would much rather be popular and successful than experience trouble and conflicts. Even though it may appear to you that the individual enjoys conflict, it may simply be the satisfaction of having an effect on the situation. Many students experience a generally powerless life so having a moment of power at school or a release of the tension associated with anger may provide them with relief or a feeling of superiority.
- People usually try to do their best given the circumstances of their lives and the specifications that pressure them; for example, young

people who make aggressive statements in school may actually be containing 75 percent of the frustration and anger they experience because of a difficult family situation.

- Certain problems are only problems because they involve ways of being that stand outside of narrow cultural standards. For example, there has been an increasing concern about the excessive number of young people medicated for attention deficit hyperactivity disorder (ADHD), especially given the subjectivity of diagnostic criteria (Nylund, 2000). Although ADHD may have a biological component, and is certainly associated with significant suffering at times, the extent to which this relatively new label is used raises questions. For example, one can easily wonder if ADHD mainly exists in cultures that have developed a narrow standard for what is a normal energy level and that require their young people to sit still in overcrowded rooms for long hours. Only fifty years ago, people were simply considered energetic or, conversely, sedate, and many of these people still led productive lives; a pathological label would not have been applied to this state of being. This is not to say that medication should never be given. Some young people can clearly benefit from medication. Rather, we are acknowledging that we have worked with many students who were medicated because they protested or did not fit in the system. Once they underwent therapy and explored different ways of being, medication was successfully discontinued, which in these cases confirmed the inaccuracy of the biological diagnosis (see Chapter 10 for a case example).

If you truly believe in the power of context and of its implications, even in difficult situations, you can access a particular attitude in your thinking and conversations about school issues. This attitude is a combination of what we call the "4Cs" of helpful conversations: compassion, curiosity, collaboration, and contextualized perspective.

Compassion

The narrative approach assumes that people most often have good intentions and that given an experience of choice, they would most likely engage in respectful behaviors. As stated earlier, we believe that there is always a reason why people do or do not do something. A true commitment to this belief also allows educators to believe that there is another more preferred version of that same individual—a caring and successful person with whom it is possible to connect. This opens the door to unconditional compassion and renders sharing and exploring safe and genuine. Consider the following statement of sharing and exploration: "So, Debbie, if I understand correctly what you said, when you get in trouble you feel powerless and that gets you to call people names, even though that's something you don't really value for yourself."

Curiosity

Adults and young people are considered experts in their own experiences. Educators' expertise lies in the ability to ask helpful questions and explore new possibilities by taking a stance of not knowing and being intrigued by students' thoughts, values, hopes, and dreams. The curiosity and interest discussed here comes from a place of genuine caring and interest, as you would have in other relationships. This is particularly important with young people who are not often given the opportunity to talk and explain their experiences to adults but are rather asked to justify themselves, give the right answer, or listen. Consider the following example of genuine caring:

> *Help me understand what happened. What was the first thing that popped into your mind when you saw Richard walking toward you? Were there Mad Feelings getting you to think, "I'll get him this time," while the other part of your brain did not want trouble? What was the earliest sign that Mad Feelings were getting to your body? Did your fists tighten up or your heart start racing?*

Collaboration

Collaboration implies that educators seek to minimize the power imbalance between them and students. Given that most people have struggled with some form of disqualification in their lives, it is important that the collaboration process include conversations that do not replicate the previous contributing factors to the problems. This often means giving up the expert stance and engaging in a collaborative, cooperative journey of exploration. In doing so, a special kind of partnership is created, where power is shared and where each party makes valuable contributions. In such a context of respect, educators would, for instance, verify whether it is okay with students for educators to ask certain questions or inform other people about the problem. They could even coauthor certain written documentation if necessary. Educators and other adults subsequently treat students as knowledgeable, interesting, and worthy, despite the behavioral problems. The following example illustrates this collaboration:

> *Would it be all right with you if I summarized our conversation by writing "Gabi was overtaken by Anger, which prevented her from thinking about consequences? She is concerned by this development in her life and has decided to reflect more on this problem. She really doesn't want it to continue taking over her life as she realizes that it brings much less fun and more worries."*

Contextualized Perspective

Keeping the broader context of a situation in mind is essential because it implies thinking sincerely about the larger sociocultural perspective (gender, race, class status, etc.). Deconstructing or examining cultural influences on individuals' responses to a situation is critical if we are to truly attempt to understand and improve disrespectful patterns of response. This process challenges the common simplification of human behaviors in our own minds, communities, and dominant cultures. Deconstructing provides a space to analyze the context of students' lives and relationships as they evolve in particular locations and at specific times. The following questions provide an example of a deconstruction:

> *What do films and television say about how boys should be and how girls should be? What effect does that have on girls? On boys? What is lost if people start accepting this? What does it mean if being tough is important? How does that affect friendships? What are other ways of being popular that are not represented in the media? How has this conversation affected you?*

Although none of these characteristics may seem new to you, it is the act of considering all four aspects at the same time that gives a different flavor to your conversations.

CHIPPING AWAY AT THE PROBLEM WITH A POWERFUL TOOL: EXTERNALIZATION

When you understand that most problems are created by people experiencing a lack of options in the context of their lives, it then becomes logical to talk about problems in an externalized way. Externalization of problems is a fundamental concept in the narrative approach. This practice, developed by Michael White (White & Epston, 1990), is based on the idea that problems, just like unwanted habits, may develop because of a series of life circumstances. Externalizing implies that the problem is perceived as distinct from the person's identity. As such, a person will not be talked about as an angry person or a bully but rather as someone struggling with anger or disrespect. In many ways, this practice resembles the medical model of helping a well-intentioned person manage allergies or anxiety. As discussed in Chapter 3, people often perceive problems as out of their control, even if it may not seem so to an observer. By externalizing problems, educators recognize that problems are not indicative of who students want to be but are reactions they can learn to control.

Effects of Externalization

Talking about problems in externalized ways has several major effects:

- Externalization shifts students' perspectives in profound ways. Instead of hating themselves, students suddenly start hating the problem. Externalizing promotes hope and agency. In this process, a space is created where students are less burdened, less para- lyzed, and more able to take actions against the habits of bullying and disrespect.

- When a problem is externalized, it becomes a tangible entity that is namable, contained, and clear. This new perspective allows students to take a stand against it and take responsibility for their behaviors of disrespect and bullying (often for the first time). People learn to control the behavior, as opposed to the behavior controlling them. In other words, externalization makes the effects of the problem more visible, enhances the necessity of taking action, and renders students more capable of making different choices to change their lives.

- As the community starts to see the problem as a separate entity, everyone starts noticing students' special talents, values, and intentions. The focus shifts from blaming students to working as a team and noticing students' efforts against problems. For example, educators may become more aware of the times when a student could have engaged in disrespect or bullying but didn't.

As illustrated in the following table, externalizing the problem using the 4Cs of helpful conversation offers numerous advantages that are clearly distinct from traditional practices of authority.

Effect of Traditional Practices of Authority	Effect of Collaborative Conversations
• Students may change because of fear or by desire to please an adult.	• Students change as a personal choice.
• Motivation is external (punishment or reward).	• Students become clearer as to why they want to change.
• Surveillance is often necessary.	• Surveillance is not necessary; students are usually committed to their own choices.
• Relapse is common, especially when students are left alone.	• If mistakes occur, they do so infrequently and generate self-evaluation.
• Frustration and resentment may grow with added punishment, which generally increase the likelihood of engaging in disrespect and bullying behaviors.	• Self-confidence usually grows as the students become more successful and aware of the preferred effects of new behaviors.

- The consequence—and not the lesson being taught—may dominate the students' minds.
- Students become increasingly upset, resentful, and alienated by their relationship with educators, which they often experience as disrespectful or humiliating.
- Students do not clearly and meaningfully articulate for themselves how and why they could react to situations differently.

- Congruence of one's values with preferred identity usually dominates students' minds.
- Students experience respect firsthand and increasingly respect educators for treating them as worthy people.

- Students become very clear and articulate about negative effects that are important to them and the unique ideas enabling them to act differently.

Internalized Versus Externalized Problems

The externalization of problems is often difficult to grasp at first. A good way to understand this concept is to apply it to your own life and consider, for example, your personal relationship to anger. Many of you may recall having done or said something under the influence of anger that did not quite fit with how you prefer to be. Later, you may have regretted your actions, felt guilty, and promised yourself to not do this again. Imagine, however, someone talking about you as an angry person, and this forming your reputation. This might trigger more frustration and a sense of being misunderstood or misrepresented. This frustration increases the likelihood that you will engage in angry behaviors again, even if you do not want to. In other words, the way the problem is talked about creates a context of resentment, which increases the chances of the problem happening again.

Now imagine externalizing anger. You would create a thorough list of effects that anger might have on multiple aspects of your life—you would notice when it takes over and when it does not, what it gets you to do, think, and feel against your preference. You might eventually be frustrated at the problematic aspects of anger and make a decision that, given its effects, you do not want to let it rule you in those particular ways anymore. Through supportive externalizing conversation, you might identify the first signs that lead to an anger problem and explore ways of choosing a preferred direction. This process of articulating, noticing, and making choices about the effects of the problem and simultaneously about the way you prefer to act ultimately allows you to take responsibility, be clearer about personally relevant options, and have preferred experiences of yourself in difficult interactions.

Externalization Exercise

Choose a problem that has affected you. It can be anything, such as an emotion (anger, anxiety, impatience, depression, frustration, self-hate, boredom, distrust, fear, shyness, etc.), a thought (critical voice, blaming, perfectionism, comparison, self-doubt, evaluation, ambition, etc.), or a habit or behavioral pattern (teasing, inter-rupting, dominating, rushing, irresponsibility, disrespect, etc.). Explore how this problem has affected you in the past and how you've seen it affect other people by answering these questions.

1. How does _____ affect you?

_____

_____

2. What does _____ make you do, say, think, and feel?

Do: _____

Say: _____

Think: _____

Feel: _____

3. When and how did you first notice _____?

_____

_____

4. How does _____ affect your relationships?

_____

_____

5. How does _____ make you feel about yourself?

_____

_____

6. When are you most likely to resist _____?

_____

_____

Can you remember an example this past week where you could have given in to _____ but didn't? What did you do to avoid _____? What were you thinking and doing as the situation evolved?

_____

_____

_____

If you want to be creative you can also further the externalization of the problem by personifying it. Children respond very well and quickly to such an approach because they have not been immersed as long as adults in a self-blaming model of thought. They talk about the problem as if it were an invisible criminal or a ghost. (There is no need to use the word *ghost* in therapeutic conversations, unless it playfully fits the students' understanding.)

The exercises on pages 58 and 59 (previously published in Beaudoin & Walden, 1998) is a favorite of many, young and old. It has to be student generated in a non-intimidating conversation to be meaningful.

Name:

Crimes:

Reward:

WANTED

This Community of Support has issued a search warrant against the following problem. Any information helpful in unmasking this dangerous criminal will be rewarded.

Name: Pushing Habit

Crimes:
Triggers frustration really easily
Blinds students from the consequences
Makes you think that you don't care about what people will say
Paralyzes your mind so that you forget everything else and focus only on your anger
Puts a great deal of sudden energy into your arms and hands
Gets you to hate other students and think they're wrong or they deserve it
Makes you feel that you are treated unfairly
Think that others, students and teachers, don't like you anyway
Gain a reputation as a troublemaker even if you don't like that
Makes you feel bad about yourself
Get in a lot of trouble at school and home
Have adults on your back and suspecting you all the time

Reward:
Less trouble
More fun, privileges, and freedom

DEALING NARRATIVELY
WITH DISRESPECT AND BULLYING

Let us now apply these concepts to educators' interactions with students.

First, explore your usual response to these situations. Remember a recent unpleasant exchange you had with a student who struggles with behaviors of disrespect or bullying.

What did you say?

_____

_____

What did the student say?

_____

_____

What did you reply?

_____

_____

How did it end?

_____

_____

What were your intentions in responding that way?

_____

_____

What were the effects of your comments on the problem?

_____

_____

So, if the problem included Mad Feelings, did your response make the Mad Feelings increase or lessen?

Were the effects in line with your intentions?

_____

_____

What were the effects of your comments and this interaction on you?

_____

_____

Could you have intervened with less authority?

_____

_____

A NARRATIVE RESPONSE

We want to be clear that we do not believe that conflicts are pleasant for anyone or that there are any magic solutions. What we are proposing are simply different ways of thinking and interacting that may minimize the unpleasantness and frequency of these events and increase young people's ability to solve these problems on their own.

During an externalizing conversation, individuals feel heard and understood and become less invested in self-defense or blaming because the focus is naturally placed on an externalized experience of the conflict. In other words, the conversation is structured in such a way that the problem is located in the conflictual interaction itself, as opposed to inside any of the protagonists. An individual can then relax more, relate the experience in a more genuine way, and gain an interesting perspective of the multiple views and effects of the situation as well as the numerous contributors to the conflict. Such conversation can lead to a much broader range of possibilities, not only in terms of a solution but also in terms of the experience of self and others. The most helpful role educators can take is to create a context where students can reflect on their experience, examine their position, and broaden the scope of their perspective.

The following is an example of one of many possible scenarios on a school playground. An attempt has been made to explain the choices and thinking process of the adult to make visible the narrative process. We are aware that not all interactions would follow such a flow. In addition, most educators would not have the time to engage in this entire discussion the first time they attempt to use these ideas. This conversation would result from a progressive and systematic commitment to these practices over time (as illustrated by the classroom project and the case example presented in Chapters 9 and 10). We simply want to give a thorough example of an externalizing dialogue that illustrates the application of these concepts. We invite the reader to keep in mind the philosophy and its intentions, rather than the specific wording of questions. This being said, imagine that you are walking on the playground at recess when two visibly upset students with a conflict between them come running toward you.

Jonathan (running and upset): Tannor called me a name. He always does that. He's so mean.

Tannor (running and upset): He started it; he messed up my drawing on the ground.

Adult (gently and calmly): You both seem really, really upset. Why don't you come and walk with me to that picnic table over there and catch your breath.

- Moving the conflict away from a blaming and individualized conversation, while still hearing and validating both students' experience
- Setting a tone of compassion and staying with their experience

Adult (walking, with a tone of compassionate curiosity): Do you two often fight at recess like this? I thought you were good friends and even neighbors.

- Analyzing the context and history of the relationship, power differential, and possible problem story or reputation and attempting to conceptualize the factors that contributed to the conflict
- Not attempting to find out who started it because this would provide only an incomplete snapshot of the issue
- Asking questions that come from a place of genuine curiosity and broader scope

Jonathan: Yeah, but I don't want to be his friend anymore.

- Students still upset and stuck in an attack–defense pattern of blaming each other

Tannor: I don't either. You always break my things; the other day he broke my bicycle at home.

Jonathan: I didn't, you . . .

Adult (interrupting): Hold on. Can I interrupt here? I really understand now that you are both very mad at each other for a series of incidents.

- Becoming clearer that the students have a history of relatively close friendship and have become pushed away by a problem
- Maintaining a collaborative stance

Adult: What is it that happens to both of you when you play together these days? Do you get taken over by frustration, impatience, anger, or some kind of resentment? I'd like each one of you to think and answer this. What happens inside of you?

Tannor: I don't know . . . I think I get frustrated.

Jonathan: I just get mad.

- Attempting to externalize a problem that gets between them (In this situation, the question is structured as a multiple choice rather than open-ended question to ensure that students move away from the focus on each other. If an adult is alone with a child, or if these two had less anger between them, it would be preferable to let them come up with their own words for an externalization right away.)
- Informing students that they will each have an opportunity to answer

Adult: So frustration and mad feelings take over your play?

Tannor and Jonathan: I guess . . .

- Anchoring the conversation with specific externalizations

Adult (next to children sitting at the picnic table): What are the effects of Mad Feelings and Frustrations?

You know I talk to a lot of students who lose really good friends when Frustration and Mad Feelings take over because it gets them to do things they don't really want to do or say words they would rather not say. Mad Feelings and Frustration actually get a lot of people, adults and children, to do things they regret later. If we are clear that there won't be any punishment here, I'd like each one of you to tell me one thing that the Mad Feeling or Frustration gets you to do that you'd rather not do.

Jonathan: Well . . . I guess the Mad Feeling does get me to break his stuff on purpose sometimes. I don't know why I do that . . . it's sort of mean.

Tannor: Yeah . . . and Mad Feelings get me to call you names. I'm sorry.

- Mapping the effects to a certain extent (Limited time and context will determine how much can be done.)

- Mentioning possible outcome of the unresolved problems to increase their awareness of the bigger perspective (i.e., losing friend)
- Inviting students into an externalized conversation where they can take responsibility for their own relation to the problems
- Minimizing the risk attached to self-exploration and revelation by demarginalizing their experience (it also happens to other kids and adults, and people say things they do not intend to say), removing the threat of punishment, and making it clear that each of them will be involved in this collaborative process

(Continued)

(Continued)

Adult: Can each of you tell me what's the very first thing that lets you know that Mad Feelings or Frustration might be sneaking into your friendship? Like today, think back to what was going on inside of you at the beginning of recess. Did you feel something in your body, like a lot of energy, or what were you thinking in your head?

- Continuing to map the effects of the problems on students' thoughts, feelings, behaviors, and relationships in different places and times (Note that the rest of this conversation can be pursued at another time or with someone else such as the counselor. The next steps are to simply follow a narrative map—increasing students' awareness of how the problems slowly sneak into their minds so that they can stop Mad Feelings and Frustration earlier over the course of the next few interactions.)
- Later on, it will be important to bring forth their preferred identities in how they like to be as friends and articulating why it fits better with their values and intentions (After frequent explorations such as this, students need less help processing ensuing conflicts.)

ADDITIONAL OPTIONS

- Give young people a choice as to what would be most helpful at the moment (e.g., talk to a third party or to the protagonist, be left alone, write about the problem).
- Create a context for young people to discuss the matter quietly and on their own (without an adult, if possible) and see if they can come to a resolution.
- Offer the possibility of each one of them bringing a best friend into the room for support.
- If an adult has to be involved, stay in touch with your own biases and make sure to listen carefully to each person's story.
- If an adult or a trained peer mediator is present, try to gently structure the conversation in an externalized way to reduce the blame and defensiveness in the room.

In general, it can be said that perspective is the opposite of most problems. Perspective can therefore be useful in the solution process. Problems tend to narrow our views. Understanding and gaining perspective make visible many options that were initially in the shadows.

SUMMARY OF THE PRACTICE OF EXTERNALIZING

Externalizing	Comments
A problem that is experienced as a feeling, behavior, or thought can be talked about as an external entity: • *Feelings.* What did *Anger* want you to do? • *Behavior.* When *Blaming* happened, how did you feel inside? • *Thoughts.* Is the *Critical Voice* most likely to sneak into your mind at school?	Make sure that you use the students' words for describing their own experience. If students focus on external events (e.g., teachers yelling), first thoroughly acknowledge the difficulties of the experience; then, when students are sufficiently heard, gently bring the conversation to the effect that this event might have had on them and what they might end up doing that they would rather not do.
Map the effects of the chosen externalization on all areas of life (e.g., feelings, thoughts, behaviors, identity, hopes, dreams, activities, performances, sleep, eating, relationships with parents, teachers, and friends).	Make sure that you are in touch with the students' experience and not simply bombarding them with a redundant, formulated effect question.
Have the students make a statement of position. Invite them to reflect on the effects and decide if they want to change the situation.	Leave yourself open to curiosity if, after reflection, the students say they do not want to take a stand against the problem. Explore the costs and benefits (if any) of the problem and whether there are other ways to get the same benefits with less cost.

COMMON QUESTIONS ABOUT THE EXTERNALIZATION PROCESS

"Wouldn't Externalizing Make Students Feel Less Responsible for Changing Their Behavior?"

Externalizing promotes responsibility because each individual is accountable for his or her relationship with disrespect and bullying. Externalizing assists students in becoming acutely aware of the effects of these problems so that they can take a clear stance against disrespect and bullying. After inviting students to notice the multiplicity of effects of a problem behavior, they will usually be asked what they think about all these implications and whether or not they want to do something about it (the process and timing of this is critical). In this process, students usually articulate that these behaviors are incongruent with the way they want to be in the world. A context is thus created where students, after a thorough reflection on their lives, choose by themselves to change these behaviors. People are usually much more committed to a change when they have clearly articulated the problem for themselves and decided without pressure to take action.

"Is It Really Worth the Effort? Will the Changes Be Significant?"

Some teachers like to have a reputation of being strict and might have a difficult time changing their reactions to student conflict. However, the change in teacher response will have a profound effect on student behavior. The changes will be significant for many students—specifically, students will obtain a sense of empowerment and an increased connection with their own sense of responsibility. Also, you will develop closer and richer connections with your students, who will respond to your requests because they appreciate you, not because they fear you. You will also be less likely to have one or two students rebelling and hating you as a teacher. Overall, as you and your class integrate these ideas progressively, the year should be more pleasant and less demanding for you as a teacher.

"One of My Students Was Severely Abused Two Years Ago and Isn't Any Longer. Would Externalizing Abuse Be Helpful?"

Experiences of abuse cannot be externalized; they are already external events. If abuse were to be externalized without further steps, it could be harmful to students because the event has already happened, and the person is unable to change that. An educator can have a conversation about the effects of the abuse, however, and how some of these effects may affect the young person's present life. Examples of such effects are self-hate, fear, and anger. After time has been spent acknowledging and hearing the suffering, it is definitely possible to externalize and significantly minimize their presence in students' lives. For example, you might ask the following questions: How did the abuse affect you? Do you feel self-hate? How does this self-hate affect your day? What does self-hate get you to think when you are at school?" In other words, you can't change a past event, but you can change the influence this event might still have in the student's present experience.

"What Are Your Favorite Externalizations
With Perpetrators of Bullying and Disrespect?"

It is dangerous to develop favorite externalizations. Certain problems and their relevant externalizations tend to occur more frequently; examples of these are "Mad Feelings" and "Frustration." In each culture, there are some problems and their effects that educators see more frequently. However, it is critical that educators ensure that externalizations come from students' experience of problems and not those imposed or created by educators. Although educators may feel comfortable with a certain externalization that seems to capture their observation of a problem, a student's experience of the situation may be totally different. Each person's experience is unique, and the externalization must incorporate the nuances of each student's experience of the problem. Imposing a favorite externalization on a person's experience can only lead to a disconnected and unintelligible conversation that will not be useful. In other words, even though some problems may be common, each person's experience of it is unique.

"What Kinds of Things Can We Externalize?"

In externalizing, two main factors need to be taken into consideration:

1. The most useful externalization is often the person's experience of the problem. By experience, we mean a pattern of behavior, a thought, or a feeling. Eventually, all of these aspects of experience are talked about in relation to the problem. Although problems affect people at the levels of cognition, emotion, and behavior, people focus at first on one level. For example, young people and their parents often focus on a behavior that is problematic. An educator may want to playfully externalize Sticky Hands for stealing, Sneaky Poo for encopresis, and Mr. Energy for hyperactivity. Older students, especially girls, may tend to focus more on their emotional experience of the problem, such as Depression, Self-Hate, Worries, or Boredom. Whatever is externalized, it has to be meaningful to students. Eventually, the externalization and its implications must stand in sharp contrast with the person's values and preferred identity.

2. Because the externalization must come from the student's experience of the problem, educators must choose a word that was actually used in the student's description of the problem. A word can be chosen at first as a temporary externalization, and, as the problem is more articulated, the educator and student can switch to an even more relevant externalization. Ideally, the externalization should capture most of the person's experience of the problem. Even though problems are created by a complex web of

sociocontextual molds, most people experience their problems as a real part of themselves. With bullying, for instance, it is sometimes difficult for students to separate what they truly want for themselves from what they have learned to see as desirable, such as being tough. Early on, problems can certainly be talked about as being part of a person if this idea seems to capture the students' experience more closely. Educators, however, must do so carefully and remember that problems ultimately come from a limited sense of options in a certain context.

Whatever is externalized, it has to be meaningful to students; externalizing conversations are useful when they follow people's experience of emotions, thoughts, and behaviors. We explore this important concept more in depth in the next chapter.

5

Being Respectful and Open to Students' Experiences

Connecting with experience is truly an art. It is the glue that makes all of the practices discussed in this book integrate in a useful and effective manner. Two conversations with similar content can have radically different effects, depending on whether experience was attended to or not. This is particularly true with students who struggle with disrespect, anger, and bullying because these young people almost always feel unheard, misunderstood, disrespected, and alienated.

For example, the word *respect* is often used extensively by educators who desperately try to impart this concept in students' minds. Many students—especially students who struggle—have told us, however, that the word is an adult concept that is not totally clear to them. They may be able to recite a learned definition of the word, but it is usually not connected in any meaningful and useful way to their lives. This is similar to the distinction between being taught about the values in Nepal in class versus actually living there. One type of learning is intellectual; the other is experiential. We illustrate the details of how to connect experience with the learning of the word *respect* in the Bugging Bug Project (Chapter 9). For now, we expand on the general concept of experience by exploring its application in students' and educators' lives. Understanding this concept allows educators to make many other lessons of life and reflections more relevant and meaningful to students. In this chapter, we do the following:

1. Define the word *experience*.

2. Explore students' and educators' experience of school as the contextual backdrop of disrespect and bullying (the process of connecting with students' experiences is greatly enhanced if educators can be in touch with the challenges of their own personal survival at school, past and present).

3. Discuss the particular effects of disrespect and bullying on students' and educators' experiences.

4. Explore practices to access and address these experiences.

DEFINING *EXPERIENCE*

This was my first meeting with a teenage boy, Teddy, who was pushed around by other students at his new school. He sadly told me that not only was he treated better at his previous school but that he also preferred the school in itself.

"Really? Why?" I asked.

"Because it was on the top of a big hill."

"Oh! It must have had a beautiful view; I really like mountains and views myself," I said enthusiastically, as an accomplice of sorts. He didn't reply, and I suspected that I had gone off in my own experience. Having caught myself, I humbly asked him what he liked about the hilltop.

His face lit up, and he replied, "It was really cool to go down the stairs with my skateboard."

Even though we both loved hilltops, our experiences of hills and the reasons why we appreciated them was completely different. As mentioned previously, entering into another person's perception of the world, their thoughts, and their meaning-making process is one of the most difficult practices to learn, especially when important differences exist, such as age, race, and socioeconomic status. This is also particularly hard to do in schools because of lack of time, similarities between students' behaviors, the hectic pace, and a differential of power. It is also easier to simply make associations to our own memories and ideas and assume that we know. Adults often think that they know what a young person was up to, what was meant, or what a particular behavior implied. Yet, young people make sense of the world in a remarkably creative way that is colored by their own life. Even the most experienced therapist or educator can never predict the meaning a young person will ascribe to an event. Take the following examples:

Baby Ika (two-years-old) is fascinated by a construction site where a pool is being dug out. While her mom focuses on the hole getting bigger, Ika excitedly exclaims, "Mommy, Mommy, look . . . the tractor is making a big, big, BIG sand castle."

After a day of playing with the waves on the beach, Amelia (two-and-a-half-years-old) watches the beautiful ocean sunset with her mom and dad. After a few minutes, she becomes increasingly concerned and finally says, "Mommy, will the sun really get all wet?"

Marie-Nathalie was talking about the Sticky Hand problem (stealing) with a third grader when he excitedly told her that he was going to take a plane to Mexico during the upcoming holiday. Sensing the young person's enthusiasm, Marie-Nathalie became curious and asked him if he had taken planes before, which he had. She then asked him what he liked about taking planes (this time wisely refraining from saying something like "I know! Take off and landing are pretty exciting, aren't they?"). With a grin half the width of his little face, he whispered, "I love the peanut bags."

Examples such as these may seem obvious, but they are often hidden in complex conversations of suffering and problem-saturated stories, especially with older students. Adults' errors are also not always visible and harmless. For the journey to be helpful to students, professionals must make sure that they are being respectful and open to students' experiences. This includes students' own personal account of events, how the events were lived given the context of students' lives, what specifically stood out to them, what it meant, how they understood it, and what it implies as far as they're concerned. In other words, attending to their experience implies understanding as much as possible what it is like to be in the students' shoes and walking the context of their existence. Change and exploration can only happen from that starting place.

EXPERIENCE OF SCHOOL

The Experience of Students Who Engage in Disrespect and Bullying

As discussed in many sections of this book, students who struggle with problem behaviors do so because they are trapped in unhelpful ways of being which are supported by a variety of contextual pressures. These students are usually unhappy and experience a great deal of frustration and resentment. They often feel that adults are unfair and never see their point of view. For these students, the traditional school practices of focusing on achievement, competition, evaluation, and rules create a context that invites more frustration and alienation. In addition, as discussed earlier, well-intentioned educators may try to address the issues by operating under common assumptions (e.g., students make the wrong choices, students choose willingly to be this way, students should have a better control of themselves, students deserve punishment). This may also inadvertently increase the occurrence of problems. The trouble they get in at school is usually intensified at home with parents adding another level of punishment (imagine having a bad day of conflicts at work and coming home to a partner who also criticizes you for the same issue).

For these students, school becomes an oppressive context in which they feel inadequate, constantly criticized, and pressured to be someone they can't be. Even if they would much prefer to be a model student, at that moment in time they just can't be calm and perform well given their experience of contextual blocks and anger. In the worst-case scenarios, these students feel incredibly resentful and are unable to concentrate or pay attention. They often have little hope of changing everyone's bad opinion of them. None of their more subtle efforts and successes was ever noticed, so they don't believe things can ever be better. Ultimately, they fail more frequently in the face of ever-increasing pressures placed on them to perform academically, control the problem, and fit the expectations of school.

The Experience of Adults at School

Understanding these experiences is more easily accomplished if educators can relate personally to students' experiences by either remembering some of their lives as students or connecting with their current sense of pressure at school (even as adults).

Educators as Students: Questions to Revisit the Past

What was your experience of school as a young person? Most adults can recall having picked on someone when they were young or having had a bad relationship with a particular educator. Think about a time when you were at your worst at school, how could an educator have labeled the problem? If that educator had only seen the problem and not the rest of your potential, what would have happened? We invite you to reconnect with some of those experiences if you can, as well as your relationships with certain teachers. We have written many questions in hopes that you will connect in more depth with a least four or five experiences. Take a few minutes to consider the questions. The answers to some of these questions could surprise you and provide you with valuable ideas to assist one or more of your students.

- Can you remember a specific occasion when you, as a young person, mistreated another student?
- Who was the student?
- Do you remember why you mistreated the student (not why the person deserved it)?
- Was it congruent with the kind of person you saw yourself as being?
- In which ways were your actions incongruent with your preferred ways?
- Do you recall what problem or contextual pressure might have influenced you to act in such a way?
- Do you recall anything about the school environment that might have made such behavior more likely? (We are aware that school contexts are very different nowadays.)
- Was any adult helpful in assisting you to reflect about those behaviors?
- What is it in particular that this adult did that was meaningful? (Adults usually intervene in many different ways, some of which are useful and some of which are not; beware that even if you remember the punishment in the situation, it was not necessarily punishment that fostered change but maybe simply some of the words that were said.)
- When you were a student, who was your favorite teacher?
- What did this teacher do that allowed you to connect with him or her?
- Do you remember a specific time when your life was difficult or when you had a problem and this teacher helped you through?
- What was it about this teacher's attitude that matched what was important for you then?
- What is it that this teacher saw in you then that may not have been visible to others?
- Was this teacher's view of you helpful in promoting your preferred self or the best in you?
- Did this teacher give you chances to overcome problems and succeed?
- How did this teacher influence your own development as a teacher?
- Which educator did you most dislike?
- Were you most likely to engage in a behavior when you wanted to please an adult you respected or when you wanted to avoid the adult's frustration?
- When you did or didn't behave to avoid an adult's frustration, were you more likely to try and sneak around and still do it once in a while?
- When you think of your relationship with a current student who struggles with disrespect, in which ways are you replicating what was useful to you? Is it helpful to connect with your favorite teacher or does it push you further away from the student?
- What are this student's special talents and preferred ways of being?
- Are you able to see the multiple facets of this student or at least trust that there are beautiful hidden aspects of this student?

We hope that you were able to reconnect with some memories and that these connections contribute to your helping a student in your class. If you were unable to connect with memories, acknowledging your experience of present school struggles, in itself, can also be very insightful.

Educators as Adults in the School System

Being an educator is an exhausting profession with an often unrealistic amount of responsibilities. Educators are always supposed to know it all, not have any personal needs, and be ready to handle any unhappy student. Because educators have so much to do all day long, any complication during the day can be very frustrating. There's nothing like feeling behind in the curriculum and having to constantly deal with outbursts of what seems to be unnecessary disrespect and trouble. These behaviors can push educators to exasperation.

When educators face disrespect, they are usually pushed into the position of trying to control students' behaviors. Educators spend long hours analyzing why the behavior happens and what they can do to contain it. They also keep in mind that their actions are models for other students. In this process, many educators end up questioning themselves and taking actions that they would rather avoid, such as constantly taking away needed recesses. Many educators end up feeling resentful at the situation, powerless in changing it, inadequate in their repeatedly unsuccessful attempts to handle it, and unhappy in their job. In the end, they feel like they are increasingly failing at fulfilling the pressures placed on them as educators—pressures to focus on the curriculum and not waste time, to control students' actions, and to model behaviors in prescribed ways.

Although many of the struggles are triggered by the problem of disrespect, some are also due to the pressures placed on educators by the traditional school system.

Isomorphic System

A portion of the school experiences of educators and students can, ultimately, be somewhat similar to one another. The experience of stress and impossibility reported at times by educators often resembles students' dissatisfaction with school. As illustrated in the following table, schools can be described as an isomorphic system, with each level functioning according to a very similar structure and set of pressures. Pressures placed on principals and teachers, and strategies to address them, are discussed in our book *Creating a Positive School Culture* (Beaudoin & Taylor, 2004).

The context and pressure of school shape everyone's experience in a similar way, and the hectic pace of it all often makes it difficult for people at one level to realize that the challenge is similar at other levels. People become so busy surviving their own pressures that they may be unaware of the shared experience. Ultimately, all of these pressures are experienced as blocks to a variety of possible ways of being that may be more fulfilling to different individuals.

Contextual Pressure	Teachers	Students	Common Effects
Perform, perform, perform	Teach as much curriculum as possible, focus on academia, waste no time, and minimize sharing and discussing of personal experiences.	Learn a large amount of curriculum quickly, ignore your feelings or deal with them quickly, constantly improve yourself.	Adults and students cannot take time to fully address the problem in a meaningful way. Educators and students feel a sense of inadequacy and rarely feel a sense of completion or accomplishment because there is always more to do. Everyone feels they must do better regardless of what's going on in their lives.
Stay in control	Control your class happenings and your students' behaviors. You will be evaluated on how well you control student behaviors.	Control your needs, feelings, and behaviors at all times in socially acceptable ways, even if you are burning inside.	People may feel discouragement, frustration, resentment, disconnection, and a desire to drop out at times.
Fit the mold	Be a good role model; share only the aspects of your life that fit the dominant culture; teach only in a way that is prescribed.	Be sure to please everyone (adults, peers, and parents), even if they each have different standards and expectations.	It is difficult to identify one's preferred self or perform one's preferred identity freely; many people don't know each other on a genuine level. A narrow set of aspects is visible and valued, and there is no time for personal sharing.

Although the effects of these pressures are very similar from one level to the next, people's sense of power to resist and address them can be different. Students, who are at the bottom of the hierarchy, may experience a heightened version of the effects because of their limited freedom to choose, leave, protest, or modify the pressures. In general, they cannot speak of the pressures and assume that they will be heard. Educators who become too overwhelmed or dissatisfied with the system can always decide to change their lives or career and go elsewhere. Students can't leave, at least not in any socially acceptable way. Students do not have any options, other than rebelling or subjecting themselves even if they are unhappy.

By making visible these aspects of the current educational system, our intentions are to increase educators' awareness and perspectives so that they can make informed decisions about the ways in which they want to relate to their students.

Never forget that you were once a student and don't forget what it was like to have your life constantly bombarded with adults' requests and expectations, even if they did not fit at all with your personal values, intentions, or desires or what you could actually conceive yourself as doing.

OVERLAPPING EXPERIENCES OF THE PROBLEM

Patterns of Interaction

In sum, then, both educators and students end up feeling trapped in a system that pressures for certain ways of being (school) and frustrated because they are dealing with a problem that is exacerbated by its very existence in that system (disrespect or bullying). All parties become trapped in an unhelpful pattern of interaction, where they do more of the same thing, feel increasingly stuck by their contextual blocks, and increasingly fuel the problem cycle, as illustrated in the following story and in Figure 5.1.

> *Oh, what a vicious cycle we can have going in our classrooms at times! I often think of Bruce, a student I had many years back, who would act out, make animal sounds during quiet times, and bring inappropriate objects to school. Bruce's classmates had reactions, which ranged from being mildly amused, to feeling fully irritated, excluding Bruce from any activity. On the days when Bruce was absent, the dynamics of the class would be so calm and productive . . . all day long! My reactions ranged from compassion for his struggle to annoyance at his inability to behave and belong. Knowing he needed consistency, I would follow through on discipline each time. My disciplinary tactics would either have a more gentle, understanding tone (when I felt more compassionate) or be harsher (when I felt cross or embarrassed because he and I were both acting out of control and upset). I started to notice that students would quietly ignore Bruce on the days when I would handle discipline in a more positive way, and on the days when I lost patience, they ended up more sarcastic with Bruce and each other. I realized that I, as the teacher, hold the context of the class. I noticed that students will mirror how a teacher responds to a student with a problem.*
>
> —Joann Rosatelli

This teacher's story illustrates two points: (1) the increase in frustration of all involved when a student and a teacher are trapped in a cycle of disrespect, and (2) the teacher's ability to set a more positive tone by being aware of a vicious cycle.

Figure 5.1   Students and educators get trapped in problem cycles of interaction, inadvertently supported by the context.

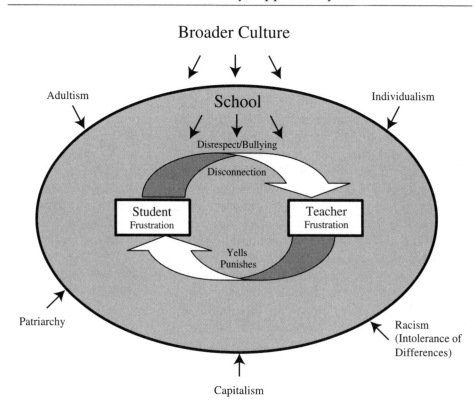

ADDRESSING THESE EXPERIENCES

Accessing Young People's Experiences

If our goal is to foster responsibility and life-altering changes, it is critical to not become trapped in our own mind and to remain open and curious about the student's own experience of events. Specifically, educators must attempt to do the following:

- Take a stance of respectful curiosity, as discussed earlier, and connect with a compassionate understanding of the context contributing to a limited sense of option.
- Externalize problems.

- Think of questions that will help students articulate their unique personal experience.
- Respond with questions in the same landscape as the discussed experience (i.e., if students talk about feelings, ask more feeling-oriented questions; if students talk about intentions, respond with questions about intentions).
- Use students' language and perspectives in conversation. Make sure to use as little adult vocabulary (e.g., the words *responsibility, respect, maturity*) as possible, unless the students use these words (which probably implies that the students actually know what they mean to them).

For example, the process of correcting a student adept in name-calling may eliminate the unwanted behavior in front of the adult, but it would not change the student's actual thinking about another student or even about the behavior of name-calling. The student may simply register the following, without much further analysis: "Adults will correct me if I name-call in front of them." For the behavior to change in a lasting and meaningful way, the student's experience of the behavior must be entered. A link must be created between the student's life, thoughts, feelings, values, and the behavior: "How did you come up with these words?" "Where did you get the idea of calling someone that? Did that happen to you?" "Why is it that people call each other names like that at school?" "What do you think of yourself doing that?" If you engage in such conversation and there is a possibility of consequences at the end, students' experience will be one of fear, in which case nothing terribly personal will be said other than that which may reduce the likelihood of punishment. The issue of discipline must be eliminated, and students must feel safe to turn inward and explore or reflect on their actual experience.

Connecting With Your Own Experience as an Educator

Have you ever done something against your better judgment as an educator? What contributed to that decision? It is worthwhile for educators to take time to reflect on the pressures they operate under and to name, or externalize, a problem for themselves, too. The questions listed in the problem exercise in Chapter 3 can be used for this purpose. In addition, drawing a sketch of the possible vicious cycle between self and the student struggling with disrespect or between the students struggling with conflicts may yield some new perspectives of the problem. When the pattern becomes clearer, it becomes possible to explore the early signs of its occurrence and develop a code with the student so that prevention strategies can be implemented. For example, a teacher who was collaborating with our agency developed an excellent understanding of a student's struggle (Discouragement) and the vicious cycle previous educators had fallen into. After a narrative conversation, she eventually developed such an excellent understanding of the externalized problem that she could actually anticipate challenging moments. With this new awareness, she took the habit of discretely giving the student brief little notes with comments such as "You're almost done!" or "You can do it," which had the effect of short-circuiting Discouragement and empowering the student to persevere in his work. The student was so touched by this caring gesture that he secretly started a scrapbook with the notes and kept it in his desk at all times. Within weeks, this student, who had a history of power struggles and incomplete work with previous teachers, turned completely around and progressively became more successful.

Addressing the Vicious Cycle

To chip away at the vicious cycle, each party must examine his or her own inadvertent contribution to the pattern and do something different that has a greater likelihood of reducing the externalized problem. They must move away from blaming each other and into a deeper understanding of the problem between them. In other words, a similar problem (such as Frustration) can be externalized for both parties, and each can become aware of the unhelpful effects of Frustration on his or her own behaviors and thoughts. The enemy then becomes the externalization, Frustration, and not the student. The goal then is to reduce Frustration and not to contain the students (the students will contain themselves once Frustration shrinks).

By this process, we do not mean breaking school regulation and completely eliminating consequences for behaviors. Rather, we suggest you think carefully about how your decisions affect Frustration and see if it is possible to maneuver in the situation in such a way as to reduce, when you can, the constant addition of more resentment in the student's life. For example, sometimes it can be useful to let some smaller events go unreported if you can and let the student know that you dislike seeing him or her in trouble all the time. Young people can feel very grateful for your support in these situations; they'll appreciate you and try harder to push away the problem behavior. They will be more likely to see possibilities beyond their respective contextual blocks. Other times it may mean letting a student know that you really don't want to call parents to report the problem behavior but that you have to (but only if you genuinely feel that way). This process can also include an acknowledgment that you are both stuck in a system that doesn't allow you to do exactly what you would prefer. Sometimes it is even interesting to ask students, genuinely, what they would do if they were an educator and had a student who struggled with disrespect and bullying.

Application

Once in a while, Marie-Nathalie receives a request to work with students who refuse to talk to any adults about their involvement with bullying. Sometimes these students come in under duress and simply sit with their back to Marie-Nathalie or angrily warn that they will not talk or listen. This oppositional situation can resemble the interactions between teachers and these students, who angrily state they hate school and everyone in it. Although connecting with experience is important in all meaningful interactions, it becomes the only way to have any conversation at all with these young people, who have obviously been profoundly alienated. Applying the ideas discussed in earlier chapters of this book, a conversation with these young people often proceeds as follows:

Student (angry): I don't want to be here, and I won't answer any of your questions.

Adult (gently and slowly): It sounds like you have been through this many times already and are fed up. I guess I'd be really fed up too if a bunch of adults had been trying to force me into changing.

Student: Yeah, I sure am.

The student's experience is one of anger at adults, a desire to not be there, and a feeling of exasperation with this process. The adult attempts to connect with the student's experience by putting herself in his shoes and acknowledging how annoying it must be to be trapped into talking one more time (about something he's ashamed of) to an adult stranger who will probably want to teach him something. Depending on the student's reaction, one can either choose to pursue this by wondering about how many adults have tried to moralize him or what he hates the most about talking to an adult.

Adult: What would you rather be doing if you didn't have to be here?

Student (hesitating): Probably skateboarding with my friends.

The adult knows that when she doesn't want to be somewhere, she knows exactly what else she could do with the time. It is easier to talk about one's passions than about one's struggles.

Adult: How long have you been skateboarding? Do you do tricks and stuff?

Student (getting more into the conversation): Yeah, my friends have shown me a bunch of tricks on a half pipe.

The adult expresses her curiosity about the student's hobby and himself as a person separate from the problem. There is more to this student than the problems, and the adult is interested in bringing that forth. This also makes him feel respected and perceived as a whole person rather than simply a bully. The adult also notes that he has

Adult: Cool! Do you have many friends who do that with you?

Student: Yeah, there's three of us.

Adult: Do they come to this school?

Student: No . . . I wish . . .

Adult: Would that make a big difference if they came here?

Student: It sure would.

Adult: Do they see you differently than what people think of you here?

Student: Yeah, they think I'm alright.

Adult (gently): What is it that people here don't understand about you?

friends and is therefore able to make good connections sometimes (as opposed to students who don't have any friends at all and are isolated with their problem).

The adult lets him know that the problems are not necessarily a representation of who he is and who he wants to be. She acknowledges that the context contributes to what he does and how people perceive him. She also wants to stay as far as possible from any conversation about his wrongdoings at this point because she's sure he has been submerged by that before and it obviously hasn't worked. Connecting with his experience of being misunderstood and alienated needs to happen before anything else can be explored. The adult is wondering if he is engaged enough in the conversation to take the risk of telling more about these struggles (it is a risk given his experience).

Student: I just hate this school. Teachers are always on my back, yelling and accusing me of everything, and others take advantage of that at recess and blame everything on me. It's so unfair. It makes me mad and I can't think of anything else for the rest of the day.

Adult: That sounds terrible. How does that affect you? Does it make it hard to pay attention in class and do your work?

The adult is connected with compassion and his experience of the vicious cycle within the context of school. She's connecting with her own experiences of having been stuck in classrooms and required to pay attention, even when she was boiling with feelings inside. Note that this connection with her own experience is in the background and not discussed because she wouldn't want it to take the focus away from his unique experience and suffering.

(Continued)

(Continued)

Student: Yeah. I'm always lost and behind.

If the student's experience had reverted back to reluctance and fear (to focus on his struggles), the adult could talk in generalized terms about students who are mad instead of him directly to make the conversation safer. For example, "When students struggle with mad feelings, how are they treated by others?" "When students have mad feelings, do they have a hard time paying attention in class?"

Adult: Most people would probably be lost and behind. What have you tried to make things better?

Student: I've tried ignoring the others at recess and not getting mad, but why bother because the teacher always thinks it's me anyway if there's a problem.

His experience seems to be one of discouragement (assuming good intentions and relying on the fact that most people who struggle with problems have tried to find a solution and experimented with the few options that did come to their minds despite the contextual blocks).

Adult: So this problem has gotten the teacher distrustful or suspicious of you?

Student: I guess . . .

Adult: Do you think the mad feelings have started giving you a bad reputation?

The student is starting to externalize a problem and mapping its effects. The conversation, now that the student is engaged and connected with his experience, will proceed according to the map discussed in earlier chapters of exploring the effects on behaviors, thoughts, feelings, various relationships, identity, future, and so on.

Student: Yeah. Everyone thinks I'm this mean bully, and I'm not.

Adult: What do the Mad Feelings get you to do that you don't really want to do that made you earn that reputation?

Once adults enter students' experiences, connect with them, examine the context, and externalize a problem as an unwanted way of being, change is finally in motion.

How can educators ensure that progress will continue and that preferred ways of being will survive the multiple challenges that young people face?

6

Making Changes Last for More Than a Week

Change is a sequence of moments in time, not a single event.

THE DANDELION PROBLEM

As children we all appreciated the bright yellow flowers we saw in the yard. We may have even collected them and offered them as a bouquet to our mothers, fathers, or grandparents—until one fateful day when someone said, "Ugh, those are weeds!" That day, we learned to categorize flowers as good or bad flowers—and most likely never picked a bouquet of dandelions again.

As an adult, you may realize that this is a social construction (in fact, dandelions have recognized medicinal properties) and want to relate differently to the dandelion. But, is it possible to develop a passion for its beauty? It would be very difficult to erase the social training. At best, you could minimize its influence on your thoughts and feelings, but you would always remember that it is a weed in society's flora.

The same can be said about many other experiences. For adults, it would be hard to change our perception of what is attractive in each gender. It would be difficult, for instance, for people in our culture to find the tiny lotus feet (about four inches in length) of Chinese women attractive, even in our culture of fifty years ago. It is difficult for many citizens of other countries to understand that young women who are unhealthy and sometimes close to death due to starvation are the occidental symbol of beauty. In sum, it is challenging to change a way of being that has been present for many years and supported by a powerful context. This is also the case of young people who have learned, lived, and survived disrespect and aggression for many years.

THINKING OUTSIDE THE BOX

Another example to illustrate the complexity of thinking outside a given frame is the common puzzle below in Figures 6.1 and 6.2. In this brain-teaser, we are instructed to attach all of the xs using only four lines and without lifting the pencil.

Figure 6.1   Attach all the xs without lifting your pencil and using only four straight lines.

X	X	X
X	X	X
X	X	X

Most people look at this puzzle and struggle. It is difficult to solve because our mind is locked in a certain way of thinking that has much to do with childhood learning and societal influence. We are taught to stay within the lines when we color, connect the dots to make a picture, and, generally, think within the box. For some, not quickly figuring out the solution might leave them feeling inadequate, unintelligent, and simply incapable, especially if they are working within a group. Some people may not spend much time wondering about the problem at all. Others may not get stuck by the conventional problem-solving methods and find the answer, which has to do with going outside the dotted lines. Yet even with that hint, most people become lost as to how to function outside of a dotted line.

The trick, as many know, is that the lines must leave the frame to connect all of the dots. This implies, then, that we must see the box and even conceive of the possibility of exiting it to find the solution (see Figure 6.2 on page 86).

In this context, the puzzle is just a simple game that has no implications in our lives. Grades, punishments, and intimate relationships do not depend on us going outside of the box. There are no emotions cluttering our minds and no one waiting for us to change our thinking, yet it is hard to break out of the confines and change our limited thinking (specified thinking).

The next time you feel impatient about a person's slow change, try remembering your struggle to move outside of the puzzle box or try putting a bouquet of dandelions on your table and appreciating it. Change is a process because it is difficult to notice our limited thinking in the first place. Once we know it is limited, we may have difficulty finding another way to think or act, and, finally, even when we find the new or preferred way of being, it can be challenging to hold on to it. The only way change can happen is through gentle exploration of one's different ways of being; with support, time, witnesses, and restorying; and with a constant revisiting of the justifications for the preferred self. But how can we identify this preferred self and sustain progress?

MULTIPLE SELVES: WHO IS THE REAL PERSON?

From a social constructionist, narrative, and brain research point of view, people have many selves. No one self is more real than another. This statement is contradictory to many popular psychology handbooks and traditional Western philosophies, which assume a core personality.

People's experiences of themselves are constructed in relationships and evolve over time (Gergen, 1985; Hoffman, 1990). Relationships, particularly if they are with influential people, provide the canvas for making meaning from experiences. In other words, we could argue that people who live in a vacuum would have a very limited sense of self, if any, because no one would be affected by their presence, and no one would be available to reflect an experience of them. These people would have no base to experience themselves as clever or funny, for example, without an interaction with another being that would allow them to ascribe that interpretation to those particular ways of being.

If the self is constructed in relationships, then each individual has multiple selves that reflect different experiences of self-in-relationships (Gergen, 1985, 1991; Hoffman, 1990). These different selves exist in the past, present, and future. Particular versions of these selves are brought to the forefront of experience by the context and the presence of certain people in a certain space. Among the many possible selves, some are preferred to others in terms of their effects on relationships and their congruency with one's intentions (and others are less preferred). For instance, many people experience themselves as shy in certain relationships and very outgoing in others.

Figure 6.2   The solution requires that we go outside the confines of the box.

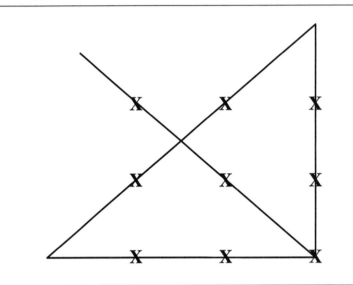

Similarly, young people can be experienced as very kind and loving in certain relationships and very angry or aggressive in others. In fact, many educators and therapists meet parents who are baffled to hear about their children's misbehavior in school. Because of the traditional antagonistic relationship between parents and educators, we often assume that these parents do not know their children very well. In reality, this difference in experience is often the result of young people's multiple facets. It is quite common for a person to engage in behaviors that may appear to contradict their intentions. In reality, these behaviors are simply different versions of selves that are brought forth by context. The only influence teachers can have, then, is to engage students in reflection and assist them in understanding, articulating, and eventually choosing the self that is more in line with their preferred ways of being. This becomes even more complicated when someone is trying to change. Indeed, when adults and especially young people are trying to behave in a more preferred way, witnesses to the behavior will often be doubtful of the effort and mistake the new behavior for a pretense or a manipulation. The protagonist, trying to change, may also feel uneasy in the new way of being, even though it is preferred.

It is difficult for everyone involved to believe that the person, even with genuine intentions or with success at resisting a problem, has developed a new, preferred identity. It is actually almost impossible to believe. The change can only become significant when it is integrated into a story.

STORIES

A story consists of a sequence of events in time as opposed to an isolated event. Everyone has stories about their identities. You can think of yourself as shy and relate a list of moments in time that made you think of yourself as such. You also can have a story of yourself as determined and share a series of events that allowed you to draw that conclusion. Both of these examples are stories of identities, even if we don't usually think of those accounts in that particular way. It becomes important to see stories for what they are when dealing with people who are unhappy with themselves or how they are perceived. By definition, stories are composed of the following elements:

- one or more protagonists
- a purpose
- a series of actions (at least two events, which are the presence or absence of a behavior, thought, or feeling, such as the presence of Kicking or the absence of Disrespect)
- linked events across time

Story Exercise

To help clarify this concept, consider an example in your own life. Think of a problem that you have overcome and fill out the open-ended sentences below:

I used to have a problem with _____

_____

I think it started when _____

_____

In fact, what happened was that _____

_____

And then _____

_____

(Continued)

(Continued)

I became more _____

_____

The   worst   time   was   probably   when   _____

_____

If I were to name one person who might have inadvertently supported it, I'd say

_____

_____

Without realizing it, this person supported the problem by _____

_____

In that particular context of my life, I could not see any other options because

_____

_____

Can you recognize the protagonist, purpose, actions, and time? These elements are in problem as well as preferred stories. Without realizing it, your presentation of a problem automatically takes the literary form of a story. Try presenting a version of the problem without telling a story—it is difficult and perhaps impossible.

Storying a Preferred Identity

Since problems always become embedded in stories, preferred identities must also be storied. The influence of problems must be contrasted with the preferred identity. In other words, a problem is first externalized, and a map of its effect on thoughts, feelings, behaviors, relationships, and identity is thoroughly completed. The student, then, becomes invited to make a statement of position. Students progressively are invited to articulate and contrast their preferred way of being in the same manner (illustrated in Figure 6.3). In so doing, however, careful attention must be paid to the use of language and the natural tendency of our mind to fill in the blanks.

CREATING STORIES THROUGH LANGUAGE

Our language and process of communicating are structured by subjects, verbs, and protagonists and actions. Language is not simply a tool to communicate an experience; language actually constitutes experience. Can

Figure 6.3 The problem story is contrasted with the preferred story. Students must first be invited to articulate the effects of Bullying and Disrespect on several aspects of their lives and then assisted in identifying alternative experiences that are more preferred and congruent with their values.

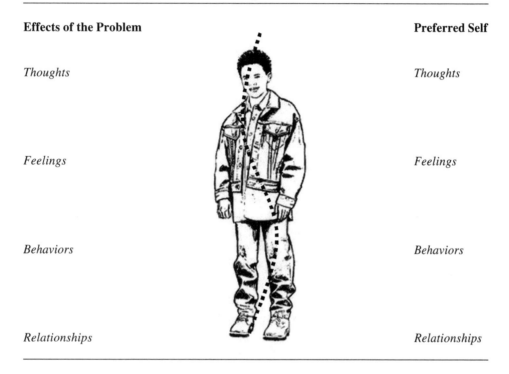

Effects of the Problem

Thoughts

Feelings

Behaviors

Relationships

Preferred Self

Thoughts

Feelings

Behaviors

Relationships

you think of an experience outside of language? If we didn't have a word for *shaved*, we would not perceive shaved versus unshaven people. Similarly, Ilongot people in the Philippines have an emotion called *liget*, which consists of anger, energy, passion, possibly tearfulness, singing, distraction, and a readiness to "slice the head of a neighboring tribesman" (Rosaldo, as cited in Gergen, 1991). We do not have a single word for such emotion; thus, that emotion does not exist or rather is not recognized in our culture. We have the words *tomboy* and *misogynist*, but words with the exact opposite meaning do not exist in English. Consequently, those characteristics are not distinguished as identities. We perceive people and create stories about self and others that are heavily structured by the language and connotations of our culture. Language is a cultural tool that forces us to think inside a box.

MENTALLY FILLING THE BLANKS

It is common knowledge that witnesses of accidents or crimes relate different versions of the same event. This has a scientific explanation:

People always have an incomplete view of an event and, without realizing it, mentally fill the blanks in their mind in a way that seems coherent to them. This process is very much colored by people's understanding of the situation—by the cultural discourses that have shaped them and the meaning they ascribe to the situation.

Take this event, for instance:

> Alex took the garbage can out by the driveway.

In itself, this event does not mean anything; it is simply an event. Now, here is the event with additional actions:

> Alex took the garbage can out by the driveway. Mother could arrive from work any minute now. Quickly the brightest porch lights were lit, and the dog was let out. Alex then rushed to the living room window and waited expectantly to see her arrive.

This series of events is now looking more like a story. It links together many events. You may find yourself developing feelings for the protagonist. These feelings would probably be clearer if more details were given about the character. Yet even if limited details were given about the protagonist, your mind probably created a visual image of the scene. What did you imagine: adult or youngster, male or female? Your characterization of the protagonist depends on the cultural scripts you have integrated about which gender and age group would take the garbage out. You are also probably ascribing intentions. Why do you think he or she is doing this? The story does not specify socioeconomic status, gender, age, race, or intentions. Is mother arriving by foot, car, bus, or bicycle? Your mental image is biased by your own life, and it may not even occur to you that it could be different. Your mind has probably filled up those blanks as well as countless others.

If the story stopped here, you would probably ascribe an identity to Alex, even with such little information (only four sentences). That is the power of events linked together in a story. So far we have only described actions. We continue the story by adding goals and intentions:

> Alex took the garbage can out by the driveway. Mother could arrive from work any minute now. Quickly the brightest porch lights were lit, and the dog was let out. Alex then rushed to the living room window and waited expectantly to see her arrive. He knew all these gestures would make her furious.

The knowledge of goals and intentions often deeply affects people's perception of another. Meaning is suddenly made of the situation in a powerful way. Notice that initially you most likely ascribed a positive connotation to the behaviors and suddenly switched to a negative connotation after discovering their meaning. Curiously, however, problem behaviors, and their negative effects, never actually reflect a person's true values and preferred identity. They usually only reflect that a problematic pattern of interaction has developed in a certain context. Most of the time, the context is invisible to us unless we seek to grasp it by exploring relevant questions and by assuming that, given an experience of choice, this young person may actually not engage in those behaviors. The end of the story provides a glimpse into the variety of factors that may contribute to the complexity of a problem behavior:

> Alex took the garbage can out by the driveway. Mother could arrive from work any minute now. Quickly the brightest porch lights were lit, and the dog was let out. Alex then rushed to the living room window and waited expectantly to see her arrive. He knew all these gestures would make her furious, and when she was furious she required that he eat in his bedroom. He could then avoid the angry conversations with his mother's new partner and just quietly listen to his favorite music.

PERSPECTIVES CREATE STORIES

Many stories are possible about the same event, depending again on subculture and perspective. The unfortunate events in the life of Marie-Nathalie's client, Leslie, strikingly show this point. Leslie was twelve years old when she was referred to therapy. She dearly loved her father, in spite of his tendency to be intensely angry, and had been completely devastated by his death two years earlier. She had been fairly depressed since then, not only because she lost her father but also because she lost her mother to the workforce, which she had to enter to provide for the family. Her grief and sadness made her more vulnerable to constant bullying at school, and her grades fell. One day, she finally decided to take her life and attempted suicide. After she was released from the hospital, she was referred to Marie-Nathalie for narrative therapy. Two weeks after Leslie started working on sadness, a popular boy from school raped her. Leslie shifted from sadness to intense mad feelings and started to have conflicts at school with teachers and students. Because she reported the rape, students further bullied her at school, and she was subjected to a traditional police interrogation: an interview with a nice officer and another interview with an officer who challenged her story and accused her of lying.

Leslie became full of rage, and, unable to contain it all, she started to superficially cut the skin on both of her arms several times per day (as she had seen a friend do). The school staff became concerned and recommended hospitalization, which multiplied the amount of rage and powerlessness that she was experiencing in her life. Someone had taken her body by force, others had interrogated her with force for hours, the gossip in school about her was out of control, her feelings felt out of control, and now she could not even go home and felt forced into a hospital. If the school staff had considered that the experience of being forcefully disrespected and rendered powerless was causing the cutting, they might have made different choices. All these dreadful events came as a succession of horror, which, unfortunately, culminated with her grandfather's death a month later. Leslie started getting into more trouble and came under close surveillance from many different people in different fields, who each had a different story of the events, including Leslie herself, as shown in the following description:

- *Leslie.* Leslie considered herself a loser and a bad person. In her twelve-year-old view, if everyone saw her as a loser, and if all these bad events happened to her, then something was deeply wrong with her. Moreover, she experienced herself as hateful toward herself and the world and felt guilty for the destructive reactions she had in many situations. Her mind was full of confusion and intense feelings too difficult to contain or understand. (Causality was located within her because of individualistic assumptions as well as the patriarchal context where women commonly feel responsible for everything wrong happening around them.)

- *School.* The school engaged in the common assumption that if a student has problems, her parents or, specifically, her mother must be doing something wrong. The school staff was very antagonistic toward Leslie's mother and quick to blame her for most incidents (e.g., regarding the rape, they felt Leslie's mother didn't ensure her safety; regarding the cutting, they felt Leslie's mother was negligent for failing to remove the blades; regarding Leslie's anger, they felt Leslie's mother didn't support her daughter enough). They required a psychiatric evaluation and medication.

- *Psychiatrist.* The psychiatrist approached the situation with his own biological bias: A person who shifts from angry moods to depressed moods must be bipolar. He consequently prescribed a heavy dosage of an expensive medication. This simply further enraged Leslie, who felt once again powerless, misunderstood, and unable to control her life, her experiences, or her body. It also further reinforced the idea that something was profoundly wrong with her. This again completely disregarded the context of Leslie's life.

- *Therapist.* As a narrative therapist, Marie-Nathalie approached the situation from a contextual analysis and believed that Leslie's rage and depression were completely normal given the events in her life. In fact, Marie-Nathalie would have been more worried if Leslie had faced all of this in a calm and unaffected way. Therapy focused on the following four areas:
  1. Hearing Leslie's acute suffering and her perspective, which she reported few others did.
  2. Raising questions to assist Leslie in seeing the bigger contextual picture of events as opposed to self-blaming.

3. Externalizing mad feelings so that Leslie could manage them in a more constructive way.

4. Attempting, whenever possible and relevant, to make visible another story of herself, the story of a Leslie who is kind (e.g., she took care of her grandfather for hours during the weekend), courageous (e.g., she was often concerned about what was just and fair for others and would stand up for it), and generous (e.g., with her family and friends) (see Figure 6.4).

All of the descriptions in Figure 6.4 are simply different perspectives and stories of the same situation. None of these can be seen as an objective truth per se about Leslie's identity.

Figure 6.4   An illustration of Leslie's preferred story.

Effects of the Problem	Preferred Self
Thoughts	**Thoughts**
I hate school, everyone.	*I wish people were fair.*
I don't care about life.	*I don't want to hurt anyone.*
Feelings	**Feelings**
Impatience, anger	*Caring for others, compassion*
Frustration, self-hate	*Guilt, regrets of problem behavior*
Behaviors	**Behaviors**
Self-cutting, vandalizing	*Helps mother, grandfather*
Smoking, high-risk behavior	*Patient, playful, good babysitter*
Relationships	**Relationships**
Distrust from adults	*Appreciated by grandfather*
No friends, conflicts	*Good with animals*
Identity	**Identity**
Bad person	*Caring person*

AN EDUCATOR'S QUESTION: IF TRUTHS DON'T EXIST, HOW DO WE KNOW WHICH STORY TO TRUST?

From a narrative perspective, what really matters is people's preferred ways of being, the effects that each one of these stories have on protagonists' lives and people around them, as well as an awareness of the cultural assumptions that color the perspectives.

Stories Have an Automatic Refill System

Have you ever noticed how hard it is to make yourself stop thinking that someone does not like you? Because uncertainty is hard to tolerate for many Westerners, our focus naturally becomes one of proving or disproving a belief. As such, if you assume someone does not like you, you notice any event that may support your assumption and inadvertently use it to extend the problem story. If your focus is such, then other neutral or even positive events may go unnoticed. Apply this process to school. If teachers have a problem story of themselves as incompetent or unable to handle a class, they will most likely notice these types of moments more so than others. If students believe their teachers do not like them, then every comment will be taken as a criticism. It takes awareness and effort to step outside of the automatic refill system and notice other events.

Stories Have a Past and a Future

Most people have an explanation for how the problem developed and perceive the future as evolving in a similarly problematic way. Some parents say, "This defiance problem was evident at birth." Of course, you can take any child and say there were some struggles soon after birth. The difference is the meaning that is ascribed to the struggles and whether or not the meaning is linked with a series of events giving it the form of a problem story loaded with significance. Given the power of time, it is imperative that new stories be revisited in the past and extended into the future to have any likelihood of surviving.

Intensity of Events

An event that carries some experiential intensity is much more likely to be storied than a neutral event. That is, if you have an overall good and peaceful day except for fifteen minutes of intense conflict with someone, the more intense—and in this case negative—experience will most likely dominate your memory. You will struggle to understand and make meaning of the incident. You will fit the events in some narrative structure that most likely makes you the victim or the perpetrator. Most people and young people in particular have a story about being victims because they know their intentions are not to harm. This process is also due to the traditional narrative structures of stories (i.e., the bad person and the poor victim) and to an individualistic view of human interaction, which reduces complex relationships into a dichotomy and attributes causality to an individual.

Nevertheless, intensity of events has important implications. In schools, the experiential intensity of problems is rarely matched by an equivalent intensity of appreciation. For young people who are frequently in trouble, this means they can only develop a very negative story of themselves and of the schools unless efficient interventions redirect the situation. For educators, this means that they can quickly burn out if they continue facing frequent, intense problems of disrespect and bullying. A vicious cycle is quickly established between an exasperated teacher and a resentful student, who both have very elaborate problem stories of the other.

Multiple Life Arenas

When a problem story infiltrates different spheres of life, it can quickly take over as a dominant identity. Consider the following story:

Russ was a teacher and had a fascination for nature, which he respected and protected thoughtfully. After working for a couple of years, he and his partner decided to permanently move to a rural area. He found another teaching job, and they bought a house. Although he loved his new location, he became quickly aware of the different values that were held in his new work environment. Specifically, tension grew with a particular coworker and a few students. Soon, they nicknamed Russ City Boy and teased him about various issues. Russ quietly held on to his values.

One weekend, Russ cleaned his field and property by burning a small pile of wood. Having accomplished a lot, he extinguished the fire and went to rest inside his house. In the meantime, the wind picked up, revived embers, and started a small property fire. The City Boy label became painfully present in his mind. The two most important contexts of his life, work and home, were suddenly linked together by a potentially negative identity label loaded with meaning. Each event separately would have been uncomfortable, but the proximity in time of the events and their direct association with an identity could have triggered a huge amount of self-doubt.

Fortunately, Russ was able to hold on to the contextual issues at hand and, most importantly, to hold on to his preferred identity by connecting with people in his life who did not believe in the City Boy label. Russ knew that people are who they are perceived to be. If his partner, friends, coworkers, and family members had all developed the problem story of City Boy, it would have been nearly impossible for Russ to escape the problem identity. In this situation, Russ was able to stay connected with his preferred self by interacting with people who saw, validated, and recognized his preferred self. He was able to choose to be with friends and loved ones and to visit contexts that brought forward his sense of agency and confidence. The City Boy story was soon abandoned as he moved on to other work environments, with his own sense of self supported by others.

Students' Narrow Life Arenas

Young people are not as privileged as adults when it comes to escaping problem identities. On one hand, they have less power to determine their own identity given their age and dependency. On the other hand, they also have fewer contexts to rely on; school and home usually dominate their lives, and these contexts are heavily interconnected. If a problem identity develops at school, it quickly invades relationships with parents. If a teacher accuses a young person of being a manipulator, parents often become watchful of such symptoms (and of course many situations can easily be interpreted as such). This leaves the young person with very little possibility of holding on to a preferred self.

Effects of Problem Stories at School

In schools, problem stories are particularly devastating because they can be held by a large number of people over many years and become a very serious obstacle for anyone wishing to change. Consider, for example, the following situation:

> Little Johnny (third grader) takes the cool pencil away from the student next to him. You witness the gesture. What do you say or do?
>
> _____
>
> _____

Now, take this a step further:

> Little Johnny (third grader) takes the cool pencil away from the student next to him. You witness the gesture, and you remember that his previous teacher complained the whole year about his stealing behavior. What do you say or do?
>
> _____
>
> _____
>
> How are your responses different?
>
> _____
>
> _____

For many people, the response in the context of a problem story is much harsher and often more punitive.

If the student changed and was simply looking at the pencil, he is likely to not understand such a harsh stance and will interpret the teacher's reaction as an unfair dislike for him as a person. When a student feels that way, other problems quickly develop, such as discouragement, sadness, anxiety, not wanting to come to school, opposition to authority, and so on. Thus, a problem story often leads to an increasing number of problems.

If the student has not changed and is still struggling with a stealing problem, he will dislike the new teacher immediately, and his resentment will reduce his motivation to change. Students, when empowered to do so, are known to accomplish a lot to please an adult whom they love and admire. The problem story can simply eliminate this new possibility for change.

When sharing information about students, educators must be keenly aware of the type of information shared and the implications in the new relationship. A cost-benefit analysis must be considered as well as the manner in which the problem is represented. Often, the problem story, frustration, and discouragement of one teacher trickle down to the next teacher, with very little space for innovation and hope.

Summary of the Characteristics of Meaningful Stories

• Meaning can be independent of the actual behaviors that generate it. Johnny's story illustrated this process. In school, for example, two students can say exactly the same comment or joke, with different interpretations by different teachers. An actual behavior may have a specific meaning with one person and a completely separate one with another.

• No event is remembered outside of meaning making: What is experienced during a day will be related to someone else only if it had meaning or if there is a search for meaning. Simple, normal activities of life, such as going to the bathroom, itching, or sneezing, for instance, are not discussed unless they come to represent a concern or an annoyance and begin to have meaning. In school, a student behavior can remain unnoticed and meaningless for one teacher and be completely annoying and pathologized by another teacher.

• Meaning is always ascribed to events experienced with intense affect (this does not mean that unaffective events are not meaningful). When people experience a situation with intense affect, they find an explanation for it, whether or not this explanation is realistic. For instance, in school, when a student becomes withdrawn or negative, everyone—students and teachers—comes up with their own personal theory or explanation for the situation.

• Once meaning is ascribed, it is very difficult to modify it unless compelling contradictory observations are articulated into a rich alternative story. For example, if you develop a story that a student is a troublemaker, then it will be a very hard and slow process to start trusting the student.

• Meaning is more powerful when similar conclusions are drawn in different contexts of life. If a student in your class struggles with disrespect and you find out that a previous teacher (or the parents) also faced those same issues, you are more likely to get hooked into a very powerful problem story about the student.

- Meaning colors what is noticed and what isn't in the course of life. When you perceive students as having problems with bullying, you are less likely to notice their more subtle gestures of kindness.

- Meaning is greater if it is built on a historical foundation and has an estimated trajectory in the future. When educators hear for a couple of years about a student with bullying issues, they are more likely to ascribe meaning to the history in a way that pathologizes the student's identity and even projects the story in the future. For example, Marie-Nathalie worked with a principal who became exasperated with a boy's trouble habit and would, in personal conversations, share her conviction that he was going to become "one of those murderers that we read about in the newspaper" (see Geoffrey's story in Chapter 10). This sad comment indicated this principal's profound hopelessness about assisting the student, the extent of the effects of the problem story on her, and the huge challenge that lay in front of this student, who wanted desperately to change, despite his inability to successfully do so early on.

AUDIENCE: YOU ARE WHO YOU ARE PERCEIVED TO BE

Remember the last time you gave a speech or performed in front of a large audience of adults, perhaps at graduation or in another context. You might have practiced at home. Imagine that you did an outstanding job at home but perceived disappointment or even criticism from your audience during the public performance. Would you be able to hold on to your identity as a great performer based on the home performance? This may sound like a silly and simple question, but in reality it is not. Of course, the answer is no; the performance in front of people would carry much more weight in your self-evaluation than your private experience of yourself. This is particularly true if the audience is a group of people who have status or some form of power in your life. Another example would be to remember receiving admiration or appreciation for an aspect of yourself; once noticed by another in a meaningful way, the existence of that aspect of yourself is more likely to become real and tangible (unless you struggle with a critical voice brushing the compliment off). If students are never told that they are being kind, funny, or clever, the option to think that of themselves will not even exist (see the Bugging Bug Project in Chapter 9 for meaningful examples of this process).

You are who you are perceived to be. If everyone in your life perceives you as a mean individual, it would be very hard for you to believe that you are a thoughtful person. A group of people somewhere, somehow, would have to mirror that perception of you for it to have any real substance. This observation is very important and holds many implications in schools, which are a significant audience for young people's lives. Sadly, schools are organized in such a way that more often than not they become an audience for problem stories of young people's identities. More students are acknowledged at recess or at the principal's office for problems than for helpful behaviors that bring public, meaningful recognition. When a student is publicly noticed several times misbehaving, he or she not only develops a problem story of her- or himself but also countless other students gossip about the student's problem. How can students possibly change when efforts and intentions most often remain invisible, while problems are broadcast to large groups?

You may think, as an educator, that you make great efforts to acknowledge progress. But honestly, how often do you wake up in the morning appreciating the absence of a flu or an ear infection? In the hectic pace of life, we focus on problems when they are present but quickly forget to be grateful when they are gone. As a result, and most unfortunately, before progress is even noticeable to the outside observer, a motivated individual will have subtly made several attempts to change his or her life with limited success and acknowledgment. Many give up before observers notice and appreciate the efforts. This is particularly true for observers who have suffered from the problem, are somewhat frustrated, and stuck in their own version of the problem story. Stories held by school audiences can become the main obstacle in an individual's effort to change, especially when the individual is a student with very little power in the system. This issue is further addressed in Chapter 10.

THE THREAD OF NEW STORIES: RECAPITULATION

Externalizing

As discussed earlier, externalizing problems allows one to take a critical stance against problems and create a space for a new story. It empowers young people to take a stance against the problem, not against themselves.

Mapping Effects

Mapping includes exploring thoroughly the various effects of the problem in students' lives. Skilled questions can quickly assist protagonists in seeing the effects of the problem, notice how it infiltrates their lives, and make a decision to explore other ways of being.

Statement of Position

A statement of position includes clearly articulating one's reasons to change, making a decision to do so, and developing confidence and hope in one's ability to engage in preferred ways.

Connecting With Values

Articulating and connecting with one's values in challenging circumstances is vital in creating a preferred story. Sarah, for instance, used to struggle with anger and negativity and engage in power struggles with adults. As she became clearer and increasingly in touch with her values of compassion, perspective, and respect, she became what she called a *spring person*—a person who is affected by the struggles of life but is able to bounce back quickly to her values and behave in a congruent way.

Digging for Successful Choices and Actions

Life is rich in events that are forgotten and unstoried. Imagine if you were to consciously remember everything you saw, every choice you made, and every step you took. It would be quite overwhelming. Yet as difficult as this may be to believe, everyone—even the person whose life is most saturated by problems—has moments of being their preferred way. Compassionate conversations allowing the retrieval and understanding of those moments (unique outcome) can be powerful building blocks of change.

Developing an Audience

Witnesses of new developments are paramount to move the new story into existence. It is only through relationships with others that a person will be mirrored their preferred self and its effect (for more on audiences, see Andersen, 1987; Dickerson, 1998; Freedman & Combs, 1996; Friedman, 1995; White, 2000; White & Epston, 1990; Zimmerman & Dickerson, 1996).

REAUTHORING ALEX'S JOURNEY

We now revisit Alex's story. A narrative discussion with Alex revealed that he strongly valued the relationship with his mother. In fact, he appreciated her openness, thoughtfulness, and her presence. On the other hand, he felt quite uncomfortable with the tension generated in his relationship with his stepfather and discovered that conflicts between them almost always led to long arguments between his mother and stepfather. Although he had tried to please his stepfather on several occasions, he always failed. Alex then resorted to behaviors that, in his mind, created the least amount of tension in the house and, therefore, the best outcome for himself and his mother. (Beware of the switches in your mind—are you now blaming the stepfather? The story could go on with his perspectives as well.)

Externalizing conversations made everyone's behaviors and their effects visible. These outcomes were then contrasted with everyone's intentions, and a storyline of successful family moments was developed. Grandparents who knew Alex as a thoughtful person were invited to trace the history of Alex's kindness and how they had witnessed that aspect of him in many other circumstances.

COMMON TEACHER QUESTIONS: NEW WAYS OF THINKING

"I'm Always Nervous When a Student Changes After Therapy and Then Therapy Stops. What Will Keep the Student Going?"

Usually, therapy is stopped when students are well anchored into their preferred ways of being, have connected in depth with their values, and are seen as successful by others. A therapist's goal is to empower young people, their families, and their teachers to be at their best without the therapist. Ultimately, therapists want people to become their own therapist and develop their own tricks to solve life problems. Therapists prefer to avoid dwelling on each little example of life and focus more on the big picture of people's experience of themselves and their contextual blocks. As such, therapists often terminate therapy with celebrations, guests and witnesses, and documentation that will remind young people of their possibilities, successes, and choices.

Therapists might give a certificate of progress that outlines strategies the students developed and used, summarizes their story of success, and renders it available for others who struggle. Therapists might also ask students to act as experts for other students struggling with similar issues, make a video, perhaps coauthor a booklet of advice, or, for little ones, draw their story as a cartoon so that they remember their journey and its preferred outcome.

"What Can I Do With a Class That Has Gone Through Programs but Has Not Changed?"

Sometimes we hear teachers say, "I am at my wit's end with this class. They have gone through three renowned programs on respect and have learned about problem solving and 'I' statements, but no change ever lasts."

It can be discouraging for a teacher to face an entire school year with a class that seems to not respond to interventions. After many attempts, the group of students themselves can become perceived as uncooperative or hopelessly disrespectful. Yet, the limited outcomes of these programs are common because the general process by which most are implemented is the same: teaching a curriculum of responses to life situations. This limited success is due to three main reasons:

1. While didactic teaching of subjects such as science or mathematics can be successful to a certain extent, teaching responses to life situations is automatically limited because a subject may be in a different emotional state when the need for this material arises. In the scientific world, this is known as the physiological laws of state dependent encoding. As numerous studies have shown, mental access to learned material is state dependent. In other words, if didactic material is learned in a quiet setting, it will be much more likely to be retrieved in a quiet setting. Have you noticed how difficult it is to remember certain events in the midst of great sadness or frustration? Specifically, you are more likely to remember sad events if you are sad and upsetting events if you are upset. You are less likely to remember joyful events or intellectual lessons when you are upset.

2. A second factor that limits the success of these programs is their lack of relevance to each student's unique life experience. Numerous students walk out of these classes very capable of reciting an intellectual definition of respect the same way you would define, for example, *galaxy*. However, when asked to explain the concept in their own words or to give a personal example, students are usually speechless. As clearly stated by Olsen Edwards (as cited in Fleming et al., 1997):

> *Language is an approximation, and it is far more approximate for children than it is for grownups. I think one of the big mistakes of adults is to think that if a child can say something, they understand it. Conversely that if a child can't say it, they do not understand it. The match between what they've experienced and the words they are capable of using is not great. (p. 37)*

3. Finally, a third factor that limits some of these programs is the process of giving scripted solutions to common scenarios. These scripts are useful to certain students (usually model students), but invariably they are not useful to students who most need assistance. This is mainly because these scripts often simplify the complexity of situations, peer relationships, and the implications of certain responses over time. Similarly, you might have had the experience of talking briefly to a coworker or a friend about a situation and been given advice, of which none fit realistically with your life.

"What About the Teen Who Is Full of Hate? I Have a Young Man Who Scares Me and Makes Me Wonder About His Potential for School Shooting."

Can these gentle conversations and externalizations really make them change? Yes, we would argue that gentle externalizing conversations are very likely to help these young men better understand their frustration and make visible their actual preferences as illustrated by the following first conversation between Marie-Nathalie and a seventeen-year-old Asian American young man.

MN: I like to start by getting to know people outside of the struggles. Feel free to ask me questions, too. I'm comfortable explaining my questions or clarifying things. Also, I'll be taking notes on some of the things you say that I want to remember. Is that okay with you? We can look at them together later on if you want. So, what do you like to do for fun?

Al: I like to play guitar. I play in a band.

MN: Cool, have you been playing for a long time?

Al: Ya ... sort of .... I started four years ago.

MN: Do you play songs you write yourself or ...

Al: Ya, I also write the songs for the band.

MN: What do you usually like to write and sing about?

Al: Well, all sorts of things ... usually about how shitty life is.

MN: What is it that makes life shitty for you?

Al: Life has no meaning. I don't value anything; I don't value grades, work, or people. I hate everything, especially people.

MN: Since when has this Hating been around?

Al: I don't know ... maybe two years.

MN: Anything in particular happen two years ago?

Al: Ya, my girlfriend left me but I don't really think about her anymore. It just started me analyzing things. I analyze things a lot and get really angry, especially at stupid guys at school. I just really want to sock them sometimes.

MN: So, when Anger and Hating are around, you want to sock people. Anything else you start thinking in those moments?

Al: Euh ... I don't know ... mostly I think how much I hate them and how much I really want to hurt them ... I have nothing to lose.

MN: So does Hating takes over your entire brain in those moments?

Al: Ya pretty much.

MN: What percentage of the time is Hating around like that?

Al: I don't know ... probably 80 percent of the time.

MN: Is Hating there mostly at school or also at home?

Al: Everywhere, all the time.

MN: How does this Hating thing affect your friendships? Does it turn against your buddies too?

Al: Euh . . . not really. Well I only have two friends really and they hate people too.

MN: What happens when you get pissed off at your friends? It must happen sometimes?

Al: Ya, well I just tell them. I don't lie and I also control it.

MN: I was wondering about that. You told me that Hating takes over 80 percent of your brain and wants you to hurt people physically. Yet I've been told of only two incidents where you punched someone at school. What is it that stops you from hitting people more often?

Al: I don't want to go to jail.

MN: So, is there a part of you that's able to remember that and keep things under control?

Al: Euh . . . ya . . . I guess . . .

MN: Can you share an example this week of a time when Hating would have wanted you to hurt someone and you controlled it? What did you tell yourself in your mind to not act on it?

The conversation with Al continues in an empowering way where he shares some of his values for nonviolence and the influence of a respected uncle who stands up for himself in calm and controlled ways. It turned out that Al was really acting more on his values for Peace than his feelings of Hate most of the time, but had never articulated his values before. Subsequent meetings focused on further exploring how he best contained Hate, what actually reduced those feelings, and his own solutions to situations where he chose non-violence.

As we discuss later in the book, the only reliable and lasting way for everyone, students or adults, to change serious problem behaviors is to discover their own relevant and meaningful solutions as they are engaged in a discussion of their experience of the problem.

Part II

Applications
and Examples

Success Stories of
Overcoming Bullying and Disrespect

7

Listening to Students' Voices

In writing this book, we were very interested in exploring students' ideas and their experiences. So many books are published about students, without their actual voices or experiences being represented. We would like to give voice to students to avoid replicating the process of adults analyzing or evaluating young people's experience, instead of asking them directly about their perspectives. If we truly want to improve schools and reduce the occurrence of bullying and disrespect, then we must understand how the recipients of schooling are affected by the numerous practices and procedures in place in the name of their best interest. Based on these ideas we surveyed 160 students of different ages about the issues of disrespect and bullying. We also had lengthy interviews with many others about a variety of issues, from disrespect and bullying to things they appreciate about their teachers and principals, to class management, to areas in need of improvement in school systems.

First, we provide the results of the survey and then share the personal interviews with students.

DISRESPECT/BULLYING SURVEY

In this survey, we focused on two areas: (1) issues of bullying and (2) student–educator relationships. Questions were open-ended to extract themes and elicit a wider range of student experiences. What follows is a summary of the most significant questions and answers.

When asked if they had been teased, called names, or pushed around at school, 111 of 182 middle school students (61 percent) replied "yes."

Several students gave us examples of incidents that happened in the two weeks prior to the survey:

"A [negative] petition was sent around about me."

"I was pushed in the bathroom."

"I was called a baby for needing a yard duty."

"I got teased for adults helping me."

"Just name-calling, exclusion, and minor pushing. No biggie." (This makes one wonder what constitutes a "biggie.")

We asked middle school students to compare bullying in elementary versus middle school:

"Middle school bullying is hard and more brutal."

"It's covert; less people tell a teacher."

"It's more persistent and rougher. People are ready to fight."

"There are more racial slurs and cursing."

"Middle school bullying is more about looks, personality, and popularity. There is pressure to keep up with current music and fashion trends."

We were curious as to how the students dealt with the tension and hardship of bullying. Students' top three answers included the following:

- Ignore it and stay calm (42 percent of students polled).
- Rely on the support of true friends (13 percent of students polled).
- Use music to calm down (11 percent of students polled).

Other strategies mentioned included the following:

- Use humor as a distraction tactic.
- Stand up to the aggressors and beat them up.
- Talk it out with the mean person.
- Use prayer.
- Remember certain ideas to get through, such as "Kids are just jealous," "I know what they say about me is not true," and "What comes around, goes around."

When asked the open-ended question, "What adult do you like to talk to when you are mad or sad at school?" 53 percent of students polled reported "my teacher." Other personnel of note that students would confide in were counselors, principals, and librarians, and they also reported parents. Of interest to us, as proponents of community involvement, was the large number of students who reported wanting parents present for support in the event of some grief. Also of note, 12 percent of students polled wrote "no one," which demonstrated either a need for privacy and reflection or a disconnection from adults and/or peers.

Since more than 50 percent of the students reported feeling drawn to speak to a teacher in times of hardship, we were curious as to why. What draws a student closer to a teacher? Two main answers were given:

- Of those polled, 54 percent reported feeling closer to a teacher who is emotionally available and makes an effort to relate to a young person and discuss relevant topics that they hold in common. The young people we surveyed are attached more to those teachers who are kind and full of humor and who help students understand themselves better.
- Thirty-eight percent of students polled reported feeling close to a teacher when they are being academically helped, congratulated, and complimented.

We wondered what students would like adults to do when students are upset about an issue. Four themes emerged from this questioning:

- Remain calm and reassuring and acknowledge the young person's mood (25 percent of students polled).
- Give the young person space and time to think (25 percent of students polled).
- Communicate honestly; understand and believe the young person (25 percent of students polled).
- Intervene and stop the "mean kids" (25 percent of students polled).

Many students reported that both actions and inactions of teachers often made students more upset when they felt that teachers were insensitive, did not listen, did not appear to care, or ignored them. Students' examples of these moments involved teachers making statements such as "live with it," "don't bother me," and "solve it yourself." Others shared that some teachers were probing and did not leave issues alone, even when the student expressed a need for some space and time to think.

Young people also commented about teachers who worsened the situation, specifically by doing the following:

- embarrassing the students
- making assumptions
- being unfair
- giving the other person more power
- forcing the students to be friends

- making mean put-downs
- asking worthless questions
- not believing them

INTERVIEWS: WALKING IN STUDENTS' SHOES

The following is a conversation between the second author, Maureen Taylor, and ten students from different schools and age groups. Although the students' quotes are authentic, the text has been reorganized and structured for ease of readability.

Maureen: What do you like about your relationships with your teachers? What do teachers do to let you know they really respect you?

Meg: When they are kind to you and connect to you other than through learning.

Alex: For me, I don't feel comfortable always having to be the smaller person in front of a teacher. I like talking to them. I think having that relationship outside of working makes things easier. And I like when teachers are big enough to apologize for their mistakes.

Roberto: Teachers who treat you as an equal, not as a little kid.

Kate: When they trust you, like when you say you brought your work and they believe you [without seeing it]. If people are able to trust each other, that builds relationships. You'll be able to show appreciation for someone because you know who they are. They are not just some face in the crowd.

Alex: Every year here I have at least one teacher who I really looked up to a lot, that talks to us like an actual person, not like, "I'm a teacher, you're a student."

Meg: My fifth grade teacher was very connected to students. She was very real, in everything she did. We had fun, but when we had to get to the point we knew it.

Maureen: What's the difference between a well-liked teacher and a teacher young people don't like so much and might disrespect?

Alex: The ones they like and respect, they can talk to. The ones they don't like, they give a lot of lip and attitude and cause problems.

Gabriel: They are not just reading from a book, they know about the subject. They also try to get to know the students better.

Trang: I like teachers who look at you like a person; they don't treat you like a little kid who doesn't know anything.

Meg:	The teachers we like try to connect with us while teaching, through teaching, and they base learning on what students are really interested in and how they learn. The ones that we don't like so much are the ones who want it their way and go only by their plan.
Maureen:	Some teachers have told us they think they really need to keep control and discipline in the classroom for respect and learning to happen? Do you think this works?
Kate:	Sometimes a teacher who is strict can maintain control of their class, and the students will respect that teacher, but it's not a good kind of respect. If the teacher will maintain control of the class and still be friendly, it's better. The students feel like they are in better environment and will do better.
Gabriel:	I like teachers who give choices as when to accomplish things. Then we learn to manage time, and we have more flexibility.
Meg:	Teachers have to keep order, but when I have a teacher who is more [flexible], I may learn more from them. I had an English teacher that was like this. She let us eat and talk in class as long as we got our work done. We could get help from her or help from our peers. Everyone respected her because they like her and they also knew if they goofed off she would take the privilege away. I learned a lot more from that teacher than someone who was strict. I wasn't used to the freedom of talking like that, but I learned a lot that year and my test scores were really high because of what I learned in there.
Maureen:	What happens in the classroom when teachers have many rules and are overly strict?
Lori:	If they don't treat students with respect and they are mean, then students don't try anymore.
Gabriel:	People pay more attention to teachers they like and respect.
Meg:	People get discouraged, and then they might not do their work. If they don't know something, they are afraid to ask the teacher. If they don't know something and want to ask a friend, they might get into trouble. Their class work grades go down, and then they can't do their homework because they don't understand the class work, and they are afraid to ask.
Alex:	It earns teachers nicknames—I know that.
David:	If they are motivating and nice to you, you want to work more for them.
Maureen:	How about when you have a teacher who acts disrespectfully? How do you and other students deal with that?

Denea:	There is a teacher who is buddies with only some of the students in class. It makes us feel weird. He's talking to his group and we're sitting here questioning ourselves, "Why is he talking to them all the time and not us?"
Meg:	There was a teacher who was from a different race, and she thought most comments we made were racist. She would call our class "stupid" and put random things on the test to trick us. We would try to talk to other teachers about this problem, but they would just tell us that we'd get through it. There was another teacher who would tell jokes a lot. Then she got really strict on us and favored the classes that had more "smart" students. She would punish the classes with less "smart" students. With both of these teachers, students stopped doing their work. It was like they figured, "I'll get yelled at anyway, what's the point?"
Denea:	There is also a teacher who calls us names like "Girl" and "Butch." I don't want to be called "Girl." I have my own name. I don't want to be known as "Girl." I want to be known as "Denea"! I really hate it when he does that.
Maureen:	We have talked to a lot of principals who try to be out in the yard, playing games, and talking to students so that they are not seen as only a disciplinarian. Do you think that works to build relationships?
David:	Yes, I think it is better to have a better relationship with your principal, to be his friend rather than to fear him.
Kate:	One principal I knew had this geography club after school, so she would know a lot of the students. It was pretty neat. I think if the principal would interact more with students, they would have a better chance of getting through to them.
Maureen:	How could the principals improve the school?
Meg:	Principals should listen to the voices of students. If students have an opinion about a teacher or something else, principals or a higher authority should listen and try to make school better for students. They should take into consideration what students say and fulfill what they want. They should also try to know more people. In a big school, they know the students who represent the school, like the athletes, but they don't know a lot of the other students.
Roberto:	If I were a principal, I would get students' views, not necessarily the community's [parents and teachers]. They are from another generation and don't know what we want.
Maureen:	What kind of homework is useful?

Kate: I was reading an article in our school newspaper that was reporting what experts say about the length of time we should have homework. It's the grade level multiplied by ten, so second grade should have twenty minutes, ninth grade would have ninety minutes. Yet that's not what we have. Also, homework should be enforcing what the student has done in class. It shouldn't be, "Oh, I have nothing for today, so I'll send this worksheet home for busy work."

Lori: Teachers don't understand that we are at school six or seven hours; we don't feel like doing homework. Sometimes there's a lot of stuff going on at home too.

Meg: Doing things that make me think. One teacher has us take notes out of the book, which is not useful. In fact, it's a waste of time.

Maureen: Do grades accurately represent the work you do? Other ideas on how teachers can get feedback on student's learning?

Lori: I worked hard one time doing a history assignment. The only thing the teacher found to tell me was that I wouldn't get points because it wasn't written with a pen. I never tried any more because my grade really didn't reflect that I had tried.

Meg: In middle school, if I met the requirements, I got an **A**. Now in high school, if you meet the requirements, you get a **C**. You have to go above and beyond work to get an **A**. This makes me less lazy; instead of just doing things "right," you have to make sure it has great content. If a teacher circles a mistake and doesn't take points off for grammar or something, that's nice. If I make the mistake again, the points are taken off. This makes me work harder. It would help if you could get other students' input on what you could improve. It would be great to have someone's brain from your own age group to explain things.

Aly: Everything is about points this year. A lot of my teachers are giving points for participation. I understand that they want people to participate, but it seems unfair. The points don't reflect how the student is. I don't think it shows who you are as a person. My favorite class is Spanish and if I get a lower grade than I think I should receive, it is only because I didn't turn in enough points for participation. For feedback on grades, progress reports are helpful, so you know how you're doing. Some teachers will also post grades every so often. This can be helpful to know if you need to work harder than you are already.

Maureen:	Why do most students answer "recess" when asked about the favorite part of their day?
Kate:	I think in elementary school there is a lot of energy. If they are sitting all day in class, they need to get some energy out. Teachers say that you can't bounce off the walls in class, so recess is the time to release that energy.
Lori:	Sitting all day is really hard. It would be cool if you could get up because you get fidgety and bored and can't listen anymore.
Meg:	It's because they are free from teachers and learning. It's fun to get out there and be free to play sports and talk to friends. If teachers had more ways to make learning fun, students would think twice about answering recess when asked that.
Maureen:	What do you think of activities in school that are of a competitive nature?
Alex:	I never felt comfortable in elementary school. When they would have a spelling bee and all eyes were on me, I would not want to do it.
Meg:	It's fun to have competition if no one gets hurt. Working in teams against another team doesn't affect students as negatively [as losing does on an individual], and it's a good tool for studying. I don't think they should have competitions about who's better than the other.
Kate:	There is a lot of competition, like who can do the best in classes. Some of it will make students work harder, but it's mostly not [motivating]. It gets to be too much when they will do anything to be the best, even sacrificing other people's feelings so they can be the best. If teachers could regulate that more, that would be better. Even if they have something competitive, if they could not make such a big deal out of it, that would be better.
Maureen:	Does getting rewards in school motivate you? How do they affect you?
Alex:	For me it wasn't about getting the candy bar or whatever; it was about trying to impress the people around me, so I can show that I'm not everything they say I am.
Meg:	I think these announcements about getting let out of class before someone else if you are quieter or cleaner almost makes it worse. Students get antsy and louder. If the class is generally good, there's no point in it. I don't think it differs how people would react; if they want to listen, they will.

Maureen: Is there time for self-reflection in school? There is so much growth that occurs in your lives, it seems like it could be beneficial to have a time and place to reflect and then plan for what's next.

Meg: We have time to reflect in French class, and we have time to reflect in our journals in English class. Although people wouldn't reflect on what they really wanted to reflect on, except in my English class. We trusted her and had confidentiality. We could tell her what we wanted her to read and she would respond and never tell anyone about what we wrote about.

Kate: Sometimes you really don't have time to think about what you've learned, because there's always the next test to think about. I think that we are so busy looking forward, we don't have a chance to look back. [Self-reflection] would help people to realize that they have come a longer way than they think and they can accomplish stuff.

Meg: Also, when I was in middle school, I was a peer helper. During the training we had triads, which means we went into a room with two other students and had ninety minutes to hang out, get comfortable, and talk about friends and feelings. It was great to have that time to reflect and talk about things with people your own age.

Maureen: Can you speak of collaboration in school?

Aly: When people say [collaboration], they think of people their own age, but I think it needs to be with people older and younger. It's helpful to know people in all age groups and not think, "Oh, I can't know her; she's too young." When we did pumpkin carving with the kindergartners, they thought we were helpful; they learned we weren't big scary fifth graders. More of that should go around the school.

Meg: Me and my peers do work together out of class. I do think that we learn a lot this way because it is a lot more interesting to listen to one of your friends than to listen to a teacher. I think students collaborate in many ways. One being in classes. My math teacher puts us in table groups to interact with other students if we have math problems. Other examples of how students collaborate are during recess and lunch, on the phone, in notes, through gestures, and one of the huge ways is online. I think that we also do socialize a lot while we talk about our work, and it helps us because we can work and learn and still socialize at the same time.

Aly: Oh yeah, also, in PE, we are all on the same side. We don't want to run! (laughs)

Maureen: What are the top three things that make school satisfying?

Kate: Understanding teachers who understand balance, students that will accept you for who you are, and not too much homework.

Alison: Friends, friends and *friends* (laughs)! Actually the teachers make me want to go to school, too. Some are really eccentric and fun; others try hard to connect to students and you can tell that they care.

Maureen: What would the ideal school be like?

David: Less teasing.

Meg: It would be a place where students could do what they want because they would have [trusting] friendships with the other students and the teachers. The principals would know most students and have connections with them. The people would have good relationships because the school would be smaller and people would really know each other.

Denea: If we have an environment where we could be ourselves. We feel like we always have adult eyes on us. We feel like our group is being watched or like our friends' group is being watched. It's not like we are doing anything wrong. We need a spatial bubble.

This last student comment is in fact loaded with meaning. In this section, we wanted to make apparent the pressures placed on students, what students relish about the student–teacher relationship, and why that spatial bubble is very desired by young people. In general, students thrive in environments where they are heard and respected, are connected to adults and peers, can collaborate with each other, and are not excessively pressured to perform, compete, or control every aspect of their experiences.

We encourage readers to have similar dialogues with students. Young people can offer a fresh perspective, honest feelings, and innovative ideas to improve your school. We have included examples of questions in Resource E. In Chapter 8, we shed more light on the cocreation of a school climate that fosters respect, appreciation, and tolerance. Additional ways to connect with your students and to reduce the tension and disrespect between students and educators are also discussed.

8

Cultivating Respect, Appreciation, and Tolerance in the School

W e propose a focus on different aspects of education: curiosity, self-awareness, cooperation, connections, and respect for perspectives of all ages. Unlike other philosophies that may offer similar goals, the narrative approach pays particular attention to the process and the experience of the learning rather than simply the outcome. This implies an analysis of context, power, and cultural discourses and recognizes the subjectivity and relativity of ideas. Flexibility and perspective become necessary ingredients in all respectful interactions, student–student and educator–student.

In this chapter, we present antiproblem values to promote in the classroom (appreciation, collaboration, etc.) as well as numerous examples of practices that foster a climate of belonging and respect. Many of these ideas have been successful in other schools and come from the generous sharing of hundreds of both educators and students. We invite you to sort through all of the ideas, embrace some and make them your own, and leave others behind. Ultimately, these ideas should not be taken as exercises to implement but rather as inspirations to discuss with your school community, where a clear commitment can be generative of many more ideas to bring forth the best of your school community.

CONNECTION

Schools are often presented as the ultimate cradle of socialization for young people, and teaching is considered one of the most social professions for adults. Interestingly, however, conversations with adults and young people often reveal a profound sense of alienation, isolation, and disconnection that is further intensified by the innumerable possibilities for relationships. In other words, there is nothing worse than feeling alone in a crowd, and this is true for both adults and students, particularly students who struggle with social issues, such as disrespect and bullying. Given the structures in the system, how then can connections be enhanced in schools?

By *connection*, we mean a process of being open and accepting of another as a whole person, with his or her multiple versions of self. In this compassionate process of honoring each other, we find the best brought out in each individual. Connection is about *being* together as well as doing joint activities.

Connection prevents serious problems between students, such as fighting, competition, disrespect, and bullying, and it prevents boredom. Students need to be connected with their peers and teachers in a meaningful way that brings forth their preferred selves. Connection helps them be tolerant with each other, accept diversity in the classroom, and enjoy their extensive time spent at school (Fleming et al., 1997).

One educator shares her thoughts:

> It is not just about the academics. If you ignore the social aspect, students will still pick it up. It's on the agenda whether or not you choose to address it. If you address it, they'll learn something you want them to learn, as opposed to it just being random. How you choose to run your classroom is part of the curriculum—how democratic you are, how much input you get from students, who you call on. Students notice all of this; they are learning ideals such as "students are not supposed to be heard" or "students' voices are important." Students are social creatures and you need to incorporate that into the classroom. They learn socially and they are very interested in each other. Why not build on it? They want to do it anyway. I think they are more responsive when you do this.

This was also reported repeatedly by the nearly 200 students we surveyed or interviewed: Their most important recollection of school was the connections they had made, usually with students, sometimes with teachers. When asked about the best time they had at school, 72 percent attributed it to the relationships that they had with teachers and friends, involving playing, school spirit, and social time. Their worst time at school involved relationships 54 percent of the time, and this was reported as being due to fighting, trouble with friends or teachers, and bullying. Connections are reported as the single most important aspect of the schooling experience for students, yet it is probably the least discussed aspect of the curriculum.

Promoting connections between students and teachers offers several advantages. This practice . . .

- Empowers students to try their very best:

  I try my hardest when I feel connected with the teacher and when she cares about me as a person.

  —Middle school student

- Builds self-esteem and allows them to try and make mistakes:

  . . . school is supposed to provide a setting where our performance has fewer esteem-threatening consequences than in the real world in the interest of encouraging the learner to try things out.

  —Bruner (1996, p. 37)

- Provides a safe classroom where students can be spontaneous:

  I really love Mrs. X; I know I can always raise my hand and ask a question.

  —Elementary school student

- Encourages students to be their preferred self, to stop trying to please or fit in the mold:

  It makes a difference to me because I can stop worrying and focus on my work.

  —Elementary school student

- Fosters enjoyment of school, renders work meaningful, and increases performance:

  What's the point of doing all this irrelevant work if I don't even like my teacher?

  —Middle school student

- Promotes an increased commitment to attend, participate, and reciprocate:

  Students want to give back, especially when they've been hurt and were helped. They want to become [teachers], counselors, and police officers. Do you want to know why? That was who helped them.

  —Middle school principal

- Inspires students who have visions of themselves as adults:

> *When my teacher respects me, I believe more that I can achieve my dream of being a biologist someday.*

—High school student

In sum, meaningful connections reduce disrespect, comparison, isolation, marginalization, and competition between students for teachers' attention. How can educators connect in such a meaningful way with their students? This can only be achieved if educators are willing to be genuine and put themselves forth as human beings. As discussed in the following table, students are very clear about their preference for connections, which mainly occur when educators are genuine.

In Their Own Words: Students Speak of Their Preference for Genuine Teachers

- "I know teachers are not always happy; being perky all the time isn't real."
- "I prefer teachers who let me know how they are feeling."
- "If a teacher lets us know how she is feeling, then we'll shape up."
- "When a teacher shares personal experience, it creates an interest between the educator and students on a personal level. That encourages us to do our work."
- "If a teacher is open, then students will be open too and be less afraid to ask for help."
- "I like teachers when they are who they are."
- "I prefer teachers who talk to me as a real person."
- "I think it's really cool when teachers talk to you often about basic things, not just academics."
- "When teachers share what's going on in their lives, it's less hard to understand them and we can be easier on them."

Connecting is not something you do as an exercise; it is an experience that you bring to a deeper level that is truly meant, lived, and believed, rather than scripted in a politically correct way. It is essential to know more about a person than just the surface, or what you envision of them. For example, Maureen knew a student who was known around campus as highly competitive and argumentative. He had a reputation for causing trouble at recess and for being disruptive in the classroom. One day one of the teachers witnessed him helping a little girl who had fallen off her bike. Many faculty members were surprised, and Maureen was left wondering whether that helpful side of him would have been more visible at school if a deeper connection with him had been established.

Connection can help a student overcome a problem story and have a positive vision and more fulfilling dreams. Educators can create opportunities for students to make visible their preferred self and determination, even when everyone has a problem story about them, such as failing, bullying, or being disrespectful. One of the principals interviewed, Gary Stebbins, shared an example of a powerful connection he developed with a struggling student and how he provided an opportunity for this young man to make a speech in front of his graduating class, even though he wasn't graduating:

> Nick told the class that he wasn't graduating with them and why he wasn't but that he had plans for his future. His words were powerful and strong. He told them how he would turn things around. I was right there, standing beside him, putting my hand on his shoulder. The students watched Nick and me on stage; they watched the forgiveness and how empowering it was. I think it might have helped others walk back, face their own problems, and help someone else. It's all part of the healing process.

For genuine connection to happen, educators can also simply share what each student may contribute to their personal and professional lives. It could be said that each encounter with a student might be transformative for the teacher as a human being. This reciprocal sharing, the Taking It Back process, was originally thought of by Michael White (2000).

The reader must understand that the Taking It Back process is very different from the traditional practice of praising students on how they are improving, contributing to the class, or being good. This process is really about the teacher being transparent about him- or herself as an active presence in the interaction, as someone who is humanly touched and moved by interactions. In addition, this sharing must be done with simplicity and integrity to avoid creating the uncomfortable context where a student would feel compelled to take care of or console his or her teacher. The Taking It Back process does not take the focus away from the student's experience but is rather expressed at an appropriate time simply to acknowledge the student's contributions.

In this process, teachers could share their thoughts with a young person:

- The teachers are leaving work with the student's enthusiasm, motivating them to have more energy to play with their own children at home that evening.
- A conversation with the student about losing the family pet reminds the teacher that his or her own pets are precious.
- Watching the student solve his or her conflict with another student reminds the teacher to trust all students more.
- The student teaches the teacher something about his or her family and culture, and it makes the teacher realize their values are quite similar.

These are all personal reflections that teachers may often experience without ever sharing them openly with students. The Taking It Back process offers several advantages:

- It honors the child as a worthy and valuable being, regardless of grades; it affirms that the child enriches someone else's life.
- It *minimizes* the power imbalance between the teacher and child in a way that allows for a more meaningful connection.
- It reminds teachers to remain open-minded toward their students and also connected to themselves. It keeps teachers in a place of self-reflection and humility with regard to students as very giving people.

Another way for teachers to share more of themselves is to hold an interview. Marie-Nathalie experimented with interviewing teachers in front of their students on several occasions. These interviews were crafted very carefully, depending on the problem stories of the teacher or school (if any) and, in general, focused on making the invisible intentions, values, dreams, and dilemmas of the educator visible in a very touching way. When appropriate and relevant, the interviewee may be invited to share briefly about a personal struggle if it is likely to have a good effect on the students. The intention is to assist students in seeing the person behind the role as more human, well intentioned, and compassionate. It has, in Marie-Nathalie's experience, reduced hierarchy in significant ways and increased commitment, appreciation, and a sense of community.

Countless students of all ages have shared with us that their attachment to an educator, whom they had a chance to know as a person, increased their motivation to complete assignments and led them to harbor a more positive attitude. Melissa, an assertive teenager, shares her opinion:

> Last year I found out that my teacher was struggling in her personal life. Since I felt for her, I made more of an effort to do my homework and be polite in class.

Certain schools we visited promoted connections, in particular, for young people who were marginalized or came from an underprivileged background. An elementary school staff we met with in San Jose, California, has a meeting early in the school year in which they discuss the situation of a few young people with more serious needs and issues. Staff members volunteer to adopt and mentor a child who is not in their class-room. The staff member is not involved as a disciplinarian of the student but is simply involved in a meaningful relationship throughout the year.

In other schools, during staff meetings, educators decide to openly discuss the effects of engaging in problem-saturated conversation about students. In one particular school, the staff learned that problem stories of students were not helpful and decided to be acutely aware of the ways in which they portrayed and relayed certain "facts." The principal explained:

> We are realizing that what you talk about creates a story; it creates a reality. When we talk about students, how do we do it? What do we do with our frustrations? We are now looking for observable facts and seeing the conclusions we draw from those items. We are building language about how we want our stories to be. It is a slow process of change.

We want to make clear that serious thinking about connection eliminates countless problems, among those, disrespect and bullying. One suggestion for increasing students' sense of connection is that schools have an area where young people who may have fewer friends could participate in structured games, board games, or art and music during free time, such as recess. Marie-Nathalie, as a counselor and student advocate, organized structured activities at recess and lunch for all the students who were likely to get in trouble. It was very successful and gave them the opportunity to run, have fun, get some fresh air, and stay out of the principal's office. Contexts need to be created so that all students, without exception, feel connected.

Finally, educators can also foster connection by doing the following:

- seeing students as people by remembering their names and engaging in nonacademic conversations about other aspects of life
- making themselves approachable, available, and accessible to help
- keeping a sense of humor (nonhumiliating) and trust
- acknowledging young people as being knowledgeable and as having something to say, even when the contribution is not obvious at first
- expressing appreciation for students

APPRECIATION

Appreciation, as we define it, is to express acknowledgment. The intention is to be transparent about our personal experience of gratitude or admiration. Sharing appreciation is a process of genuine expression of gratefulness, without the intention to alter the recipient's behavior in any way. In schools, such appreciation is scarce. Everyone recognizes its value and craves it, yet people lack the context and means to express it in meaningful ways. Educators may be overtaken by their duty to motivate students and get into a habit of simply praising in the hope of reinforcing certain behaviors. As for students, they develop the habit of listening and doing what they are told and may not even think that their opinion or feedback has much value to an educator. Most of the time, the system is not structured in such a way to give voice or space for students to offer feedback.

It is interesting that there are so many adults organizing young people's lives and yet there are so many students who remain so hungry for appreciation of any kind. A few minutes of meaningful attention from an adult can be life altering. One of our Bay Area Family Therapy Training Associates interns recently acknowledged a student's effort as he was working hard on a drawing. The student stopped, turned, and said, "You really think that? Nobody's ever talked to me like that before." It is really sad to see marginalized students fall through the cracks despite educators' intentions.

To remedy this, Marie-Nathalie used to walk to the principal's office with students who had shared their success at resisting the temptation to engage in a trouble-related behavior. Marie-Nathalie would ask the students to share with the principal how they had reached success and why they were proud. Principals and students loved it. In the end, most principals did not become educators to have a punitive relationship with students but to see students blossom. Yet, their role and responsibilities often restrict their contact with students to a disciplinary interaction.

Two principals shared with us some of their personal strategies:

> Probably my greatest fun is to have teachers tell me of students who have done something well in the classroom. I'll have that student called down here [to the office] to either read to me or to share some accomplishment. They do come down to my office for good things.

> I make it a goal to call five to ten parents per week to comment on a positive behavior of their child. It forces me to consciously look for positives. My son's teacher used to do this, and it had such an effect on me as a mother . . . when my son would come home from school, I just wanted to give him a big hug.

There are two main areas where students are usually appreciated: academic performance and citizenship. Yet, as we define it, appreciation is also seen as going well beyond the recognition of a student's action that the educator wants to reinforce as positive. Appreciation on a more personal level is meaningful and may extend to a broader set of ways of being.

It is interesting that teachers' appreciation for students is often expressed to parents at parent-teacher conferences. If students are present, such as at student-led conferences, these interactions can be quite powerful because they involve the telling of preferred stories in front of a parent audience. A lot of beautiful comments and experiences of appreciation about students occur when students are not in the room. If the student is not present for the comments, the personal effect on the student is lost.

Appreciation can also be nonhierarchical, such as in joint celebrations. In a joint celebration, a class is acknowledging that a successful day is the result of a shared outcome; the responsibility for the successful outcome is perceived as bidirectional. In such a context, the teacher shares the effort and the outcome by being involved as an equal benefactor of the accomplishment. One teacher shared an example of this:

> *Toward the end of the day, we spontaneously ended early to celebrate. I told the class, "We had a beautiful day. I wasn't impatient. We all worked hard. Let's eat some popcorn and enjoy being together." We did. It was peaceful and refreshing.*

> —Kathleen Ryan

Appreciation between students is covered in greater detail in the Bugging Bug project in the next chapter, in which students are success spies, distribute secret notes, and plan a celebration day.

Self-Appreciation

Another important form of acknowledgment is self-appreciation. Self-appreciation develops naturally in environments that are supportive and provide various forms of approval. Schools demand such a high level of accomplishment and performance in students that it should not be challenging to ensure that they feel proud of themselves. In a context where students are proud of themselves and naturally engage in self-appreciation, there is less need of adult input. A teacher shares an example of this:

> *I try to find something for students that they have a built-in interest in, for instance, this village over here that we constructed. I didn't have to tell them that that was a good job. They looked at it and they were really proud of it. I try to get to the point where students are proud of what they do, not that they are proud simply because I'm proud.*

Indirect methods of expressing appreciation can be valuable, too. For example, some teachers ask students to state what positive memory or idea they are taking away from the day as they are exiting the room. Often this can be a very sweet exchange of appreciation. As Maureen was waiting outside a colleague's classroom one day hoping to chat briefly with her, she witnessed a beautiful exchange. The teacher asked the class to consider what they were proud of doing that day. She got down at eye level with them, and, as the line filed out of the classroom, the children spoke to her about it. The children left being reminded of their accomplishments, and this teacher was filled with stories of proud children, often sharing stories of appreciation with her or stories of something she could feel proud of having facilitated during the day. Maureen stood quietly and humbly watching this, realizing the power of such a simple act and also realizing that, when students are asked to self-appreciate verbally, it has an external appreciative effect on the teacher.

Appreciation for Staff Members

Ideal systems allow appreciation for everyone, teachers included. Given that there is a large student population, there is an enormous pool of appreciation for educators left untapped by most schools. When educators feel appreciated, they feel nourished and energized and have patience and kindness toward students as well. This reduces the likelihood of them becoming exasperated and falling into a problem cycle of disrespect with students.

The staff at Campbell Middle School exemplifies this process beautifully. Twice a year, students who wish to write a letter are given the opportunity to express appreciation to any school staff member who may have made a difference in their lives. A staff member from Campbell Middle School shared the following thoughts about this expression of appreciation:

> We have a tradition here on campus where students are asked to select people who have really made a difference for them and write a letter. Students are encouraged to sit down and write letters to different people in the school. It may be the secretary, the custodian, teachers, and so on. The student can send it to whomever they want, and if a student doesn't want to do it, they don't have to.
>
> I'll receive letters from kids who I don't really know who they are. They'll indicate to me, "You stopped and you said something to me that really meant a lot." For me, it was just an action; for them, it was something they hadn't experienced.
>
> Teachers look forward to these letters. The teachers save the letters; they keep them to read. Often they will receive a letter from someone who will totally surprise them. I seldom hear of anyone who doesn't receive one. Everyone is receiving one.

The beauty of this practice is that it also creates an opportunity to acknowledge the support staff, such as the yard duty staff, custodians, cafeteria employees, therapists, tutors, bus drivers, and instructional assistants, who often feel invisible in the system and very rarely benefit from any inclusion. This sort of practice of acknowledgment can offer the advantage of creating a sense of community to many.

Another creative practice at Campbell Middle School is that of sending singing telegrams on Valentine's Day. Those telegrams are sung by groups of students in appreciation of teachers' and principals' efforts. The telegrams are ordered by anyone on the school campus and present a very kind gesture of appreciation. A staff member shared the following thoughts about the Valentine's Day practice:

> On Valentine's Day, kids are able to send singing telegrams to other people on campus. Student volunteers [singers] are coordinated by a teacher. They'll receive a request to sing and go to that class. We'll have four or five teams of students singing in different places. We have students who are sending singing telegrams to their teachers. One day

I was stopped in the office by these three girls, who gave me a card from someone and started singing to me a cappella. It was wonderful, beautiful, and uplifting.

Although appreciation can certainly be spontaneous rather than structured, we believe a more formatted system can generate a climate where people develop the habit of showing acknowledgment. The following list shows some ways for educators to gather positive feedback and appreciation from students and parents:

- Conduct a survey on positive aspects of classroom and school procedures and projects.
- Facilitate class discussions on appreciated aspects of teacher and class relationships. (Discussions can be facilitated by the principal, a teacher, or a parent.)
- Create a playful yet sincere report card for teachers, principals, or both.
- Include a response form on notes home where parents can ask questions and share gratitude.
- Develop a student feedback team responsible for spending ten minutes with each class, midyear, and gathering students' honest and confidential feedback about their classroom experiences. (This can then be summarized and integrated for the educator to read.)
- Have a class box where students can leave notes for the principal to share with teachers at staff meetings or put into staff mailboxes.

COLLABORATION

Collaboration is the act of working jointly to achieve a common goal. It involves shared leadership and respect for others' opinions. In classrooms, this often takes the form of cooperative learning where a group project is structured to be free from focus on individual accomplishment. The teacher essentially plans the time so that mutual positive dependence is created among the group members. Cooperative learning is most successful if the teacher has spent time modeling appropriate group behavior and stresses both individual and group responsibility (Kagan & Spencer, 1994). The teacher also stresses that each group member is capable of contributing to and accounting for the group's results (Olweus, 1993).

Although cooperative learning is very valuable, we like to invite educators to extend the idea of collaboration in all areas of interactions as modeled by the adults in the school community. Playing a collaborative game once every so often isn't enough. Collaboration is most successful when infused daily.

For collaboration to genuinely develop between students, teachers must first take an honest look at the subtle ways in which collaboration is sabotaged or enhanced. As discussed earlier, competition is the most frequently used method to motivate students and while it may lead to a satisfying rush of goal-oriented action, it also shatters the deeper current of collaboration. If educators are really committed to the spirit of collaboration, they need to make a conscious choice to systematically reduce the competitive factors in their classrooms and replace them with more collaborative statements. Educators must realize that extreme and subtle methods of competition will not coexist with an integrated spirit of collaboration.

Competitiveness is not valued in all cultures. In fact, many collectivist cultures go so far as to demote an individual who might have worked alone on a novel creation in hopes of receiving glory. For example, the Japanese culture has a quote that states, "The nail that sticks its head out will be hammered." In the traditional Hawaiian culture, young people feel humiliated and embarrassed by foreign teachers' individual praise of them in front of their classmates because it implies to the students that they are not working in harmony and collaboration with their peers. Other cultures, such as the Aboriginal culture of Australia, have games, such as relay races, with the goal of all teams reaching the finish line at the same time.

Many educators manage to motivate their students and foster learning without competitiveness using other enthusiasm-producing methods. The following Table 8.1 lists common practices that promote competition between students and classes and some simple alternatives to consider.

Table 8.1   Collaborative alternatives to competitive statements

Usual Competitive Statement	Alternative Collaborative Statement	Underlying Collaborative Strategy
"I'd like to see which team can clean up first. They can go to recess first."	"I'm wondering if you can break our class record of cleaning up."	Class is in competition with an inanimate object (e.g., a clock) as a whole team.
"Team 3 has the most points for this month. Next month you will have new teammates to work with."	"Let's move teammates around, so you get to know everyone. One teammate from Team 3 please switch with a member from Team 4."	Ever-changing team membership eliminates the meaning of winning and losing.
"Class, we are going to play Around the World now. Kris and Joe, please start . . . three plus sixteen equals . . . "	"Kris and Joe, let's see if you can match each others' answering at the same time: three plus sixteen equals . . . "	Students should match the other's exact speed of speech or physical accomplishment.
"You will work on your own writing assignment, and we will end with a writing	"Partner A will start creating the story and stop after thirty seconds. Partner B will	Students will coconstruct an assignment, working as a whole class to meet a goal.

(Continued)

(Continued)

Usual Competitive Statement	Alternative Collaborative Statement	Underlying Collaborative Strategy
contest, seeing who has the most descriptive words in their story."	continue the creation of the story for thirty seconds. Alternate back and forth. At the end, we'll see how many descriptive words our class can come up with!"	
"Class, let's look at the chart here to see how many students read ten books last month. Each sticker equals five books."	"Look into your own sticker book and pat yourself on the back if you reached your reading goal" or "What is the total of books we all read as a class?"	Teacher encourages noncompetitive and more private ways of keeping records to reach group goals.
"I would like to announce the classroom awards for this month."	"Let's talk about how you have been working toward the personal goals you set last month."	Students are encouraged to set their own goals and self-reflect on their own accomplishments.

These practices of energizing activities without competition create a context where everyone wins and belongs to a community. The fun is not to put down someone but to share and build. The reader is invited to explore the numerous noncompetitive activities promoted in other books on the subject (Beaudoin & Walden, 1998; Hill, 2001; Luvmour & Luvmour, 2002). The Bugging Bug project, detailed in the next chapter of this book, is designed to foster collaboration. Yet, even the Bugging Bug project cannot succeed in an environment where the teacher maintains a very competitive climate. When students have been extensively socialized to be competitive in school, new ways of being must be patiently and persistently encouraged.

While competition can enhance motivation in a situational short-term manner, collaboration, on the other hand, can create a solid foundation that can be used in many situations. Class meetings are good examples of truly collaborative classrooms. Class meetings can focus on a variety of purposes such as group problem solving and consensus decision making.

Group problem solving is important to help students learn and become comfortable in the process of collaboratively finding solutions to existing or potential problems. Typically, the class meets in a circle so that all people can be seen equally (although many teachers just do it regardless of seating).

The teacher acts as the facilitator. Items on the agenda may be reviewing the week, cocreating class agreements, talking about problems and solutions, giving compliments, and sharing successes at improving or resisting a problem. A large part of the meeting could be devoted to the social relations within the class and the school. Issues of bullying and disrespect are natural and important topics to include in these discussions (Olweus, 1993). When students feel they are making valuable contributions, their motivation, sense of purpose, and belonging to the class can greatly increase.

Consensus decision making means that participants examine different viewpoints and arrive at an agreement that is best for all. This is more than each student just casting a vote on a classroom issue. The key to consensus decision making is that each student is aware that they may not get their favorite choice but they will have a voice in what is best for the whole group (Vitto, 2003).

The following story by veteran teacher Linda Boucher illustrates the power of a classroom accustomed to working collaboratively.

> I was once teaching in a school where only two colleagues and I shared the value of working collaboratively with students. As a result we stood out a little from the rest of the community. We didn't attempt to control students all the time and so they were a little more rowdy and rarely lined up perfectly, which didn't seem important to us. At some point, a new principal decided that he was tired with the high noise level in the cafeteria at lunch. I think he assumed our students were the culprits. Anyway, he decided to create this challenge where the classes who would be the quietest during the lunches of an entire week would win a prize. He assigned one side of the cafeteria to my colleagues and I and the rest of the school on the other.
>
> As usual, we engaged in our collaborative process with students where they determined the expectations, goals, and the value of the achievement. We had a discussion with them and raised some questions: Did they want to take up this challenge and why? What percentage of the time did they think they could be quiet (set a realistic goal)? What might help them achieve their goal? How would they like to celebrate their victory (regardless of the principal's choice of prize for them)? The students decided for themselves that they wanted to do it so they became committed to making it happen. They also decided that what they wanted for their celebration was a popcorn and paper airplane party.
>
> As a result, for the entire week, our classes were the most silent of the whole school during lunch, and we won. The principal had a lot more respect for our teaching practices after that.

Effects of Collaboration

In a nutshell, collaborative practices help students develop important life skills, enrich their connection to the group, heighten their sense of belonging to a community, and develop a greater appreciation for classmates (Thompson, Cohen, & O'Neill Grace, 2002). Working closely with peers also allows students to learn more about each other, which increases acceptance, tolerance, and trust. In the end, students in cooperative learning are mentally and emotionally engaged in class activities for a far higher percentage of the time. Students develop a joy of working with others, a sense of group harmony, and an increased appreciation for the people at school.

SELF-REFLECTION

No one does their best thinking on fast forward . . . speed kills great ideas. The faster we speed up, the less time we have to think, to incubate, to ponder, to dream . . . in schools the answer has always been more important than the thought process.

—Reiman (1998, p. 99)

In schools, young people also have to be focused outwardly 100 percent of the time. They have to focus on the comments from their teacher and their peers, adults' evaluations of their performance, other students' movements, and the classroom environment.

Worst of all, when students are in trouble, adults constantly tell them to think before doing. Yet, students are rarely given time to simply think—to process their goals and intentions—aside from when they are in trouble, in which case they usually just dwell on the frustration of being punished. Reflectiveness should be promoted in the absence of conflict, and then, in addition to its intrinsic value, it would have the additional benefit of being a preventative measure.

When young people choose on their own to have some peaceful time alone, it is often pathologized. Even if it occurs at a time when they are supposedly free to act of their own will, such as recess, many adults, concerned that the child is depressed and lonely, may even ask, "Are you all right today?" If the reflectiveness happens during class time, the label on the child may become "daydreamer," "shy," "not paying attention," or "having trouble concentrating." Our culture has a skewed vision of young people: They are not expected to be inwardly reflective in the absence of problems; they are supposed to be wild and outgoing. If they do not fit this model, adults get concerned.

We also expect young people's energy to function according to adult schedules: energetic during recess and quiet during class. If the child has the misfortune of being enthusiastic during class and quieter during recess, they run the risk of being pathologized once more. In other words, young people are allowed to be young only at certain times of the day. Adults have normalized standards about what is acceptable, and young people remain under the adult gaze.

Everyone needs time to reflect. High schoolers in particular really appreciate time to think about their lives and relationships. Time for reflection is important because it allows for refueling, connecting with a purpose, reviewing accomplishments, processing mistakes, examining congruency with one's values, and ultimately improving the self.

In other words, the main advantages of self-reflection are that it:

- provides time to explore ways of being that fit who one truly wants to be
- allows one to become grounded in one's values
- clarifies goals and intentions
- helps one learn from mistakes and plan different responses to challenges
- slows down a person to a relaxed state
- increases ability to be attentive and relate to others
- creates a space in the day to integrate lessons of life

Self-reflection can be encouraged in numerous ways and integrated in schools' practices, for teachers and students, without it becoming overly time-consuming.

The self-reflective times discussed in this book are distinct from the graded and structured writing essays that are imposed on students. This in no way means that those types of essays are without value. We are just encouraging educators to weave in an additional practice of self-reflection, which can be freer in time and format.

Our numerous visits to a wide variety of public schools have opened our eyes to the many ways self-reflection can be promoted. The following are examples of this:

- cultivating a garden for quiet reflective time
- ensuring the library is open for recess periods
- providing a journaling time for students and giving them a choice as to whether or not they wish the teacher to read their reflections
- pairing all teachers with one another so that students who express a need for some quiet time can simply go into another agreed-on class
- having an area in the classroom that a student can go to solely for alone time, to draw, journal, and daydream
- providing a small room with quiet music where students can go relax and benefit from some time out

COMMUNITY AND DIVERSITY

Most public schools, among many institutions, are disengaged from their community. In the United States, elders are segregated into care facilities and young people into day care centers. This has two significant negative effects:

- Parents and teachers end up isolated, disenfranchised, and drained from carrying in isolation the responsibility of educating young minds.
- With the additive effect of this segregation and individualism, young people learn to be driven by their own personal successes and develop very little sense of belonging and accountability to a community.

Yet, it does not have to be this way, and it is not this way in all schools. There are numerous advantages to and very simple ways of supporting educators and, at the same time, assisting students in understanding community values and the beauty of giving for the sake of giving.

Support for Educators

Support for educators, either financially or through volunteer efforts of willing helpers, is often the most obvious benefit of community relations. Related to financial support, principals and institutions that are involved with their communities often receive donations and generous gifts from a variety of donors. Sometimes a wealthy donor, knowledgeable in a school's mission, willingly wants to support a particular program. Volunteer efforts might involve retired elders or available parents contributing some precious time and energy to a variety of school-related activities.

Students' Commitment to Something Bigger Than Themselves

Students' sense of belonging can be addressed by getting involved one day a week or one day a month in community work. It is important that the projects be chosen by students or selected by students from among several possibilities presented by teachers. Examples of community action could be working at an animal shelter, serving soup at a shelter, being a docent at a museum, writing letters to victims of disaster, working at day care centers or nursing homes, performing neighborhood beautification, writing for local newspapers, raising money for saving the rainforest, helping out the custodian, painting murals on the school walls, or planting a neighborhood garden.

Participating in service projects as fund-raising activities can be more meaningful than selling cookie dough or wrapping paper. For instance, students can voluntarily choose to be part of a team that mows neighbors' lawns or assists elders for intrinsic rewards or for a small donation to the school.

Often, students are also interested in learning more about other student's lives. Maureen's class participated in a pen pal letter program with classes in other states. It is exciting for students to learn about students in other regions of the country. Other educators correspond with students in foreign countries, or write to students at nearby schools and follow up with a meeting at a park in June. One principal told us that the students at his school are learning to speak Spanish. After learning enough to read in Spanish, they are going to take a trip to another school across the city to read children's books in Spanish to the kindergartners. Another principal explained how buddy classes could be involved in meetings to share class projects and learning in each other's schools. This would have the added benefits of giving teachers a sense of community, diminishing their isolation, and increasing respect for students who are different.

Increasing community involvement is an endeavor that requires time from students, including time spent outside of school hours. Educators need to be aware that benefits of community involvement are plentiful and that reevaluating the time allotment and policies regarding homework may be necessary to allow for more diverse activities to take place.

Involving Parents

The most obvious and beneficial way to increase a sense of community is to involve parents and grandparents. Our survey of and discussions with sixty fifth graders in parent participation programs made visible how grateful students were for the presence of parents in their classes.

When my parents are at school, I . . .

- "can show them my work"
- "think they understand me better"
- "know they care"
- "know they can calm me down better"
- "know no one will hurt me because they are there watching"
- "feel more included"
- "get to see them and talk to them more"
- "have them help me"
- "feel more at home and comfortable"
- "have fun"
- "like that they are nice to me"

In addition to these observations, students also benefit from the sense of community created by the relationship between their parents and their teacher. This relationship weaves together meaningful aspects of students' lives that would otherwise be disconnected; allows them to see their parents through the teacher's and other students' eyes, giving them free space to reflect on the value of the parenting they receive; and makes the educational journey a family endeavor, where everyone is interested and involved in learning. Students benefit from a wider range of role models. This is particularly important for minority students, given that 90 percent of the educators in the United States are white (Kivel, 2002). For underprivileged students, the opportunity to witness and work with people from their own as well as more privileged communities can broaden their dreams for themselves. For students from the upper middle class, benefits arise from being exposed to people from the broader culture, and being provided with a more realistic vision of life and its struggles. These students can develop connections that allow them to see others as people, despite class or ethnic barriers, a practice that also reduces cultural insensitivity.

Valuing Differences

Being culturally sensitive is not just having knowledge of different groups. One can never accumulate enough knowledge about all groups, and even if one did, it would remain an intellectual endeavor disconnected from a significant percentage of one's behaviors. Being culturally sensitive is about developing an experience of oneself—an experience of oneself as open and receptive to differences, while at the same time holding, in awareness, the bias promoted in one's subculture. Whether we like it or not, we were programmed from a very young age to believe in certain ideas and most likely have not had a chance to review all of the content of our brains. Most people, for instance, are brainwashed by society's advertising industry, movies, magazine, TV news, and newspapers, and they integrate certain stereotypes.

What comes spontaneously to your mind when asked to visualize a president, a doctor, a lawyer, a CEO of a company, a Nobel prize winner, or an Olympic medalist? For most people, it is the image of a white male (see Resource C). Your mind is limited by what you have seen. What could be the benefits of living in a diverse environment? For many, the benefits include a greater variety of solutions and customs, more flexibility and safety, a wider range of innovations, a greater sense of community, and a life richer in possible ways of being. This must be reflected in schools for this important part of life to be integrated by all.

> To value diversity is to teach with the intention of valuing diversity and to pay attention to those things that reflect diversity in your classroom. . . . As a culturally proficient instructor, you treat learners in a way that learners perceive as respectful. This may mean using a different criterion for respect than you would for yourself.
>
> —Robins, Lindsey, Lindsey, and Terrell (2002, p. 56)

The curriculum in the United States is saturated by the stories of domination of white men. It is incongruent to tell young people that we value peace and then require that they memorize all the dates related to wars (Riesler, 2001). It is important to add a variety of perspectives in the curriculum and make visible the invisible accomplishments of those who are not white men. For example, it is important to present women who have contributed great discoveries in mathematics or science and the strong women in history who have won Nobel prizes (see the National Women's History Project, www.nwhp.org, for school materials). People of color need to learn pride in their ethnicity and honor their ancestors, which does not happen if they are constantly and narrowly presented as losers in history (see Zinn, 2001). Students and their parents need to know that Native Americans have made innumerable contributions to our world, including our political system (Bernal, 1987; Weatherford, 1988). The curriculum should also acknowledge that our numbering system, algebra, and trigonometry originally came from the Arabic cultures (Kivel, 2002). And, this is just a short list of the numerous examples that should be incorporated in our education system. Some remarkable organizations are available to consult with teachers and principals to promote cultural enrichment, both in the curriculum and school community. Readers are also encouraged to connect with the Southern Poverty Law Center in Montgomery, Alabama, an organization that actively distributes free, quality material to schools and educators interested in promoting tolerance and diversity in their community. The nuances, perspectives, and wealth of information offered by cultural awareness is truly awe inspiring and rewarding to those who take the time to seek it and live it.

> *People become more understanding of each other and more patient when differences are viewed as gifts to exchange instead of problems to be eliminated.*
>
> —Hill (2001, p. 9)

RESPECT AND SHEDDING ADULTISM

Shedding adultism requires that educators reevaluate their ways of relating with students and become aware of the delicate balance between authority and mentoring. Adults committed to this reevaluation must be willing to constantly ask themselves if the situation requires the use of power and direction or if space can be given for young people to think, explore, and be self-directed.

Misconceptions About Reversing Adultism

Addressing adultism is not about reversing the power structure. Sometimes adults struggle with conceiving different relationships with young people and can only imagine the opposite: young people ruling the situation, which is typically a terrifying thought for many. Shedding adultism involves a negotiation of decisions, based on what is best for all parties. It reduces the power imbalance between young people and adults without completely eradicating it.

Warm, genuine, nonthreatening relationships between teachers and students can have a positive effect on the behavior of students, reducing the incidence of bullying. Caring teachers who guide young people to self-control, rather than exerting control upon them, make it unnecessary for students to attempt to assert their power negatively (Gootman, 2001).

Shedding adultism is a deeper process than occasionally implementing an empowering academic exercise. It is a philosophy of relating to young people that is embedded in several subtle and more profound interactions every minute of the day.

The conscious decision to reduce the adultist practices that color our relationships with young people is truly valuable. Young people become seen in all their multiple facets of selves instead of scripted roles. One teacher described for us an enlightening experience she had:

> The other day I was playing a math game with the students and it was like I had a classroom of totally different people. They were so excited and so stimulated. Then the behaviors I started getting because of that! It was interesting because I never ever see any of that in the normal classroom where they are pretty controlled. They couldn't contain themselves. I have a demure girl in class who all of a sudden had a totally different voice. She was going "Aarrwwk!" She was telling her peers she was going to get them. I was amazed and thought, "Gee, I really need to do more of a variety of things, to see the whole picture."

When adults maintain a hierarchical and, at times, oppressive relationship with young people, they miss out on rich moments of genuine connection. They also, believe it or not, miss out on opportunities to learn.

Children and teenagers have incredible views of the world. They often see what adults' eyes have been trained to ignore and, in that sense, can offer very enlightening perspectives. Youth ask questions about discourses, the taken-for-granted beliefs that adults have such a hard time recognizing and deconstructing. For example, young people may ask, "Why do women have to shave their legs and men don't?" "Why are adults allowed to yell but not us?" Questions such as these are often annoying to adults, but they speak of underlying structures in our thought system that we generally do not question enough. Young people also remind adults of being instead of doing. Adults are often task oriented and constantly driven by the future or attempts to amend the past. Young people are who they are and enjoy the present time, which, in reality, is living. Children and teens can contribute to adults' lives with invitations to be present, creative, and observant of taken-for-granted issues, if the adult is willing to seriously consider and reflect on young people's opinions. Take these educators' accounts, for example:

My present students are three- to five-year-old preschoolers, and because they have very little self-control, I must use more structure than I really enjoy. The challenge is to remember that I don't in fact know everything—to not allow the controlling energy to stifle the children's creativity or to block me from seeing their intuitive wisdom—which is formidable, considering their very limited experience with life! When it comes to creativity, these children are in many ways truly my equals and even my teachers, and this is the way I do really connect with them.

—Beverly Prinz

I learn things all the time from kids. That's just never ending. You learn to be humble first of all, because you obviously don't know everything. There's always something more that they teach you, because they are relentless. They don't go away! (laughs)

—Diane Paul

Part of facing adultism is to recognize, once again, the value of diversity and not place individuals' worth on a hierarchy based on narrow criteria, such as length of life experience. It is recognizing that young people may have less experience if measured strictly chronologically, but acknowledging that, on a quantitative level, some underprivileged youth have seen more of life than many adults ever will, and some privileged students have traveled extensively to places many adults have not. On a qualitative level, young people's views are also different—often creative, fresh, and inspiring. When young people are treated with respect and spoken to as other worthy human beings, they develop a sense of autonomy, responsibility, politeness, critical judgment, and express articulated opinions. An elementary school principal spoke the following of respect:

There are so many programs out there that promise ... community ... self-esteem ... academic achievement. I would prefer to say, "Let's work together to see what we can do to be the best teachers we can be." That is what helps to resolve those things. In working to be a good teacher those things come into play: how you listen to your students, how you treat your students. My teachers who are respectful of their students and listen to their students get more respect back than the teachers who say, "I told you to all sit quietly in your seats!"

As this principal mentioned, educators listening and treating students in respectful ways through small means and throughout the day can go much further in promoting respect than formal programs. The following Table 8.2 illustrates the difference between messages that inadvertently have adultist effects and others that place educators and students on a more balanced playing field.

Table 8.2   Alternatives to adultist statements

Common Statements	Exploration of the Adultist Implications	Alternative Nonadultist Statements
"You think this is hard? Wait until you are an adult!"	Disqualification and hierarchy; challenging aspects of childhood are devalued when compared to adult struggles, which are much more serious.	"You can do it! Keep trying!"
"You are not allowed to play with Kevin during recess. You two keep getting in trouble together."	Imposition of external control; children and their struggles must be externally controlled instead of solved and discussed.	"Let's discuss who you think would be a positive friend to play with during recess" or "Let's talk about how the two of you can play without getting upset."
"Get used to it. It's just the way it is for third graders."	Disqualification; children's opinions are unimportant.	"I know things can be difficult sometimes. What can we do together to solve these problems?"
"You're not old enough to know algebra. Where in the world did you learn that?!"	Underestimation; students' abilities are under- or overevaluated and generalized based on age.	"I think it's cool to learn new things at any age. What do you think?"
"I am so frustrated with you; you will lose fifteen minutes of recess for pushing my buttons."	Unilateral exercise of power; children are powerless, and adults have the power to enforce orders when they are frustrated.	"I am feeling frustrated. I'd like to take a few minutes to calm down. Let's talk before recess."
"The staff decided that there will be no more tag games on this campus."	Unilateral exercise of power; children do not have the maturity to contribute to decisions affecting their lives; they are not involved in the process of finding solutions.	"There have been some injuries during tag games. What ideas do you have to help reduce this problem?"
"Come on! You have made the same mistake three times. Try harder!"	Teacher assumes that the issue lies in motivation as opposed to trying to understand student's experience or assumes that children are less intelligent and less disciplined.	"Help me understand what gets in the way of you succeeding at these problems" or "Let's take a look at these mistakes. There's something to be learned from them."
"As long as you are in my class, you'll do exactly what I say!"	Disempowerment; children are helpless to change or comment on the happenings in the classroom.	"Let's make a plan about how we are all going to deal with these issues."

When educators treat students with integrity, respectful interactions become lived experiences that are easy to replicate. When young people grow up in an adultist environment, they become resentful, fearful, and sneaky. By the time they reach adolescence, they lose their own sense of self and opinion to such an extent that their answers to most questions become "I don't know." When they are accustomed to being heard, they articulate their thoughts and share them, often in a fascinating way.

An outcome of developing a less adultist school environment is that students start owning their schools, their academic journeys, and their freedom. Giving possibilities to students seems risky, and it is, given the starting point. The risk involved in not doing so, however, is higher than the cost of opening the hearts and minds of young people.

> *A failure to equip minds with the skills of understanding and feeling and acting in the cultural world is not simply scoring a pedagogical zero. It risks creating alienation, defiance, and practical incompetence. And all of these undermine the viability of a culture.*
>
> —Bruner (1996, p. 42)

The following is a description of seven areas where educators can easily revisit the issue of respect for students. These examples do not encompass all of the multiple ways in which adultism can be shed, but rather are strategies we have encountered in our visits, reflections, and research.

Discipline

Shedding adultism does not mean eliminating all responsibilities of young people when a troublesome or hurtful habit happens, such as disrespect or bullying. Quite the contrary, people of all ages can benefit from understanding the implications of their behaviors and must be aware that there are consequences for their actions. We really encourage parents and educators to involve students in articulating the situation and its effects on others and to discuss reasonable consequences that are experienced as fair to all parties. If the consequence is not experienced as fair (as in most hierarchical and adultist ways of disciplining), then the student will simply ruminate on the frustration of it all, rather than learning and reflecting. The following is a quote from a principal, Dale Jones, who is very committed to nonadultist relationships with students:

> *When students have issues, I try to work with them and have them solve it. I'll ask them, "What do you think would be an appropriate way to solve this problem?" It's important to listen to the students and their reasons why something happened. I facilitate dialogue between students so that they can resolve things. I'll help them learn new ways of acting. It does take more time and a whole set of skills, like the ability to role-play with a student.*

The more pervasive a young person's problems, the more tempting it is for the adult to put on a white coat of authority and knowledge in an attempt to work with the child. In reality, that is when it becomes most important for adults to step back and really listen; educators must understand students' experiences not only to empower them but also to help them articulate problems and preferred ways. The irony is that when students have pervasive problems, adults tend to take more control, even though the earlier control didn't help.

It is also important to determine whether stern discipline, as a blanket policy, is necessary or not. People of all ages have different ways of being comfortable in the world (moving, dressing, eating, etc.). Sometimes doing what is truly best for young people overrides the habit of controlling and teaching in a hierarchical way, as in the following story:

> One of my students clearly needed to move around more than the other kids. So I simply let him stand up and dance from one foot to the other while working on essays and assignments even though everyone else was seated. It made a big difference for him, and I felt good accommodating his different needs. I was told later on that it would drive substitute teachers crazy and that they would get mad at him.
>
> —Joe Joaquin

Often, there is a disciplinary expectation on a school site of complete silence in a classroom. This expectation places teachers in a quandary: Should a teacher promote communication, cooperation, and learning or uphold the expectation? Consider this teacher's story:

> In the early 1970s, I was teaching big classes and had found that the students worked best in small groups. These classes fairly bubbled with energy, and it sometimes happened that the door of the classroom was suddenly thrown open by the principal or vice principal, who would stand with hands on hips and roar, "When your teacher is not in the classroom, I don't want to hear a sound out of you!" At such times I could never decide if it was worse to stand up and reveal that I was in fact present or just to wait until he finished glaring and left! Whenever I tried later to explain my methods and reasons to the administration, there was no respect for such innovation, only respect for silence in the classroom. Years later, I met one of my former students by accident, and she was very happy to see me again. She thanked me for these classes, as she had never forgotten the unique humanness of that environment in the midst of the rigidity of the high school style of education.
>
> —Beverly Prinz

Student-Led Conferences

There has been a growing trend to reduce adultism in schools by giving more power and responsibility to students. It has become clear that students are more successful when they determine their own personal goals and are empowered to find their own ways of achieving them. A good example of such practice is student-led conferences, in which students are responsible for setting their own academic goals, evaluating their progress, and presenting their outcome to their parents and teachers. There is ample research now available demonstrating the efficacy of this practice. Student-led conferences also provide an environment where students can express their pride and self-appreciation (see the numerous titles written on this subject, e.g., Benson & Barnett, 1998; Grant, Heffler, & Mereweather, 1995; Pierce-Picciotto, 1996).

Despite the research and logic behind these practices, conferences led by students require some adjustments in educators' habits and may not be fully satisfying at the very first attempt. While it is always more motivating to do something once we have decided it *is* important, well-intentioned educators often may understand and believe in these novel practices but still struggle with the habit of directing the show, inadvertently undermining the spirit of the practice. For example, a student shared with us that her teacher completely took over the conference, after the student had only spoken for a few minutes. Adults, used to having power, must constantly remind themselves to let go of the habit of ruling. This is not an easy task, given the prevalent problem-saturated stories about young people, the beliefs that support control of students in our culture, and, at times, the many years of experience in the traditional educational system.

School Government

Adultism often subtly infiltrates the thoughtful concept of creating student governments, even though their very existence is supposed to allow for student voice. An example of this is when only popular students are chosen for the position or when the ideas are those actually put forth by teachers. This reduces the likelihood that the opinions and ideas of all the young people on campus, including those of marginalized students, will be heard. One teacher describes her experience of such student government:

> At our school, there was a little student council. There was a message that kids should participate in their education, but it was only certain kids such as the good kids or the kids who "deserved" it. It wasn't seen as something that all kids should be learning.

The intention of the student government, then, doesn't match its effect since many students don't actually have a voice. Adults' overactive involvement in student government can inadvertently continue to promote educational standards and privilege students who fulfill the dominant culture's ideals, therefore excluding a lot of minority or marginalized others, whose diverging voices are ironically quite important to hear. Much more can be learned from differences of opinion than from similar ideas (Winslade & Monk, 1999). An effective, true student government should include students from all groups and allow for free expression, even if the adults, recognizing the competency and wisdom of young people, may not always agree. Take this story, for example, from an elementary school:

> *Our student council operates to let students have their own voices heard. One example of this is when our student council decided that it would be a good idea to have a vending machine on campus. The staff and parents were really against this for various reasons. We shared our concerns with the council. They considered our ideas and were thoughtful about the pros and cons. They took into consideration the fact that we wanted them to have healthy snacks and decided to research the matter. They decided they would still go forth, with some alterations in the type of food served.*

> —Dale Jones

Teacher Positioning

Traditional education usually positions the teacher up front as the one with knowledge, while the students are perceived as recipients. This has adultist implications because teachers are then assumed to be the only ones with knowledge and students are assumed to be passive recipients. Bruner (1996) made the following statement quite well (see also Freire, 1970/2000, for a classic discussion of the issue):

> *We humans show, tell, or teach someone something only because we first recognize that they don't know, or that what they know is false. It is only when these states are recognized that we try to correct the deficiency, by demonstration, explanation, or discussion. . . . No ascription of ignorance, no effort to teach. (p. 48)*

A more honoring and balanced view of young people involves recognizing their knowledge and making a space for them to also act as teachers. In such a context, they experience themselves as valuable, competent, and respected in their intelligence. It also relieves teachers who are crumbling under the pressure to be responsible for everything. Students can definitely take an active role in the sharing of some responsibilities, including the responsibility to teach others. Giving students responsibility positively empowers them, and as a result, they will be less likely to seek it destructively through problem behaviors and bullying (Gootman, 2001). "Never do to students what they can do for themselves," states Eisler (2001), who has promoted a model where students are given the opportunity to teach or coteach as equal contributors to everyone's learning. She states that in many schools, unfortunately, "education is done to students rather than with students." A positive effect of a more honoring process of coteaching is that it creates an environment where each student can become a role model of different ways of being for others (including the teacher) in various ways. This can be very freeing for the teacher and enriching for the students. In this situation, teachers redefine their roles and see themselves as mentors who belong to a community of learners.

They feel less pressure to know all the answers all the time as the responsibility of knowing becomes shared.

Mistakes

Teachers aware of lessening adultism in their class try to acknowledge the mistakes they make in their classrooms to students. When students encounter adults who acknowledge mistakes, they can learn to be comfortable and confident when dealing with their own mistakes. It is a much richer lesson of life to learn the limits of one's knowledge and competency and to be able to acknowledge these limits as natural. Whether students notice or remember the educator's mistake is not of such importance as the powerful effect it can have on them to interact with an adult who is genuine, honest, and has integrity.

Grades

If adults also step back a little on evaluation, students are able to be more reflective of their own behavior and simply freer to be. Take the example of having students give themselves grades as part of a grading procedure. Students, unfamiliar with this process of evaluating their work, may struggle to come up with a self-appraisal. They may tend to be harsher on themselves through fear or unfamiliarity or because it is their experience that they are always evaluated in harsh ways. Conversely, they may overvalue their performance because it is a rare opportunity to give themselves high ranks. When students become more comfortable with this process, they become more realistic and increasingly engaged in useful self-examination.

Names and Titles

In many schools, students are called by their first names, and adults are called by their last names. The intention of this system is often to create a structure for respect and authority. Think of your own school: Does this practice really have that effect? We would like to share the following excerpt from the Web site of the Christa McAuliffe Elementary School (2003) in Cupertino, California, where the staff decided that everyone should be called by their first names:

Why do students call teachers and other adults by their first names at McAuliffe?

We recognize the value of relationships based on mutual, genuine respect. We respect each other for who we are, rather than simply for what position we hold.

In the real world, we do not call colleagues by their last names. Doing so puts an unusual twist on relationships by formalizing them and making them hierarchical.

By using their first names, the adults invite students to feel comfortable with them; they invite them into an environment where we all work together, collaboratively. Students learn that they are not entitled to less respect because they hold the job of students, rather than that of teachers, or because they are children, rather than adults. In the security of these relationships, children gain experience trusting adults and taking risks that help them grow.

TEACHER QUESTION ABOUT SHEDDING ADULTISM

"Doesn't It Seem Like Having Students Speak Up for Themselves All the Time Could Cause Some Kind of Revolt?"

Students must face consequences for their behaviors. What we are questioning is not this concept but rather the process by which consequences are decided and the extent to which students are involved in both the explanation of their stories and the determination of a consequence. Shedding the excessive use of power involved in adultism is an invitation to give up some of that authority to young people so that they become more self-directed and develop an internal sense of accountability. A sudden shift from a very adultist to a self-directed environment is indeed likely to create a context where the young person might indulge in freedom. The process should be progressive, involve conversation, and accept that some mistakes will be made in the exploration of new ways of being. We cannot expect students to immediately be self-directed if they were never given a chance to develop that aspect of themselves in their younger years. The ideal situation is one where young people are raised throughout their childhood as responsible people and increasingly capable of dealing responsibly with freedom and choices.

In some ways, shedding adultism involves a conscious awareness of respecting young people in the same manner that you want to be respected or that you would respect another adult. This may sound clichéd, but many educators holding this belief sometimes contradict it during interactions with students.

Again, shedding adultism is not achieved through an exercise or a promising program. It is really about reexamining one's personal stance and habits of relating to young people. It is a process of reevaluating, minute by minute, whether an action is congruent with intentions and values of being respectful to people of all ages, even when we do not initially like young people's ideas.

We have reviewed these wonderful and rich ideas to foster respect, appreciation, and tolerance in schools. Now we explore the actual step-by-step implementation of this philosophy in classrooms with the Bugging Bug project.

9

Dealing With Disrespect and Bullying in the Classroom

The Bugging Bug Project

This chapter describes a variety of innovative classroom practices to address bullying and peer abuse in schools. While many of the activities listed are described here in their elementary school format, most of these activities have also been facilitated in upper grades with some adjustment. Through honoring activities, students are invited to reflect on the effects of bullying and make personal choices to promote appreciation, tolerance, and collaboration in their classrooms. Elementary school versions require a lot of creativity and a careful attention to children's mastery of language while middle and high school versions require sincerity, trust, and flexibility. Facilitating these programs in any grade level requires a genuine interest for young people's ideas and experiences.

It is interesting to note that, traditionally, bullying habits have been addressed by educators and therapists by working alone with the child; talking in the privacy of a closed, confidential office and meeting each referred child separately. It can be argued that these individual interventions are typically slow and minimally effective, leading to considerable redundancy in the work of educators and therapists because most problems in schools with disrespect occur in the context of relationships in the classroom or other public areas, such as the playground and in a large portion of student interactions. Based on these ideas, we believe that disrespectful behaviors must be addressed in the context where they occur. One such context is the classroom. It has been our experience that working in the classroom is extremely valuable and powerful for teachers and students because it promotes a collaborative approach where all the students are on the same team in an effort to promote respect.

The classroom project discussed in this chapter was designed to create a sense of collaboration, connectedness, appreciation, and tolerance. It consists of a series of experiential activities and discussions aimed at bringing forth respectful practices from a group of students. This project was *never* facilitated in the same manner from class to class. Rather, the facilitator would develop a thorough understanding of the complex problem dynamics for each class and create a series of logical steps to address the intricacies of their unique subculture. In this process, only five or six of the activities presented below could be used and maybe some others would be created. In this way, each class ended up with their own 4–8 week curriculum addressing their unique pattern of interaction.

A REVIEW OF THE NARRATIVE IDEAS THAT GUIDE THIS PROJECT

This classroom project is an integrated application of all of the ideas discussed in this book. It is not just a series of exercises that one can simply implement in the class, but rather a philosophical journey that addresses contextual factors promoted by teachers while at the same time inviting students' preferred ways of being. Specifically, some of the contextual factors discussed earlier include competition, evaluation, external rules, performance, individualism, adultism, and intolerance of differences. This project is therefore about reducing the presence of these contextual blocks by inviting teachers to minimize them and, at the same time, foster a climate of collaboration, team spirit, adult–student respect, and a valuing of differences. A good metaphor to illustrate the importance of this joint process is to imagine growing a precious flower deep in a forest. You may engage in all of the best growth-promoting activities in the world, such as watering, fertilizing, and weeding, with a devoted commitment. But in the end, the flower will not grow as long as the environment remains unsupportive of such development. We truly believe in and have witnessed the beauty of classroom transformation when teachers make the commitment to reflect on their own involvement with these contextual issues.

As for students, the initial work is to assist them in becoming aware of the effects of bullying and disrespect on themselves and others. To achieve this, a problem is externalized so that it can be examined without blaming or passing judgment on anyone. Although it is preferable to let students choose a relevant name, the Bugging Bug was playfully used in several classes to allow entire elementary schools to become a team against it. In middle and high schools, words such as Disrespect, Meanness, Anger, Harassment, Gossip, and Cliques are often used. After students map the effect of the problem on their own lives and become aware of the implication, they are progressively invited to make their own decisions as to the kind of person they each want to be and why. The subsequent activities become a journey into enriching their preferred story of a respectful person. The weekly focus on discussing respect renders the class's commitment concrete in the mind of each student. It also allows all students to progress in their own way and become increasingly aware of the advantages of and their personal preference for respectful interactions. Toward the end of the project, an audience (the class, principal, parents, other students, etc.) is created on several occasions to witness the individual preferred stories and validate them.

Even though the project is written as a week-by-week curriculum, the facilitator is expected to adapt the project to the specific needs of each unique group of students by varying the order of presentation of the activities, extending or shortening the length of time for certain steps, skipping some exercises, and creating new ones. In fact, more than the activities themselves, it is the process of honoring and connecting with students' experiences that is the underlying key to the success of this project. Although we have included a large list of possible activities, not all need to be implemented to transform the classroom. In fact, if no changes are visible after four or five activities, it would mean that an important contributor to the problem has not been recognized, or that the teacher's practices are not congruent with the philosophy, or that these activities are used as concrete recipes as opposed to guiding new ways of thinking and relating. The teacher would then need to take an honest look again at the use of competition, for example, or the effects of certain interactions. Given the amount of possibilities presented here, we hope that our readers will be able to simply choose and adapt what is useful to them. Maureen's comments have been added to express her experiences as a teacher cofacilitating this project and to offer insight to educators who wish to implement this project alone.

SECTION 1: EXTERNALIZING THE PROBLEM

Maureen: Daily, my class teased, excluded, argued, insulted, and pushed each other to the limits. This particular class of students had a reputation that had followed them from their previous grades. For four years, they were known as a difficult class to teach. The group was known for having many dynamic personalities but few

(Continued)

(Continued)

positive role models. The students who had good citizenship and were academically focused were quiet about it, almost embarrassed by their successes. It was considered cool to be in conflict with each other. The students were quite concerned with their social standing and were critical of anyone who acted out of the norm, the norm not being scholarly, respectful, and kind. This overtook any drive the students had for being curious about learning or mastering an interesting subject. Each of the students was affected by the context of this class, and it was difficult to get through all the academic material because of the battles that occurred. Loneliness, anger, competition, and sadness were all very present.

As their teacher, I was fighting fires one at a time. I consider myself a compassionate person and tolerant of a range of behaviors, but I was rapidly losing patience and any drive to make school a fun and exciting place to be. At the beginning of the year, teaching this group of students was pure survival. I went home at night exhausted and discouraged. I felt like the job I was doing was more than sufficient, and the students were just a problem to endure for the months to come. I felt that I had limited time and resources, and I became impatient and raised my voice often. I became half-hearted in my teaching and frustrated with the outcomes, which fueled the belief that their reputation had announced. I tried team-building exercises to build some cohesiveness and began giving rewards for the smallest acts of kindness and courtesy. The team-building exercises I introduced were enjoyed by the group because it was a break from the regular routine; however, the students faked their way through by learning what expected correct answers should be, gave rote answers when asked for feedback, and weren't genuinely positive in their contributions. It wasn't honest growth. Within hours, they were teasing and insulting each other again.

I felt a need for some kind of intervention because I was aware that their behavior affected my attitude, and, in turn, my attitude influenced their behavior. It was a vicious cycle. I also knew that I wasn't living with my values, philosophy, and teaching style in this classroom. I lost some of the rapport that I naturally have with students, and I hid my enthusiasm for learning because I was tired. I was at a loss for what to do. I sought Marie-Nathalie and the Bugging Bug project.

Week 1: Connecting With the Teacher

In this project, collaboration between teacher and facilitator is critical. The teacher must become interested in the ideas and the process for the program to be helpful, regardless of who actually requests the program (i.e., principal, parents, administrators). The first week is thus spent getting to know the teacher on a personal level and gathering information about the difficulties in the classroom. This is done informally as well as formally, in the same way one would be curious and gather information about a new teammate. It is helpful, for instance, to understand how and why the teacher got into teaching and which values are important to him or her as an adult relating to students.

An exploration of how the teacher understands the disrespect in the classroom, how the teacher is handling the disrespect, and whether or not the teacher's practices of handling disrespect fit with his or her initial vision can give direction to the program. The teacher can define differences within the class that are not being respected. This connection with the teacher is the foundation of the program because the teacher must be engaged and eventually comfortable enough to examine his or her own teaching practices that may inadvertently contribute to a vicious cycle of disrespect (e.g., challenging adultist practices). This is not to say that teachers should be blamed for the disrespect but rather that they are a powerful part of a context where the problem happens. Throughout the program, the facilitator touches base with the teacher weekly to catch up on new developments and plan relevant exercises.

> *Maureen:* This time spent reflecting before the program began was valuable. Marie-Nathalie and I had some conversations about adultism, competition, and the frustration I felt. I was trying to understand what I was inadvertently doing that contributed to the students' impatience for and intolerance of each other. I knew there were patterns of interaction in the classroom that caused an anxious, competitive context for all. As Marie-Nathalie described the format and philosophy of her program, I could see that it was aligned with my values and with how I really wanted to relate with my students.

If a teacher is facilitating this alone in the classroom, he or she may have feelings of isolation. Because it is necessary to remain open and examine the teacher's role in the context of the class, teachers may face some difficulty exploring their thoughts and emotions alone. It could be very helpful to pair up teachers or to have the teacher consult with a trusted colleague. It would be validating to have another teacher with whom to counsel. There are a few different ways to approach this:

1. Complete the program in the teacher's classroom, solo.

2. Collaborate with another teacher, running the program in the teacher's own class but conferring with the colleague weekly on issues that arise.

3. Collaborate with another teacher, running the program with both classes together. (Classes could be in the same grade level or in different grade levels.)

4. Collaborate with another teacher, running the program in each other's classrooms. (Students often appreciate visitors in their classroom. Teachers could feel a fresh start with a new group of students is desirable. Teachers will also get the reward of coming back into

their own classroom to hear their class retell their experiences, sharing what was exciting and important to their experiences, reinforcing it, and owning it as their own.)

Week 2: Valuing Diversity

What If Everyone in the World Were the Same?

The first visit in the classroom involves engaging the students in a discussion about how the world would be if everyone were the same. Typically, this idea triggers a lot of reflections from all students, and the discussion is easy to facilitate. Questions asked are adapted to the age group and grade level. In some instances, multiple-choice questions yield much more participation and understanding than open-ended questions, especially with younger kids, groups, or students who are not accustomed to having space for their voices. For example, in elementary school, it is helpful to ask questions such as "Would we have more solutions to a problem or fewer?" or "Would you have more toys and games or fewer?" In a high school, it would be more relevant to ask questions such as "How would music be affected? Would we have more groups or fewer groups?" or "How would sports be affected? Would we have only one type of team?" The facilitator should make an effort to acknowledge contributions and ideas of all students and to invite students' ideas about these issues rather than facilitating a lecture about diversity.

Promoting a context where students can articulate their own thinking about diversity is much more likely to have the effect on students of understanding the concepts and behaving accordingly. This being said, however, it is important that the facilitator ask these questions from a place of genuine curiosity and not with an all-knowing or moral attitude. A great question can be experienced in a negative and disrespectful way when coming from a position of all-knowing as opposed to one of authentic interest. When everyone's ideas have been voiced, the group summarizes the advantages of a world with different people, with a particular emphasis on students' actual experiences of these advantages. A process of dynamic questioning, such as in the following excerpt, can be initiated: "How many of you like pizza? Raise your hands! Well, pizza comes from Italy. How many of you like burritos? Raise your hands! Burritos come from South America. We are so lucky to have Latin people living in our country." The questions must be relevant to the students' age group and directed to items experienced in their day-to-day lives. With teenagers, for example, it may be worthwhile to associate popular teen public figures with certain categories. The same can be done with other items, such as the radio, which was invented in Holland; the telephone, which was invented in Canada; and automobile gasoline, which comes from oil from the Middle East. It is generally helpful to write students' ideas on the blackboard as it honors and recognizes the ideas as being valuable for everyone, and it reduces the power imbalance associated with adults as the only ones to have ideas worth writing up. The facilitator's stance in itself contributes greatly to promoting an atmosphere of acceptance and respect.

What Are Differences?

When the class clearly understands and owns the concept that differences are valuable, the facilitator can address the specific differences that contribute to the richness of the class. To begin, the facilitator asks the students to generate a list of major differences (race, religion, language, country of origin, etc.), making sure to include those differences that the teacher has noticed to be targets of teasing or bullying. The next step becomes a dynamic process of honoring the unique differences of individuals in the classroom by category. So, for instance, the facilitator might say, "Those of you who have a name that no one else has in your classroom, stand up," and everyone applauds. Or the facilitator might say, "Those of you who have a disability or know someone who has one, stand up," and again everyone applauds.

It is important that the facilitator be sensitive in the choice of categories and not overestimate the long-term safety issues associated with students identifying themselves as a member of a particularly marginalized or oppressed minority. For example, in most schools, it is preferable (unfortunately) to avoid inviting gay youth to identify themselves, especially those whose sexuality may not be known. Even though students may be genuinely interested in valuing diversity and in becoming more respectful, the culture has trained most of them in prejudiced ways, which take time to be uncovered and deconstructed. The classroom may feel very safe when the facilitator is there, but when the facilitator is gone, students may regret their visibility or may forget the novel idea of tolerance. The formulation of these questions must therefore be thought of carefully. The way a question is presented can open or close the space for the verbalization of disrespect and can have powerful counter effects to what was intended. For example, appreciation for certain invisible categories can be addressed by naming popular representatives of these oppressed minority groups instead of asking for students to identify themselves as members of these groups.

Maureen: Learning about diversity is fundamental in the classroom. I believe you can never do enough through the year to celebrate diversity. Read biographies; celebrate holidays and share cultural stories; talk in other languages, including sign language; honor inventors from all races; have kids share information about their ethnicities; have real skin and hair colors available for art; have cultural days, sharing music, art, and recipes from other cultures; and have the class environment reflect on the value of diversity by decorating with art, puppets, and musical instruments all of different cultures, among other ideas.

What Happens When Differences Are Misunderstood?

Once differences have been appreciated, students are questioned as to what happens when people don't understand or are afraid of differences. The problem is named and externalized early on in the conversation. Examples include Disrespect, Intolerance, and Disconnection for older groups and Bugging Habit or Bugging Bug for younger students. Sometimes a name will be more abstract, such as Black Cloud, Harsh Part, or Acid 9. For the name to be useful in any way, it must be meaningful to the students and connect with their experience.

An extensive discussion of the effects of the problem (Bugging Bug, Disrespect, or whatever name was chosen) is critical for two reasons. First, for students to actually want to take a stance against those behaviors, they need to have a clear understanding of the effects that such problems have in their own personal lives and in the lives of their peers. Second, becoming aware of these effects can reconnect them with their sensitivity and empathy toward others. It can be assumed that if people really understand and connect with their own painful experiences as well as the pain some of their attitudes inflicted on others, they would probably refrain from doing so. Questions that can be used include, for example, "What does the Bugging Bug get kids to do that deep inside they don't really want to do?" or "How do kids feel when the Bugging Bug gets them to do something mean?" The process of asking questions is particularly important to keep students actively involved and interested. A sufficient amount of time must be allowed for this section as the facilitator must make sure that most students have externalized the problem and noticed its effects.

With younger kids, it can be helpful and fun to illustrate the Bugging Bug's effects on kids by doing a brief skit. The skits can be about a student noticing that someone is different and having a debate in his mind between the Bugging Bug and his preferred good conscience. This debate is represented by two people standing behind and over each shoulder of the student volunteer (who usually just listens). The person playing the Bugging Bug (usually the facilitator) must remember to be mean without marginalizing certain students in the class. It would be hurtful for a facilitator to play a Bugging Bug making remarks about kids who are obese or of a different race for example. It is preferable to keep the skit's dialogue on the effects of mean versus respectful behavior. In other words, the person playing the Bugging Bug might encourage a student to be mean because, for example, it will be funny or will make the student popular, or the Bugging Bug might say the student won't get in trouble since everyone dislikes the other student anyway. The person playing the preferred self (the teacher or another student) might encourage the student to be respectful because, for example, he or she wants to be known as a kind kid or because the student doesn't like to be hurtful, or the preferred self might say the student should try to know the other student before passing judgment.

If a Bugging Bug puppet is used during the skit, it should not represent any specific known character or be excessively cool or attractive. This could inadvertently bias the project by transforming the unwanted character into a popular hero. It is also important to avoid a concrete bug (e.g., a bee), which may result in younger kids becoming confused and exterminating the actual living insect in the neighborhood of the school.

Sometimes kids really believe in the externalization and genuinely believe that a real bug sneaks in their head. This is usually more of a concern to adults than to kids themselves. For kids, the idea of a real bug makes a lot of sense given that they really don't like to get in trouble and do mean things; it is logical that something gets them to do it. At the same time, however, the responsibility of the child in pushing the Bugging Bug away must be emphasized and explored in depth. As discussed earlier, adults can be reassured by knowing that this concept does not eliminate accountability but rather empowers students to make choices and clarify their preferences.

Using both the term Bugging Bug and the term Bugging Habit (or simply Disrespect) may also help older students, who may be skeptical of and disconnected from the idea of a bug. The goal is to help students separate the problem from their individual identities so that they may take a stand against it; whether they conceive it as a habit or an actual external object is irrelevant.

> *Maureen:* Already they could see that the problem wasn't them personally. The problem was externalized outside. A student known for malicious gossiping, manipulative flirting, aggressive soccer playing, or bullying wasn't only that identity. Suddenly that problem was the Bugging Bug, and there was a whole person there who had a lot to offer our class. The students were beginning to be open to understanding how their negative actions were hard on each other.

Another practice that can assist a facilitator in staying close to students' experiences is an anonymous question box that can be set up in a corner of the class. Anonymity can open a line of communication between the facilitator of the program and students who may be uncomfortable about talking in class. Students can be given blank cards to write questions or comments that can be addressed in the next meeting (once again, specify that student names should not be mentioned in a blaming way).

Discussions often need to be followed by an individual reflection, such as a homework or classroom assignment, to ensure that all students have the opportunity to connect the project to their own life experience. When this is not done, the facilitator runs the risk of reaching and involving only those students who actually have a voice, while further alienating students who most need the project. The facilitator needs to be sensitive to staying connected with most students in the classroom. Paralleling class discussion with individual reflections has two advantages: It facilitates the inclusion of students who may have a harder time understanding verbal material because of a language difference, a learning disability, hyperactivity, or other issues, and it can greatly assist the facilitator by providing useful information about what was understood and what needs to be reviewed. In other words, it helps the facilitator stay closer to students' experiences in the next discussion and readjust the next step of the project if necessary. Students can also be invited to notice how the Bugging Bug affects them during the week to increase the likelihood that the conversation be evocative the next time.

Maureen: For a homework assignment this week, have students write their reflections on the following questions: What is the Bugging Bug? What effects does it have on you? What does the Bugging Bug get you to do that you would like to stop? What do you like about diversity? This comes in handy next week when the class makes posters.

After learning about the Bugging Bug, I found it valuable to check in with the class several times this week to discuss what experiences the students had with the Bugging Bug. I often shared my stories of how the Bugging Bug visits me, such as feeling frustrated in a meeting, feeling competitive with a friend, and feeling angry while driving.

We need to extend a caution: Do not overuse the externalization such as Bugging Bug. Students can feel manipulated if it is too frequently mentioned. Also, do not use it if you are mad, unless you are sure you can hold on to the context of a nonblaming externalization and not judge the child.

Week 3: Unmasking the Bugging Bug

The next discussion can be a follow-up on students' observations during the week and their personal reflections. Specifically, questions such as the following can be asked about what they have noticed: "When and where is the Bugging Bug most likely to strike?" "What ideas does it put in people's minds about others?" "Is the Bugging Bug an important issue to think about?" "Are you willing to help increase everyone's awareness of the Bugging Bug in their school and community?"

The class can then be invited to create prevention posters consisting of a slogan and artwork. The previous week's homework can be very useful here as students artistically illustrate the result of their personal reflections. To avoid the extreme narrowing of creativity that may occur when everyone draws an insecticide bottle, the facilitator can refer students to personal examples by simply showing such a drawing as an example and asking them to do another type of advertisement that would be unique and different. The slogan can simply be the student's personal reason to avoid the Bugging Bug. Examples of slogans include the following: "Friends are more fun than the Bugging Bug" or "I value peace over Bugging Bugs."

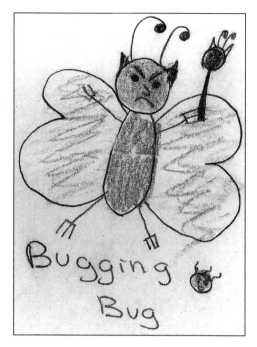

The process of creating preventive posters offers several advantages: It provides a context where students actually have to articulate their own thinking about the issue, it requires students to imagine themselves in somebody else's shoes, and it creates a visible and public document that testifies to their preference for respectful interactions.

It is preferable to not set it up as a contest, which would invite competition, evaluation, and hierarchy among students and consequently increase the likelihood of disrespect. Moreover, prizes can easily shift the focus of the project from one where students are invested in exploring respect to one where they focus on materialistic gain. Students can be given the week to work on their posters.

In middle and high school, this popular activity can also be creating pamphlets where students write more elaborate texts on reasons to oppose certain problems such as Disrespect, Peer Pressure, Discrimination, etc. In one high school where a version of this project was facilitated, a small group of male students struggling with outbursts of violence decided to publish the following quotes in a newsletter:

"One act of violence can change the whole course of your life."

"The heat of the moment can get in the way of seeing nonviolent ways of being."

"Being violent to deal with problems only increases problems."

"Society says fight for respect. I know I don't need muscle to get respect."

"In a big way, walking away (from fights) makes you stronger."

Maureen: When creating the posters or pamphlets, it is important to talk with the students about diversity. All of their ideas are valuable to the class in making it a well-rounded and colorful environment. Some young people may have more defined artistic abilities, and others may have catchier slogans, but it's important for students to express themselves and not feel competitive or feel the need to copy another's document. The teacher could consider making a poster or a pamphlet, too. Students should be given ample time to be successful at creating these documents. I gave my students two sessions to work on their design and asked them to finish coloring them for homework.

This was a rewarding process as we got to use our imaginations to create a real Bugging Bug for ourselves. Each student had a vision of what it looked like in his or her individual mind. We created our own visions, and we put dialogue to our visions of this bug.

I do speak of sending some of the Bugging Bug work as homework. This is only a suggestion. Over the years in my teaching career, I have changed my vision of what homework should be. My goal is to send home only meaningful homework in the desire for my students to have more free time (more than is given with the current amounts of homework) to play and pursue outside interests. That said, I realize there is pressure to send homework for various reasons, so here are some ideas:

- Create a word search or cross-word puzzle with Bugging Bug vocabulary that your class is using.
- Write advice to a student in another country about the Bugging Bug. Make sure you include definitions for *Bugging Bug* and *respect*. Extra credit challenge: Write your letter in code and be sure to have a key.
- Write riddles about the Bugging Bug.
- Write an advice column about the Bugging Bug problems that exist. Write both the inquiry and the response, in different voices.
- Write a story from the Bugging Bug's point of view.
- Write diary entries from the point of view of a child who is ridding him-or herself of the Bugging Bug.
- Draw a maze of the steps and the process you go through to get rid of the Bugging Bug.

Week 4: Poster Show

The meeting can start by displaying everyone's posters in the classroom, with names being randomly called to introduce their own or another person's poster or even to ask the class who would like to explain their posters. Acknowledgment (by way of applause) of each poster and the message intended is really important. If there is some time left after the presentation of all posters, the facilitator can initiate a discussion of his or her experience in creating these posters and how it affected the facilitator's ways of being. For the following week, students are invited to notice whether or not they are able to sometimes resist the Bugging Bug. This question can be presented as a mystery, as something that everyone wonders about.

SECTION 2: BUILDING ON SUCCESSES

Week 5: Individual Success Chart

This week, questions can be asked about whether or not students have noticed themselves resisting the temptation of disrespect during the week. In elementary schools, students who feel that they have resisted the Bugging Bug at least once are invited to raise their hands. After a general acknowledgment of everyone who tried, students are invited to share their successes. All students willing to share a story of their success are listened to and enthusiastically applauded one by one, in an effort to create a dynamic and energetic context of appreciation. It is important to remind students to not mention any names when sharing the event, as doing so would be a Bugging Bug thing to do. (It is often tempting to say names, as in "Jason pushed me but I didn't react and I walked away.") Since each of those statements is usually brief, every student who raises his or her hand to share a success is given the opportunity to do so and is applauded by everyone. When all are given the opportunity to be acknowledged, the facilitator can introduce the Individual Success Chart. Adjusted individual success charts are useful for all ages and even for adults. Specifically, people are invited to start writing down the times when they could have been disrespectful but chose not to be. This process offers several advantages:

- For students who struggle with the Bugging Bug/Disrespect and often end up in trouble, this process suddenly makes visible the times they could have gotten into trouble but did not. The focus shifts from noticing the unwanted behaviors to how skilled they can be at avoiding problems. These observations are encouraging and promote hope of being trouble free.
- For students who are usually victims of the Bugging Bug/Disrespect or students who discretely hold on to preferred ways of being, this process offers the possibility of making visible their commitment to respectful behaviors.
- For the teacher who may be unaware of the discrete efforts made by some students to be respectful, this brings forth good intentions and meaningful incidents that may otherwise remain unnoticed.

Maureen: During this time, I was starting to notice that my class was feeling more peaceful. I was beginning to relax, as well. This may occur at different times in different groups. We were noticing successes of our own and behaving in more preferred ways. Before recess or lunch, I would remind students that when they returned, we would spend time reflecting on our Individual Success Chart and filling it in. I would give them ten minutes or so when they returned. At first, I had a dilemma. I was worried about taking up academic time to give them time for Bugging Bug activities like this. Soon I realized that the time was worthwhile, because the activity focused them and reminded them of their preferred selves; they were then able to concentrate more on their academics. The ten minutes taken paid off.

Week 6: Strategies and Tornado Breaths

The facilitator should review the charts ahead of time to make sure all students understand the activity. Sadly, it is not unusual to read on a success chart a statement such as the following: "I got upset at Jennifer during basketball and, instead of punching her, I hit myself three times." By knowing students' experiences ahead of time, the facilitator can clarify without mentioning any names that the Bugging Bug may try to get them to hurt themselves instead of others. A discussion can be facilitated about their thoughts of self-harm. Do they see self-harm as another version of disrespect? How does the Bugging Bug convince kids to be mean to themselves? What effects does it have? Self-harm is also a powerful subject of conversation for middle and high schoolers who can be very articulate about why some young people think that it would help, why it usually doesn't, and what may be alternative ways of dealing with emotions.

In elementary schools, this meeting starts similarly to the previous one by acknowledging students who have had at least one success at resisting the Bugging Bug. This time, however, the process is followed by a discussion of the strategies students used to resist the Bugging Bug and what they need to remember if they want to do this again. Often, students are unsure of what exactly allowed them to be successful. It is preferable to not put anyone on the spot but rather to ask a series of questions to the entire class, such as the following: "The last time that you were able to resist the Bugging Bug what kinds of things were you thinking about?" "When you feel yourself getting mad, what do you remember to avoid doing something mean?" "When you feel annoyed by someone you know, what do you tell yourself to stay calm?" Asking variations of the same question is necessary when working with a big group such as a classroom because different words and sentences will be closer to the experience of different students; creative redundancy will ensure that each student can relate to at least one of the versions. Students' answers and reflections are compiled on the blackboard. Occasionally, the facilitator may have to ask for more details or rephrase an idea so that it fits, but it is important to do so only rarely, as the goal of the project is to honor students' knowledge.

Each of these strategies can then be expanded into a creative team strategy. For example, most of the time a student will come up with the idea of taking a deep breath. This is a practice that can be useful when the entire class is very hyperactive. If students do not mention the idea, the facilitator can ask them if they think a deep breath could be helpful against the Bugging Bug (or in groups needing more structure, simply share this as a strategy other classes have used). The deep breath idea can be playfully expanded as the metaphor of a tornado breath, especially in elementary school. The tornado breath is a slow, deep breath that the whole class takes together to wash the Bugging Bugs from everyone's body. The Bugging Bugs actually get caught in the tornado of everyone's deep breath and get helplessly blown out of the classroom. Students are encouraged to close their eyes while doing so to visualize the air blowing in all parts of their bodies to make sure that the Bugging Bug is not hiding in a little corner, such as a toe. Kids usually love the tornado breath, and it is not uncommon for them to start using it as a regular strategy in their everyday lives.

Note that the brainstorming of strategies does not involve applauding every contribution. An overuse of the process of applauding will automatically lead to a weakening of its meaning and power. For that reason, applauding is limited to acknowledgment of successes. After the brainstorming, students are invited to continue being good observers of their own successes and strategies for the following week.

In middle and high school, systemic applauding of others' efforts and successes is usually not very popular and may invite rejection of the facilitator. Taking a deep breath, however, can be practiced in stress reduction programs. Students can be interested in learning various methods of relaxation such as meditation, yoga, progressive muscle relaxation, etc.

Maureen: Ahhhhh whooooooo! A tornado breath . . . what a helpful thing for each one of us. Every school year in California, there is a schoolwide earthquake drill. We must duck and cover under our desks, and it can take some time and patience. Our drill occurred around the time of Week 6. The class remembered that tornado breaths were a great calming technique and began doing it during earthquake preparedness. We considered renaming the breath to earthquake breath but liked Marie-Nathalie's version. I even taught this to my toddler. Once you know it, you can't deny its power!

It can be tempting to skip doing the Individual Success Chart and go to listing strategies in an intellectual manner. This is the downside of other character education programs I have seen in the schools—these programs intellectualize ideas and force them on students. What I came to appreciate about this project is that classmates come up with strategies after they have honored their own experiences. It offers more richness of ideas and more ownership of the process. It's exciting to hear the class stories of victories—some large, some small; all are important. During this week I also facilitate a short discussion around the question: "What would our class be like if we were Bugging Bug free?" I congratulate the class because they are making strides toward that goal and ask them if anyone would like to congratulate another student.

Week 7: What Is a Team?

Once again, the facilitator invites students to share their successes at resisting the Bugging Bug, applauds each example, and then expands the list of team strategies. Thereafter, questions can be asked about the meaning of being a team:

- How do you define the word?
- What makes a team successful?
- What are the advantages of being part of a team?
- How would your class be different if you were treating each other as teammates?
- Imagine that your team is playing soccer or basketball—would you want to yell at someone who makes a mistake and misses the ball, or would you want to be supportive of the person, help the person out, or say something like "good try?"
- What would be important for you in a team?
- How would you like your class to be a team? What would you like about it?
- How would your class be different if you were treating each other as teammates?

When students have a good understanding of the implications of being a team, several activities can be implemented. A name can be determined for the team by either asking students for suggestions, writing them all on the blackboard, and combining them somehow (e.g., the first syllables of each possible name) or randomly drawing one of the names out of a basket containing all the suggestions. During the following week, students can contribute to the drawing of a big paper flag and try to be a real team against the Bugging Bug. They can also create team recipes for baking an imaginary respect-inducing cake.

Week 8: Defining Respect

The meeting can begin with the class sharing their experience of being a team. If students felt unsuccessful at working as a team, more time can be spent exploring how the Bugging Bug interferes and what students would prefer to do. For example, how does the Bugging Bug prevent kids from supporting each other in school? When you make a silly mistake, what would you like your teammates to do or say? What needs to happen for this class to become a team? It is easier to ask students what they would like others to do when they make a mistake than to ask them what they want to do when someone else does. The first formulation opens more space for tolerance and compassion and closes space for blaming and punishment.

As students progressively become experts at unmasking the Bugging Bug, working as a team and noticing their successes, the discussion moves toward respectful ways of being. For example, the class can be invited to brainstorm on how they would define respect if they were to write a dictionary. This exercise can be hard for many students, even older ones, because this word is often used intellectually with little connection made to actual life experiences. Students usually have to be prompted several times using questions such as the following: "Try to remember the last time you felt respected. What was the other person doing?" "How does it feel inside when someone respects you?" "When you want to show people that you respect them, what do you do?"

Again, it is important that the facilitator be comfortable asking the same questions several times with different words to reach as many different students as possible. While an individual meeting would provide the therapists with the knowledge of language meaningful to each student, classroom work does not provide such luxury, and the facilitator—more or less alone—has to come up with the initial wording that will touch students' personal experiences. As mentioned earlier, it is very important to avoid the general adult temptation of lecturing and explaining the word to students as it would simply maintain their disconnection from the meaning respect has in their own lives. It is preferable to accept an initial meager definition and send students on a mission of exploration of the word and its meaning.

Specifically, students can be invited to interview at least two adults about their experiences of respect. The facilitator or the teacher could type a list of suggested questions that students can expand if they want. Examples of these include the following:

- How do you define respect?
- How did you learn about respect as a child?
- Who was the most respectful person to you?
- When did you decide that you wanted to be a respectful person and why?
- How do you hold on to respectful ways when you feel upset or annoyed?

Unfortunately, in our busy world, some adults get annoyed by having to answer too many questions, and it is preferable to have students choose about three questions that intrigue them as opposed to setting them up with a frustrating interview experience. Only if the interviewee is interested should the other questions be pursued. Requesting that students interview at least one parent offers the advantage of inviting parents not only to participate in their child's school learning experiences, but also to reflect on the issue of respect toward young people. The other adult chosen can be one who students experience to be particularly respectful to them. It can be really interesting for them to connect with this adult on a more personal level and deepen their understanding of how one develops preferred ways of being. The interview creates a context where meaningful adults can share some of their life experience without imposing the conversation and without being moralizing. In many ways, it creates a forum for adults to be accountable to young people about the effects of their ways of being.

Maureen: I suggest that the teachers get involved personally by asking themselves these questions and also going through the process of interviewing a close adult friend or relative. By reflecting on your own life, you will be prepared for next week's activity when your class interviews you, but, more important, it can get you closer to remembering your experiences as a young person. By interviewing another adult, you can more closely understand the process your students are experiencing and also learn more about someone you care about.

Week 9: Interviews

Students report on not only what they found in their interviews but also what they think about these ideas and whether or not they feel these ideas can be useful to them. Questions can be covered one by one, giving students who wish to share the opportunity to do so, or the discussion can be opened up so that students respond to whatever interested them most. Retelling the interviews increases the likelihood that the experience will be meaningful and connected to their personal lives. This discussion allows students to move from the position of observing these ideas to one of owning the ideas in their own unique and personal way. Once everyone wishing to share has done so, the definition of respect discussed the previous week can be extended with students' new ideas.

Several Interviewees Speak Out on Respect

When you were young, who was most respectful to you, and how?

"My mother would listen to my problems and treat me like an equal."

"My friend always listened to my ideas about how to play games."

"My teacher wouldn't gossip about me and tell people I wasn't good at something."

"My father let me make my own choices."

"My parents always told the truth and helped weak and old people."

> *As an adult, what do you do to try to be respectful?*
>
> "I am always kind to others and give credit when it's due."
>
> "I make sure that people know I value them, by listening."
>
> "I try to help others who need it and not emphasize it too much."
>
> "I try to do the best and right thing that there is to do."

Students are given the opportunity to interview their teacher and facilitator regarding their personal experiences with the Bugging Bug and respect. This particular activity is powerful and often one of the most remembered. It can easily take an hour and may need to be the activity of the following week. It can be set up in a variety of ways. The teacher and facilitator can interview each other first and then ask for reflections, questions, or comments from the class; a small group of volunteers (maximum of about six or seven students) can choose to come up front and sit in a half circle with the teacher and facilitator and ask questions one after the other; or, if many students want to interview the teacher and facilitator, the interview can simply be opened to the class at large. Helpful questions to ask in this context include the following:

- Did the Bugging Bug/Disrespect get you to do things you didn't want to as a child?
- How did it affect your friendships when you followed the Bugging Bug/engaged in Disrespect?
- How did you learn that you didn't want to follow the Bugging Bug's ideas? How did you come to take a stand against Disrespect?
- Did a teacher help you discover respect?
- Did this teacher treat you in a way that made you want to be respectful?
- What did this teacher do exactly?
- Were there other adults around you who helped you learn to be respectful?
- Were there some adults with whom it was hard to be respectful?
- As a teacher, how do you hold on to respect when the Bugging Bug is in the classroom?
- How do you try to remain respectful when something upsetting is happening?

To some facilitators, this interview may appear to be risky, especially with teachers invested in hierarchy and discipline. Such teachers, however, are often the ones who will most appreciate and benefit from the experience because it reconnects them with their own memories of classroom oppression as well as their initial visions of themselves as teachers. In Marie-Nathalie's experience, most teachers actually seem to be very open and interested in the process, which may appear safe given his or her connection with students by that time and a willingness to subject oneself to the questioning as well.

Several Interviewees Speak Out on Respect

What does it mean for you to be respectful, or, how do you define respect?

  "Respect is the ability to listen and accept other people's opinions."

  "Paying polite attention to others shows respect."

  "Being kind, considerate, and a good listener."

When you get upset at someone, what do you try to do to resist being mean and disrespectful?

  "Patience is the best of all virtues. I try to put myself in someone's shoes and understand the differences."

  "I remember what it feels like to be treated in a mean way."

  "I take a deep breath and say, 'Bless you.'"

The physical arrangement of this activity is tricky. Students can simply keep their regular seats or be invited to gather in a circle. Inviting all students to sit together on the floor can create a more intimate atmosphere for sharing precious personal stories. However, such proximity also increases the likelihood that the Bugging Bug/Disrespect will interfere sooner or later and get some students to play tricks on each other (such as untying shoes). With such proximity, the actions of only one or two uninterested students can quickly snowball and interfere with the other students' ability to pay attention. In elementary schools, it can be helpful to wonder whether or not the class could actually work together as a team and achieve fifteen seconds of complete silence. Students can close their eyes while doing so to prevent the Bugging Bug from getting everyone to look at each other and giggle. This challenge is usually received with great enthusiasm, and the facilitator must be prepared for numerous requests to repeat the activity with longer silence times. To ensure that the activity is successful, it is preferable to keep the increments short—fifteen seconds, with a maximum of a minute and a half. If the activity is to maintain its significance and usefulness, it is preferable to not repeat it more than once, despite students' excitement about it. Interest for silence can dissipate quickly if overdone.

The interview inevitably increases the connection between students and their teacher. After this activity, many students we encountered share how they now perceive their teacher as "being more human," "more like them," or that they felt they "could do it too since their teacher did it as a kid." Teachers generally comment on how wonderful it is for them to share some of their life stories with their students. For many this experience renews their commitment to being respectful with their students and reminds them of what it was like to be young and misunderstood by adults.

Maureen: The interview that took place in class in which the students interviewed Marie-Nathalie and me about our lives was pivotal. It was a critical point in our success as a team. They were able to sit together and ask very deep questions about our experiences with respect and disrespect. They were able to enjoy a very human side of me. I know that is when they all really bought into a trusting relationship with their teacher. I could almost see the gears in their minds turning: "If our teacher is being so honest with us and values us so much that she would share personal thoughts, memories, and emotions with us, then she must believe in us. We are dear to her." It was exciting for me to see their drive to learn more about human nature and their pure curiosity when interviewing me. The fallout from this session was phenomenal. The environment in the class was peaceful for quite some time to follow. We were getting to know each other as real people, with rich and varied personalities and experiences. There was a lot more lighthearted humor in the class, and people didn't take things so seriously or personally. I found that I worried less about the students and trusted them more to make positive choices in their daily actions. I saw the students more as allies to encourage, rather than foes.

Week 10: The Bugging Bug Versus Respect Photo

Students can be asked whether they've noticed if their team is becoming more respectful: Do they see any difference between the times when the Bugging Bug is there and when respect is there? Usually, students have been noticing progress for some time and are excited about it, especially since it usually leads to more playtime one way or another. After recording students' observations, two consecutive photographs can be taken: one playfully depicting the classroom when the Bugging Bug is there and one representing how people stand with each other when Respect is there. Ideally, the facilitator and the teacher should be in the photograph since they are members of the team. Students absolutely love these photos and are very eager to see them. A copy of both photographs is usually given to each student. An artistic montage can even be done during the week with paper frames and titles for each picture.

Poem on Respect

Respect _____ .

Example: "Respect bridges people together like the rainbow bridges earth and sky."

Respect is _____

Example: "Respect is acceptance and tolerance."

If respect were a person, _____ .

Example: "If respect were a person, I would like to spend a lot of time with him or her."

I like respect because _____ .

Example: "I like respect because it allows me to get along well with everyone."

When the world is more respectful, _____ .

Example: "When the world is more respectful, there will be fewer wars."

In preparation for the following week, the classroom can be invited to create poems on respect, either as a classroom or as a homework assignment. Specific questions can be distributed to assist students in the writing of metaphors.

Week 11: Team Poems

After briefly checking in with everyone about the writing assignment, the facilitator can ask students to mark their favorite poem line on their own paper. Once everyone is ready, names can be randomly drawn and each student given the opportunity to read his or her favorite line. This exercise works well with some guidelines: First, names are drawn randomly to avoid the boredom of being the last one called on, such as when desk rows are used to call on students; second, it is fun to give the challenge of applauding each contribution for as long as the teacher takes to write it on the board; and, third, each student must choose only one short line even if the student likes the entire poem, otherwise the final text will be too long.

After everyone makes a contribution, the text can be used as it is, or students can reorganize it by suggesting which parts should be at the beginning, the middle, and the end. In elementary schools, students can also practice reading it as a group with some claps and rhythm (like a rap) or with students reading their own lines. Students are then ready to copy their team poem on their photograph montage.

Maureen: Here's an example of our class's poem:

Respect is to be nice to everyone,

experience respect and be happy you have it, respect is very useful in every sort of way.

If respect were a person, it would be welcomed everywhere. I would want him in my family,

that person would be almost perfect.

Respect should be in everyone and around everyone; respect means people are nice to each other for their best. When I respect people it makes me feel nice inside. Be kind to people and they will be kind to you. When the world is more respectful,

we will all get along better . . .

There will be less fighting and hunger . . .

there will be more friends.

Respect is like gold for our feelings, for our families.

I respect my family because they care for me and support me. I respect my sister because she is nice to me. I respect my brother because he's the best.

Respect is something that comes from your heart. You have to be gracious, you have to be kind. Respect is when people come together, it makes love. What would we do without respect?

Week 12: Secret Success Spies

Now that students are experts not only at noticing and resisting the Bugging Bug but also at noticing and understanding respect, they can be invited to be secret success spies to recruit an audience for the new preferred story. (Although we encourage teachers to choose and reorganize the program in a way that best suits each unique environment, it is highly advisable to have established a clear externalization of the problem and its effects and have students practiced in spying on their own personal successes before engaging them in secret spying. The reason behind this is that it is usually easier to notice one's own efforts, and when problems have been long-standing, it can be challenging to suddenly become appreciative of others. If not enough time is spent facilitating the earlier steps, students could still be under the influence of the problem and simply believe that students who struggle don't make any efforts or don't have any successes. This outcome would support the problem and feed frustration and disrespect instead of challenging it.)

In the classroom, each student is responsible for secretly noticing two students' successes at being respectful and fighting the Bugging Bug/Disrespect. This activity can also be done with upper grades by reducing the playfulness aspect of it and increasing instead the emphasis on how difficult it is to appreciate others' efforts and successes. One has to be a really attentive observer to notice another's avoidance of a problem. For younger students, a specific form can be created and made available to students at all times to document the successes they witness. The following is an abbreviated example:

A Comment From Your Secret Success Spy (SSS):

Dear _____ ,

Today I noticed that you resisted the Bugging Bug!

When?_____

Where?_____

I think that the Bugging Bug wanted you to_____

_____

And instead you chose to _____

_____

Congratulations!

Maureen: To organize this program, names are assigned randomly. Cut two copies of the class list into strips so that each child is represented twice. Walk around and have each student pick two names out of a hat. It is preferable to avoid pairing students who are seated right next to each other because it makes the process of secret documentation difficult. I suggest having the students discreetly show you the names drawn, so you can keep a master list of spies because sometimes the students forget who they are to spy on. Each day, choose a practical time of the day when students can be reminded of their spying responsibilities and given a few minutes to complete their success note. For example, it can work to remind students just before recess that they will be given five minutes to fill out their success notes after returning to class. Recess, with its numerous trouble possibilities, is an ideal time for many students to resist disrespect and the Bugging Bug. I had the students give the secret notes to me so that I could verify that all students were receiving at least one, once in a while. It wouldn't take me long to tally who was noticed resisting the Bugging Bug on the master list. Then I would sneak the notes onto the students' desks before they arrived in the morning. This process is particularly important to ensure that no one has been inadvertently unpaired or that, for instance, a student did not receive any notes because both of his or her secret spies were sick or out of town that week. At one point, I had to ask a child discreetly to take over spying for another spy who was absent frequently and also was struggling with communication issues. This was done quietly, and no one in class knew. It was truly a secret success.

The excitement of being a secret spy is usually enough to motivate students to be good observers of success.

Maureen: Can you expect thirty students to really keep a secret? Read here. It works!

It is helpful, however, to discuss once again the numerous ways in which the Bugging Bug might interfere with this activity. Important issues to address with students include being assigned to spy on someone whom they don't like, focusing on who is spying on whom as opposed to the successes, trying to exchange secrets ("I'll tell you who I am spying on if you tell me who you are spying on"), forgetting to give the notes, asking everyone if they are their spy, and being uncovered as someone's spy and lying about it. Usually these problems disappear with a simple prediction and discussion of them. The disappointment of not spying on a friend can usually be mediated by knowing that there will be other opportunities to spy on their friends' successes within the next few weeks. Students are encouraged to refrain from asking others whether or not they are their spy. If some do, they can simply be answered playfully with "maybe, maybe not" or reminded gently that talking about this would take a lot of fun out of the activity. Spying on someone they don't like that much or someone who struggles a great deal with the Bugging Bug can be discussed as a challenge that the facilitator believes everyone in the class is capable of taking on. If necessary, examples can be given of successes that may be harder to notice, such as calling names three times in a day instead of four; even if the problem is still there, there is less of it, and that is a success. By this time, students usually are very comfortable at noticing successes.

Some students get so excited that they cut out newspaper letters to send completely anonymous success notes. Students even make secret notes for their teacher even though the teacher is not directly assigned a spy. Teachers experience these notes as touching and validating since they often exert great efforts at being patient.

Maureen: I received a success note from a child regarding my growing level of patience with the class. Don't expect one, however, and feel forlorn if you don't receive one. Students are not used to giving teachers feedback. Please keep in mind these comments are from my experience and intended to be helpful, not to be held as a comparison to your experience (faster, slower, more or less engaged).

In many ways this activity creates a positive gaze that short-circuits the usual critical gaze present in class. In such a context, it becomes unusual for a child to run to an adult in power to tell him or her every little mistake or misbehavior another is doing. All the attention is used to notice achievements and successes. This positive gaze is renewed every day since the teacher distributes the success notes the following morning at the beginning of class. As a result, students are kindly reminded of their earlier successes.

Week 13: Sharing the Experience

By now, students are usually excited about sharing some of their success notes. A discussion can focus on how receiving the notes and knowing that people are watching for their accomplishments affects them.

Students realize that they have a lot of successes that they don't notice and appreciate that everyone is more kind and tolerant. What else are they noticing about change in the class? The facilitator may choose to either continue the process for an extra week (making sure everyone is receiving notes) or reassign everyone to new spies.

Week 14: Spy Guessing and Super Spying

The class is ready to proceed to a guessing game about who spied on whom. This process has to be facilitated with great care to ensure that the Bugging Bug will not get students to feel excessively good or bad about their guesses. It is critical to avoid an atmosphere of competition or comparison where some students win and guess right while others are fooled.

To prevent this from happening, all students are told to write down the names of five people they believe were their spies. After everyone is finished, students are called on randomly to read their five guesses out loud. The facilitator then requests that the real spy please stand up, and the entire class applauds the spy for being a successful observer. Any reference to whether or not the guesses were right is avoided. This is fairly simple to do given that the process has to unfold in a quick and dynamic way to prevent the class from being disengaged by the time the last spy is revealed.

Once the secret spies are unmasked, the class can be invited into super spying, where basically everyone spies on everyone and students are encouraged to sign their success notes. Knowing the identity of one's success observer can foster a more directed thoughtfulness between an ever-expanding number of students. Despite all of these advantages, however, students are often fond of their secret identity, and many persist in remaining anonymous regardless of directions. We allow students to pursue the activity in the way that is most exciting to them as a gesture of respect for their ideas and a willingness to collaborate in a nonadultist/ hierarchical way. Letting students choose honors their own preferences for either a visible connectedness or an invisible yet exciting and generous act of appreciation.

Several formats are possible for the documentation process, each with their own limitations:

- Many classrooms are divided into subteams of four to six students, grouped together. A team folder with the success chart of each member of the subgroup can help this format work. This format offers the advantage of making the charts readily accessible to students who, given their spatial positioning, are the most likely to notice their teammate's successes in class. On the other hand, this format can become confusing when students from other teams want to write successes or when the classroom arrangement changes.
- A book of individual charts can be an exciting and concrete reminder of the class as a team, working together to become more respectful; this method is problematic in that only one person can write in the book at a time.
- Individual folders for each student located in a central place offer the most flexibility and easy access for everyone; at the same time if they are irremovable, they can only be completed during breaks and if removable, can easily be misplaced and lost.

Depending on time, goals, classroom size, age, and arrangement, a facilitator may choose to adapt one of these ideas to his or her own context, which may even imply a combination of two formats, such as having both a subteam folder and a central success chart file. Whatever the choice, potential negative side effects of the format must be considered; for example, posting success charts on the wall could trigger hurtful comparisons and competition as to who has the most entries. An adequate balance between accessibility and individual privacy thus needs to be developed.

Aside from these logistic issues, the classroom super spying is fun and exciting. Students often check their charts to see what has been written and get excited by the documentation of successes they haven't even noticed themselves. When the students feel that they've had an important success but no one seems to have noticed, they can share the details of the achievement with a classmate, who can then document it for them.

Maureen: Here are two pieces of reflection from my classroom. First, these weeks of spying were quite fun. Please stay playful and keep in mind tactics that will promote suspense, adventure, and mystery. Second, it was very important to me to not emphasize whether students were correct or wrong when guessing which spy was observing them. The context I kept in class was that the spies did a good job observing, and their jobs were easier because the class showed remarkable effort at resisting the Bugging Bug.

SECTION 3: CELEBRATION OF KNOWLEDGE AND EXPERTISE

Week 15: Appreciation Day

After spending close to two months on developing respectful and tolerant relationships, students are excited to talk about the progress of their classroom. Initially, the goal of this discussion is to invite students to briefly publicly share successes they have noticed of their peers. However, it frequently snowballs in certain classrooms into a much more extensive process of appreciation that lasts as long as two hours. This sharing is typically much more extensive than what was documented on the success charts and in some ways makes it possible for students who dislike writing to participate.

Several tips should be kept in mind while facilitating this activity:

1. Once again, avoid naming anyone related to a misbehavior and focus only on successes.

2. Encourage students to give specific examples of the progress made, otherwise the acknowledgments remain too broad and meaningless, such as "I want to nominate Alex for being nicer."

3. Implement a playful format that will sustain suspense throughout the activity, such as mentioning the recipient's name only after acknowledging the success, for example, "There is a boy here who is much more willing to include others in basketball and who even supports others during mistakes by saying, 'Good try,' and that is Adam."

4. Keep statements brief and warmly applauded.

5. Arbitrarily choose an order by which to proceed. So many hands are up and eager to be picked that it is easy to feel overwhelmed and lost as to which student raised his or her hand first. Going around the room in circles or row by row ensures that everyone gets a fair chance to share and also allows the applauding to continue. (Students are more willing to applaud when putting their hands down does not involve the risk of missing out on a chance to talk.)

6. Invite the class to take on the challenge of making sure everyone's successes have been acknowledged so that no one is left out (which would be a Bugging Bug thing to do).

It is worth allowing the activity to continue for as long as the energy for it exists. By doing so, the facilitator ensures that everyone keeps a fantastic memory of the event and does not become bored. By this time, students have usually shared their observations on at least six or seven occasions depending on classroom size. Students wanting to share more observations can be given the opportunity to write them down.

The meeting ends by informing students that they will start their last week of super spying. The importance of documenting their observations is emphasized since the activity is coming to an end and since everyone would probably want to keep memories of their successes. The challenge now is to spy on as many different people as they can before a specified date. Students can be asked to notice successes of people they haven't spied on yet. Paying attention to people they know or like less can be discussed as the ultimate exercise in appreciation. For such an extensive activity to be successful, charting has to be reduced to a minimum and be an easy process. An effective documentation process involves providing each student with a stack of small slips containing a few open-ended sentences pertaining to the observed success. Additional blank slips can be available in a visible location. At this stage, the what, where, and when of the success can be enriched with the spy's personal reactions to it (e.g., "I was very impressed to see you do that," "I thought it must have been really hard," "I want to remember to do that when it happens to me."). A simple sentence acknowledging how one was impacted as a witness can be very meaningful and reinforcing. Students can start seeing themselves through others' eyes and become even more in touch with not only their ability to be empathetic but also the effects they have on others. It creates an opportunity for a minireflecting team with all of its valuable effects. An example of a blank success slip is shown here.

Dear _____,

I have noticed that the Bugging Bug probably wanted you to _____

_____

_____

and instead you chose to_____

_____.

When I saw you do that, I _____!

Date: _____   Place of observation: _____

Congratulations!

From your Room 9 teammate: _____

Again, it is helpful if the teacher provides a few minutes of class time for this documentation. Ideally, slips should be given directly to the teacher or dropped in a designated basket with the agreement that they will be read all at once at the end of the week. Everyone will experience reading his or her notes as surprises on a designated day. A daily countdown can be set up by the teacher around the number of people whose successes have not been observed yet. No names are publicly mentioned to avoid marginalization of students. Some teachers ask a trusted student to spy on another for a few hours to make sure everyone has been spied on.

> *Maureen:* The Individual Success Chart (Week 5) and secret success spies were very engaging. The students were thrilled to be able to tell their stories of respect and recognize others. Even an unassuming student who formerly was shut out and afraid of sharing positive ideas could make his or her quiet but important successes known. It was a safe place to do this. Students focused on a wide range of positive behaviors; therefore, it became a space where all students could be honored.

Week 16: Party

The designated date finally arrives. Students are eager to see how many and which successes were noticed. After this celebration, students are treated as experts and consultants for other classes. They are also invited to continue sharing their appreciation by simply telling their fellow classmates when they observe the successes. The class can be asked if they are willing to experiment with simply telling people about the observed successes.

Week 17: Skits

Students can be invited to prepare an anti–Bugging Bug show for their parents, the administration, and other classes. The goal of this activity is to create a context where students' expertise on the Bugging Bug and respect can be publicly acknowledged. This activity also provides a challenging context for teamwork. The show can be a series of skits prepared by subteams. It can include the following:

- performances of some of their actual successes at fighting the Bugging Bug (that have been recorded on success charts)
- interviews with the Bugging Bug itself
- playful game shows on people's knowledge of the Bugging Bug
- news reports of incidents involving the Bugging Bug
- advertisements of anti–Bugging Bug products
- a detective's search for the Bugging Bug
- examples of the Bugging Bug sabotaging a current event, such as a presidential election, the Olympics, and so on

Students are usually very excited about this project and have many creative ideas of their own. It is critical to take a few minutes to explore with the class how they think the Bugging Bug might interfere in this project because disrespect is much more likely to happen when students are excited and anxious about an event. Usually, students can easily predict where conflicts might erupt and how to solve them. Students' predictions about themselves and their own age group are usually much more accurate than adults' fantasies of them. After listing the potential Bugging Bug problems on the board, respectful ways of resolving them can be brainstormed.

Maureen: It is important to provide a safe context for brainstorming skit ideas. One way is to make groups and then have each group decide on their topic. It may be more helpful for the class to think of many ideas for skits, decide which skits they want to have in the show, and then make groups based on what each child's interest is. You may avoid popularity contests this way. I had students give me a paper with their two favorite skit ideas written on it, and students were placed in groups with those interests in mind. Everyone ended up happy. You may end up with a more diverse group of interested actors this way, rather than having each group hash out their topic and worry about the Bugging Bug visiting the groups with conflicts and stress early on. However, both ways of constructing groups will provide learning experiences.

It is often tempting for adults to organize, supervise, and structure the skits. Students as young as first graders are very able to come up with great ideas and perform them with little adult input when adults trust them to do so. Rather than supervising the skits, adults can be more helpful by reviewing performance tips, such as talking loud enough for the last row to hear, facing the audience, making sure players are visible to the audience, taking turns speaking to avoid talking over another player, supporting others' performances with solid applause, and so on.

Maureen: Personally, I was nervous about the skits. Our class wanted to invite their families and friends to our performance. I had never been the director of a school play before and had big expectations for myself. I was very apprehensive that people's judgments would be harsh. I knew in my heart that I wanted this to be a student-produced performance. I didn't want to impose my ideas on them. I wanted their creativity to flow and for them to feel ownership of this event. Yet, I was worried. What would people think of me as a teacher if the performance wasn't flawless or if it was rough and childish? I swung back and forth on the pendulum and settled within my original intention: This would be the students' performance, and I trusted them to do their best. From then on, I facilitated their discussions of what they wanted and coached them to speak loudly, face the audience, and to be their role. The rest was theirs, and we are all proud to say that they did their best.

Teacher and facilitator can also prepare an official letter announcing the event and requesting the permission to videotape. This letter should be enclosed with students' personalized and creative invitation cards to their parents and guests. The video provides parents who are unable to attend an opportunity to watch the show. It is helpful to videotape a dress rehearsal as well as the actual show to increase the likelihood that students will be proud of at least one videotaping of themselves. This rehearsal can involve showing the facilitator what has been accomplished during the week and setting up the video camera properly.

> *Maureen:* The skits were an exciting time for the students. Working together on a production that they could invite their families to was meaningful for them. The students focused on the behaviors that the Bugging Bug influences. It was safe for them to act out teasing and insulting behaviors and how they changed their behaviors. We had two increasingly troubled sessions of rehearsals, then a discussion of how to use our strategies to prevent the Bugging Bug from further invasions that were causing dissention, jealousy, and disorganization in each group. We continued with two additional trouble-free and focused rehearsal times, followed by one dress rehearsal before the big show. I think each group may demand different amounts of time, but it is helpful for the successful outcome of the skits to give them ample time to practice. They put a lot of effort into the production, and I saw useful collaboration from each group. This is about the time when they came up with the idea that the Bugging Bug is allergic to kindness and respect. This became a strong concept in our room for the remainder of the school year.

Weeks 18 and 19: The Show and Its Video

Reengaging in a discussion of how the Bugging Bug may try to sabotage the show may be appropriate. Students are usually excited, and reviewing some team strategies to relax and prevent the Bugging Bug from taking over the show can be invaluable (e.g., tornado breath). The performance provides an audience for the distribution of certificates of progress. Certificates can be created with open-ended sentences so that students can write what they are most proud of having accomplished. Students can even decorate their certificates and ask a best friend to sign as a witness or even write a sentence or two about the progress that they have noticed. These certificates can be presented by students at the end of the Bugging Bug show.

The following week, a video of the show can be carefully viewed with extra attention to the possibilities that students will feel critical of their performance. Students are usually eager to share with the group their experience of the show and their parents' reactions to it. Discussions of what they liked, what made them feel part of a team, how they avoided the Bugging Bug, and what the class should do differently if they did another show can be interesting. When everyone has had the opportunity to share, the facilitator can discuss two video-related processes: the process of watching it and the process of sharing it.

The Process of Watching

The Bugging Bug may try to make students feel bad about the video. Younger teenage girls in particular are likely to feel very self-critical about their appearances. Non-native English speakers may feel embarrassed by their accents. Certain students may be tempted to criticize, blame, or make fun of others. All these concerns need to be addressed ahead of time to ensure that the experience of watching the video is positive. Asking students how they think the Bugging Bug will interfere with the fun of watching the video, predicting self-critical feelings, and discussing what students want to remember if the Bugging Bug interferes will improve the experience for everyone. Students can also be told that most people perceive their own voices as being strange.

The Process of Sharing

The sharing of videos for home viewing is a challenging exercise in teamwork. The number of copies the facilitator is able to provide will greatly affect the process. A minimum of one copy per ten kids is workable.

> Maureen: There are two ways we have done this; however, don't let these two ideas limit your creative solutions on how to share the videos with your class.

The chain video. The organization of this process is usually done with the class and based on who lives in the same neighborhoods, who sees each other over weekends, who knows where others live, and so on. Chains of students emerge out of the discussion, and a whole plan of sharing is established. You may wish to draw names of the first students to start each chain. The students are then responsible for passing the video on to the next student in the chain. It helps to attach a list with names and phone numbers of the students on the chain, with instructions for parental support in passing the video on.

The library system. Have your video copies available to students to check in and out of the class library. This provides more accountability for each copy; however, it may take longer for the videos to circulate.

The facilitator may choose to mention that the Bugging Bug may sometimes get some family members to make a critical comment; this issue happens occasionally and can trigger a lot of sadness and shame. If it does happen, the facilitator can engage in a discussion of adults' struggle with the Bugging Bug. It is impossible to shelter students completely from harmful comments, but it is certainly possible to assist them in making different meanings out of the experiences.

Week 20: Stories

At this point in the project, students are quite comfortable with the Bugging Bug versus respectfulness and many of them have extended these practices elsewhere. Students have now become knowledgeable in all aspects of disrespect: identifying it, noticing its effects, standing up to it, developing several strategies to address it, experiencing their lives without it, and observing others' successes. All of this knowledge can be summarized in stories. A story can be read to them initially as an example of a format. Even though many students are thrilled by the idea, not all are comfortable with unstructured writing. Open-ended sentence templates of stories can be provided for those who wish to participate.

Maureen: Consider this a class writing assignment or perhaps a homework assignment. This is meaningful homework if there are supportive environments (quiet times for reflection and creation) for homework at your students' homes.

The following are two abbreviated examples of story templates:

A Bugging Bug Story Titled _____

Once upon a time there was a child named _____
who lived _____.

This kid's favorite _____ was_____, and when all
the homework was done _____.

Sometimes, however, the Bugging Bug would sneak into the kid's mind and try to create trouble. Specifically, the Bugging Bug would _____
_____.

It would also make the kid think _____.

After listening to the Bugging Bug, the kid would often end up feeling _____
_____.

The Bugging Bug sneaked in particularly often _____. One day, however,
the kid suddenly realized that _____. The kid decided that _____
_____.

From then on, when the Bugging Bug would put mean ideas in the kid's mind
_____.

This completely changed the kid's life because _____
_____.

Others, in particular _____, started noticing _____
_____.

The kid's friends were saying _____, and the kid's parents _____.

People were now thinking that _____ was a very _____ kid.

The kid also preferred to be that way because _____
_____
_____.

So the kid avoided listening to the Bugging Bug as much as possible and grew up to become a _____
_____.

My Own Anti–Bugging Bug Story Titled _____
_____

I am writing my story so that other kids can learn from my experience.

The Bugging Bug used to get me to _____ . It would sneak into my mind at _____.
It even got me to think that others _____.
I also really felt _____.

Because of the Bugging Bug a lot of negative things happened in my life, such as
_____
_____ _____.

I really didn't like these bad things to happen, but it took me some time to realize that I was listening to the Bugging Bug. I first noticed the Bugging Bug when
_____
_____
_____.

What really helped me was to realize that _____
_____
_____.

Then one day, after_____
I decided that _____
_____ _____.

My first big success at resisting the Bugging Bug was _____
_____. I even surprised myself and felt
_____. From then on, I tried very hard to _____ _____.

(Continued)

(Continued)

Now when the Bugging Bug tries to sneak in, I _____
_____. My favorite strategy against it is to
_____ .

Since I got rid of the Bugging Bug, my life has been much better because
_____
_____ .

Well that's my story, and I hope that it helps you, too, because
_____
_____ .

Week 21: Public Reading

Even though most students may have written a story, not all will be
interested in reading it publicly because of shyness. Asking for volunteers
usually works fine, and the students' teacher or the facilitator may be
available to read their stories for them. Depending on time, five to ten
short stories can easily be read and acknowledged before leaving with a
group of helpers to plan the introduction of the project in another class.
Students should be asked to fill out a feedback questionnaire to help the
facilitator improve the project and reinforce their new status of experts.

Given that students are now proud of their knowledge and experience,
these stories can be introduced as possible teaching tools for other students.
At this time, the facilitator can recruit students who would be interested in
cofacilitating this program in other classes. Gaining parental permission for
these students provides an opportunity to briefly ask parents whether they
have noticed any progress at home. A few issues have to be considered when
assigning elementary school students the responsibility of cofacilitation in
other classes. Leadership practices that promote respect and support must be
discussed. Examples of these practices include the following:

- always being supportive of younger students' contributions as
  opposed to evaluating whether an idea is good or not
- repeating or acknowledging what each student says as opposed to
  simply going from one student to the next without comment
- remaining engaged with the class as much as possible as opposed to
  talking to other cofacilitators about the younger students' comments
- talking loud and dynamically to keep younger students' interest as
  opposed to talking slowly

Roles assigned to helpers also need to remain simple, such as being
responsible for one area of a discussion or one role in a skit. Writing ideas

on the chalkboard is ideal for the facilitator because it leaves the main stage to student leaders and at the same time allows for quick assistance if needed. Responsibilities also need to be assigned based on students' special talents, and positions can be created simply to include students. For example, shy students might be pleased to have the role of camera protector, note taker, or applause supervisor.

BRIEF SUMMARY OF CLASSROOM FACILITATION CONSIDERATIONS

Classroom work requires the facilitator to be extra careful to follow students' experience, create a safe discussion format (minimizing the space for the problem to occur), sustain the classroom's interest, honor students' ideas, avoid marginalization, and minimize the violence toward the Bugging Bug.

Following Students' Experience

Following the experience of a large group of students well enough to open space for each of them to change significantly in his or her own unique way can be quite challenging. The facilitator has to be very keen in listening to what is said and what is not said and to keep track of students' experiences whether they have a voice in the group or not. There are several ways to facilitate this: (1) give individual written assignments covering the same topics that were discussed in class, (2) include a variety of activities (e.g., drawing, singing, acting) that allow students to explore issues regardless of their verbal and written skills, (3) use multiple externalizations by inquiring about the same topic with a variety of questions to attempt to connect more accurately with a students' experiences framed in their particular languages; and (4) use simple and short questions that are likely to be understood by everyone.

Creating a Safe Discussion Format

When working with issues of disrespect, one has to be extremely careful in crafting activities and discussions to prevent the problem from interfering without any methods of addressing it, especially early on. The first few meetings with the class set the tone for the rest of the project; thus, the facilitator must carefully word questions and anticipate the ways in which the problem may be triggered. Questions such as "What do you feel may be causing some problems in your classroom?" may feel respectful to the facilitator who is trying to involve students in the articulation of their experiences. However, questions such as these are likely to invite disrespectful answers, such as including a child's name, and open the space for problems to happen, such as blaming, students answering with "nothing," or disconnecting from the problems.

A more useful question is, "Other classes that I work with tell me that habits such as teasing or anger or bugging get in the way of them having fun at recess. Does this happen in this class, too?" This type of question has the intended effect of opening space for a discussion of students' experiences while still providing a structure that minimizes the likelihood of hurtful statements. When asking students to share their observations of how the Bugging Bug gets in the way, it is also helpful to specify early on that mentioning a student's name in this context is being disrespectful in itself. Another way of minimizing the space for problems is to use multiple-choice questions. These questions offer the following advantages: They involve students in active yet structured reflections, therefore reducing the likelihood of disrespect; they reduce the complexity of answering questions about completely novel ideas; and they assist students without a voice in the articulation of their thinking (i.e., help them avoid a blank or puzzled "I don't know" response).

The facilitator has to find ways to prevent intolerance as much as possible and to address disrespect respectfully if it occurs within the conversation. Often a gentle questioning of a student with regard to whether or not the Bugging Bug may have sneaked in just now is sufficient. Otherwise, classroom team strategies such as tornado breath can be invaluable.

Sustaining Interest

For classroom work to be efficient and interesting, students must experience themselves as successful in the activities. The context must be such that they can safely take the risk of sharing and exploring ideas at a pace that suits them and still emerge triumphant and excited at the end of the exercise. From that perspective, the rhythm of introducing new activities and ending previous ones must be carefully adjusted to each group and each individual in the group. Activities must be sustained long enough for most students to really connect with it but be terminated before students become bored and disengaged.

Honoring Students' Ideas

Throughout the project, an effort is made to bring forth students' own knowledge and ideas about the problem. Lecturing is avoided at all times and is replaced by questions and discussions of issues. It is important to choose questions where answers can be honored and to not overestimate the group's ability to decide certain matters. For example, it would be counterproductive to ask a group of thirty students where or when our meeting should take place; the likelihood of getting a multiplicity of different answers that cannot all be applied is high. The positive effects of involving students in certain decisions can be significantly outweighed by the disadvantages of creating a context for competition, jealousy, or rejection of ideas. This is particularly important given that for certain students, expressing an idea in itself can require a great effort; not being able to honor and support such effort can reinforce problems of disconnection and experiences of disrespect.

Avoiding Marginalization

In their efforts to refrain from not marginalizing individual students, facilitators work at refraining from marginalizing the classroom. It is important that the class understands that disrespect is a problem with which many young people and adults struggle; they are not a "bad" class and young people are not "bad" compared with adults. Posing a question about young people in general, such as "What does the Bugging Bug get kids to do that they don't like to do?" is preferable to a question about a particular class, such as "What does the Bugging Bug get your class to do?"

Minimizing Violence Toward the Bugging Bug

It is often tempting for young people and adults to express hatred and violence toward the Bugging Bug. Although some of this is unavoidable given what it represents, facilitators are discouraged from promoting violence. Students are encouraged to work on their relationship with the Bugging Bug in a way that focuses on bringing forth their preferred ways of being (understanding, patience, tolerance, and respectfulness) as opposed to focusing on the smashing of the Bugging Bug itself.

CONCLUSION

Variations of this project were conducted in over 100 classrooms in the Silicon Valley of California. It was most successful when facilitators focused on students' experiences and adjusted the activities to the specific issues of the group. It was less successful when facilitators rigorously followed the outline for the program, prioritizing the schedule over the students' experiences. Thus, facilitators engaging in this project must understand the ideas that have guided the choice and creation of the activities as well as the timing of their presentation to the classroom. This requires therapists and educators to have a good understanding of the narrative concepts behind the activities, such as externalization of the problem, restorying, creating an audience, and cultural influences that shape classroom interactions. Without this theoretical grounding, the exercises could inadvertently replicate certain structures of power instead of challenging the problem of disrespect.

In this project, students are able to develop new meanings of their preferred ways of being that allow them to make more respectful choices. When students make changes, it is not because they have intellectually learned about respect but rather because they have discovered for themselves what their preferences are in their relationships with each other. It is much more convincing and significant to realize one's own preferences than to be told what they should be.

This program offers several unique advantages. It provides students and school staff with a common language about a problem and its multiple forms. This not only allows them to become a community fighting for the same cause, but also it unites them against disrespect as opposed to uniting against specific individuals. This is in contrast with the usual situation with people being upset at students who bully but replicating the same condoned behavior by marginalizing and excluding the perpetrators of bullying.

These ideas also make it possible for teachers to reconnect with their initial attraction to their profession: the reward of helping and caring for young people, as opposed to punishing them. A few teachers now acknowledge that students' behaviors did not necessarily represent who they actually were and preferred to be, but were rather often the result of expectations, specifications, and restraints that shaped their actions into problem habits. Given this kind of reaction from teachers, it makes sense that teachers have been willing to divert precious time from other classroom activities to this project. Without the Bugging Bug around, more efficient and effective learning takes place.

10

Working With Individual Students Around Bullying

*Helping a Child Suffering
From a "Bullying Spell"*

Given the importance of addressing the context of bullying, the reader may now wonder how individual work can be helpful. Individual work can be invaluable in addressing a child's unique experience of relationships. The impact of individual work, however, can be greatly enhanced by intervening, at some point or another, in the community where bullying takes place. In this chapter, Geoffrey's story of breaking free from a bullying spell with the support of his community is told.

A PROBLEM-DOMINATED IDENTITY

Geoffrey was an African-American adolescent boy living with his single mother, a stepfather, and a five-year-old brother in a middle-class household. All the teachers knew him for his conflicts on the playground and warned other teachers in advance of the likelihood of having trouble with him in the classroom. For four years, Geoffrey had been working with several psychologists and psychiatrists on his behaviors and attitudes at school. Various medications, such as Ritalin, had been prescribed, unsuccessfully used, and discontinued. At the time of the referral, Geoffrey would typically get a disciplinary pink slip almost every day for either pushing, kicking, fighting, cussing, lying, bugging, talking back, name calling, insulting, yelling, or not doing his work. He had a reputation (which he hated) of being a bully, a troublemaker, and a mean kid. Geoffrey would often say, "Everyone is talking behind my back," and regularly, he angrily refused to make attempts at doing assignments, stating that he couldn't do it anyway. His mother was feeling discouraged, was wondering about racist issues, and was starting to feel alienated and angry at the school for constantly sending him home with complaints. At times she supported her son and at times she supported the school, never too sure whom to believe or trust.

REWRITING THE STORY IN A VACUUM

The initial meetings with the child focused on fostering an ambiance of respect and collaboration and on externalizing the problem. The concept of externalizing (White & Epston, 1990) consists of viewing problems as separate from individuals; that is, problems are not seen as being deficiencies and part of the person's identity but rather as a result of the influence of external discourses and problem stories. Externalizing has the effect of inviting clients to experience problems as other than (or outside of) themselves in a way that makes it more likely they will begin to take charge of them. It also honors individuals' separate and preferred identity, which is masked or clouded by the problem.

In the work with Geoffrey, the externalized problem was thus initially called Frustration. As narrative work proceeded, Geoffrey seemed relieved to progressively experience Frustration as an externalized problem and could notice the extensive negative effects it had on his life. The field of influence of the problem was explored with its impact on Geoffrey's behaviors and attitudes; his relationships with relatives, teachers, and friends; his feelings about himself and the kind of person he would rather be; and so on. Further, Geoffrey began noticing times when he did not engage in unwanted behaviors and incidents where he successfully resisted Frustration (unique outcomes). From a narrative perspective, these were openings for assisting Geoffrey in reauthoring his life in a preferred way.

However, although these observations were initially associated with joy, pride, hope, and motivation, Geoffrey was eventually discouraged by the lack of acknowledgment he was receiving from the rest of the community. He resentfully came to realize that despite his best efforts, he remained disliked by his peers and under constant surveillance of the school staff, who suspected and disciplined him easily for many instances of, albeit unclear, participation in trouble situations.

Marie-Nathalie held thirty-minute weekly meetings with Geoffrey and held family meetings; however, his mother's support in the evenings somehow could not counterbalance the frustration of the full days spent in the classroom with teachers and other students or the long periods spent unfairly punished in the principal's office (which of course was not the principal's intention). Conversations with teachers and invitations to notice the new developments or understand the process of restorying were also unsuccessful. Frustration was recruiting them as well, and most of the time the accumulated resentment toward Geoffrey prevented them from offering any positive feedback. Even attempts to invite his main teacher to notice just one instance per day when he resisted Frustration was in vain as his teacher, overwhelmed with thirty other students, would report that there were none. Teachers had experienced the problem as oppressive, and now they could not see the space for a different story, especially since it had forced them into a role of constant disciplinarians, which they disliked. The history of difficulties and the feelings associated with it were not dissolving automatically because of Geoffrey's small signs of progress. Geoffrey's experience of himself and the school's dominant view of him clashed, causing an incongruence. This struggle eventually had the effect of making Geoffrey very bitter and hopeless about his situation. It supported Frustration's fundamental message that Geoffrey was "bad" and disliked and couldn't do anything about it.

As a result, Geoffrey would angrily state that he hated school, hated all teachers, hated the class, hated to be alive, and that everyone hated him too. Two more externalizations, Hating and Negativity, took over everything at school and especially Geoffrey's own narrative of himself. Geoffrey was now considered a very angry and negative student and was punished even more for his increasingly frequent and violent refusal to engage in academic assignments.

A school break, a new teacher, and a new classroom were of no avail. Geoffrey could not see the problem as externalized anymore and felt that there was no Frustration, that it was just him being very bad or possessed by the devil (the only way he could make sense of the problem, given his good intentions and his desire to be good). These thoughts had the effect of creating a significant amount of distress and anger toward everyone. More serious and frequent offenses and suspensions from school started to take place, especially since the problem was convincing Geoffrey that if he was already in trouble, it was not worth trying to control Frustration any longer. Specifically, small misbehaviors quickly snowballed into major suspension issues following an elaborate series of insults that Geoffrey would yell at the authority figure. The latest victories of Frustration over Geoffrey were now a major topic of conversation among the administrators, school staff, and students. Parents of other students started calling the principal requesting that Geoffrey be transferred out of their child's classroom or that Geoffrey not be allowed to play close to their child. Frustration, Hating, and Negativity had to be renamed as a bigger problem called Trouble Habit.

As the situation worsened, it became clear that interventions needed to also focus on the audience as opposed to solely on the student's story of himself. The community needed to revise the narrative they held about Geoffrey and open space for the performance of a new narrative at the same time Geoffrey was bringing forth his preferred story of himself. The performance of the preferred story would never become real until it was circulated and received in the system.

REWRITING THE STORY IN THE COMMUNITY

New Beginnings

The problem was now renamed the Trouble Habit. Discussions around the Trouble Habit's effect were kept to the minimum necessary for Geoffrey to once again externalize the problem. The effects of the problem were acutely felt and distressing enough; they did not need to be further talked about. The therapy goal was now mainly to focus on Geoffrey's desire to escape Trouble and to bring forth, publicly, every attempt at resisting the problem (unique outcomes). The idea that Geoffrey was already supported by an antitrouble team, with him at all times in his heart, was also introduced. As discussed by Zimmerman and Dickerson (1996), virtual teams not only break the alienating feeling of isolation but also allow individuals to hold on to preferred ways of being by mentally recreating the experience of being with supportive people. In Geoffrey's life, this team consisted of his mother; Marie-Nathalie; and his favorite animal, the ostrich. The ostrich's participation became very meaningful when Geoffrey was given a photograph of a group of four ostriches that he kept with him and cherished for some time. Ostriches were discussed as being very fast, very tall, and equipped with a powerful beak that could easily injure Trouble.

Resistance to Trouble Chart

As a first step to the circulation of the preferred story, evidence of the resistance to Trouble needed to be made visible, both to support Geoffrey's experience of his few successes and to have some proof to show the school. At the very first discovery of a unique outcome, Geoffrey was invited to create a very artistic chart titled Geoffrey's Resistance to Trouble Chart and to document every time he could have listened to Trouble but didn't. Geoffrey was enthusiastic about the idea and spent a lot of energy tailoring the chart that he then chose to post on the front chalkboard of his classroom. His mother was encouraged to ask about those acts of resistance daily and to minimize conversations about Trouble. The team was going to attend to the experiences that fit Geoffrey's preferred self and refuse to be an audience for the problem-saturated story.

As Geoffrey was starting to fill his chart, the news circulated that a student study team had been scheduled to explore the possibility of transferring Geoffrey to a special education program and have him reevaluated for learning disabilities or emotional disturbance. Another wave of despair and intense worries engulfed Geoffrey. Yet, he pursued his chart, and the team now discussed only the acts of resistance and none of the pink slips. These discussions would involve questions such as the following: Do you recall a time today when you could have gotten in trouble but didn't? What was going on? What kind of things was the Trouble Habit inviting you to do? What was the first thing you did to resist it? Was it hard? How did you come up with this idea? Were you holding on to someone's image in your heart? Were you thinking of anything in particular when you were doing that? How did it feel? Is it a good thing that you were able to do that? What effect did it have on your teacher? What could have happened if you had listened to Trouble? Did you know you could be so strong? What does that say about you? What will your mom say when she hears that story? What do you want to remember about this incident? Do you think you could do it again? What would you call this strategy? The goals of these questions were to empower Geoffrey to notice his own resources against the problem, bring forth his preferred way of being, give meaning to moments of victory that would otherwise remain invisible, and to show Geoffrey the preferred effects these actions of resistance had on his life.

Invitations for teachers and the principal to notice his progress were intensified: Marie-Nathalie asked them to help Geoffrey with his chart and shared with them his latest success. This sharing would also have the effect of challenging individualistic notions that Geoffrey would change in isolation and invite everyone to collaborate in the creation of a more supportive and appreciative context that would promote his preferred identity. Specifically, every time Geoffrey resisted Trouble, the team either wrote it in a note to his teacher and principal or simply walked to the principal, administrative assistant, or the nurse's office where Geoffrey would repetitively explain what he did and what strategy he used. Those strategies were eventually all compiled into a list that consisted of ideas or thoughts that Geoffrey found useful when resisting Trouble. Examples of such strategies included remembering the consequences, remembering his mom, thinking about the ostriches, keeping distances when Trouble was around, and substituting words instead of cussing.

Plastic Surgery in the Classroom

One day Geoffrey tearfully shared with Marie-Nathalie that he had discovered that his teacher was using our meeting times to talk to the classroom about him. She had asked students to be tolerant and understanding because he "had a lot of problems but he was working on them." Geoffrey was very upset by this "talking behind his back," felt marginalized, and believed his entire classroom was gossiping even more against him. Although the teacher was well-meaning, this gesture had the effect of strengthening the experience of marginalization, isolation, and stigma that Geoffrey was desperately fighting. The problem-dominated story and its audience were once again closing the space and suffocating the new developments.

As a result, it became clear that the classroom needed to be quickly invited to notice the preferred story. Geoffrey and his mother agreed that since the classroom had been involved already, Marie-Nathalie facilitating a classroom intervention at this point could be either neutral or helpful. Geoffrey had now resisted big Trouble for three weeks and had documented six official acts of resistance. The teacher agreed to provide Marie-Nathalie with a few minutes of her classtime to do a group intervention. After introducing herself, Marie-Nathalie shared with the students that she had come to inform them that they had a hero in their classroom, a boy who had been fighting a big battle with a Trouble habit and that his experience was comparable to fighting a creature that keeps on coming back even when you think you have gotten rid of it. Moreover, Marie-Nathalie said, fighting Trouble habits is often very hard because people, even parents, don't notice that young people are trying very hard to do their best. Did any of them have that experience of trying to change and no one noticed their efforts? Hands raised. Marie-Nathalie added that despite these difficulties, Geoffrey was becoming an antitrouble expert, and, if any of them needed advice, Geoffrey could probably help them deal with their struggle. Students were then told that they probably had not noticed how Geoffrey had improved because it would have required extremely good observation skills. Marie-Nathalie asked, nevertheless, in case some of them had that highly developed skill, had anyone paid attention to Geoffrey's progress. To her great satisfaction, hands raised and students started sharing some of the new developments that they had observed. Students had specifically noticed that Geoffrey was "a better sport," "more respectful of the teachers," "had a better attitude," "hit other students less frequently," "stayed away from fights," "cussed less," and "cooperated more in games." Geoffrey, in the back of the classroom, seemed stunned in amazement.

This brief intervention profoundly affected him. The teacher reported that he was agitated for the rest of the day but remained nondisruptive. When Geoffrey was questioned about his experience, he shared mostly how surprised he had been at hearing other students share positive feedback about him. He never expected that, and even though all had planned the intervention together, he had been fearful of confirming his worst ideas about his reputation. These comments honored his progress, encouraged him to pursue his efforts, and opened possibilities for additional steps in this preferred direction.

The teacher was also affected and shared how impressed she was with students' observations. It invited her to reconsider her own story of Geoffrey and to create space for new developments. A few weeks later, she reported that since the classroom intervention, Geoffrey had "stayed on task," "persevered more in challenging assignments," "had more internal control," "accepted reprimands more easily," and "complained less often that [things were] unfair." She also started noticing that there were times when she expected Trouble (e.g., during field trips), and it didn't occur. Her sharing of these moments with other teachers invited them to be curious and pay attention to these new developments as well. Later, she accepted the invitation to treat Geoffrey as an antitrouble expert and did on one instance consult with him on how to improve a situation. She even retained pink slips instead of sending them to the principal on a couple of occasions, which had the effect of instilling hope in Geoffrey to get another chance to be the kind of person he wanted to be in her eyes. Geoffrey felt that his teacher was moving from punishing him to being hopeful and helping him fight the problem. This was very important since how a teacher thinks of a student usually affects how the student thinks of her- or himself.

The classroom intervention challenged the context in several ways: (1) it invited collaboration and support among students, which challenged individualistic ideas that one should fight their problems alone; (2) it defied the usual practice of pathologization of persons, which limits therapeutic conversations to a minimum number of people behind closed doors; (3) it emphasized that nonacademic achievements are also very difficult to accomplish and worthy of honor; (4) it reversed the gaze of evaluation to one of appreciation; and, most important, (5) it inverted the hierarchy that had been established from one where Geoffrey was a marginalized, troubled young man who should be excluded to one where he could be admired and included more. In the context of this case example, peers had inadvertently been recruited into problem watchers (Zimmerman & Dickerson, 1996), which had the effect of not only marginalizing Geoffrey and leaving him more vulnerable to Trouble, but also of creating a context where only problem-related events would be noticed and subsequently understood as an internal deficiency. Since the problem story then clearly resided in the public domain, it was necessary, even critical, that the preferred story also be announced to this audience. A narrative can survive and truly become a dominant influence on one's life only if it is recognized, acknowledged, and received in the community in which it is performed. Therefore, this classroom intervention mainly created a counter audience to the known problem story to circulate an alternative knowledge of Geoffrey and publicly bring forth his expertise at fighting problems.

Another Ugly Duckling Story:
The Importance of Meaning Making

An unfortunate effect of the classroom intervention was that the principal (who heard about its success) mistakenly believed that publicly offering compliments to Geoffrey was the secret to avoiding Trouble. Geoffrey was an extremely bright and perceptive child. He could easily detect when a compliment was given to him to alter his behaviors, and this had the effect of inviting Frustration and big Trouble in the face of a well-intentioned person. Geoffrey's ability to fight the problem was not increased by compliments but by the meanings he ascribed to situations and by his experience of people genuinely liking him. So, for instance, when the principal approached Geoffrey at the very beginning of recess and said, "You are such a good student, Geoffrey, and I know that you can be so nice," the meaning that Geoffrey would ascribe to the statement was not "she likes me" but rather "she's trying to manipulate me," and this meaning would invite feelings of Frustration, which in turn would make him much more vulnerable to opportunities for Trouble on the playground. It is important here to note that this does not imply that Geoffrey would intentionally misbehave to upset the principal (which is how the problem invited her to make sense of these actions given her own good intentions) but rather that the frustration experienced by his meaning making made him much more vulnerable to Trouble.

In sum, it was not the focus on the positive or even compliments that invited change but rather the new meanings that Geoffrey was able to develop around his experience. These new meanings came from experiences, from the raising of questions, and from invitations to reflect on his choices, not from telling him which behaviors were good or bad. It is much more convincing and significant to realize one's own preferences than to be told what they should be. The key elements of the new developments were thus what these changes meant about him as a person, about the kind of individual he preferred to be, and about people's experience of him.

Predicting the Steps Back

School staff members in general were now starting to be aware that Geoffrey could actually resist Trouble. They became very eager to not only see Trouble disappear completely but also to see academic performances improve toward average standards. Indeed, as discussed earlier, teachers and principals usually dislike the role of disciplinarian. Understandably, they want to resolve problems as soon as possible to interact with students in other than punitive ways and fulfill their social responsibilities for increasing young people's knowledge to normative levels. Higher expectations and pressure to maintain a trouble-free lifestyle became a new problem. Adults' hopeful comparison process between what was and what could be inadvertently pressured Geoffrey to perform better and faster, which significantly threatened progress. First, it inadvertently had the effect of making Geoffrey more anxious, agitated, and thus more vulnerable to Trouble. Second, it created a context that was ahead of what Geoffrey could actually do in terms of controlling the problem since he was still in the process of developing strategies to deal with every situation. Third, it threatened the support and encouragement that the school staff was now offering since any setback was further interpreted as being intentional since everyone knew he could actually resist Trouble.

A month-long Freedom From Trouble Chart was created, with Geoffrey graphically displaying the process of moving forward with occasional setbacks. Predicting some instances when Trouble might prevail and showing this chart to the relevant school staff relieved Geoffrey from the increasing pressure placed on him to succeed. This discussion involving everyone ensured that teachers and the principal would understand Geoffrey's experience and the natural process of change. It also reassured Geoffrey that he could now trust that he wouldn't lose all the new and appreciated support if Trouble were to get the upper hand once in a while. This chart was kept very carefully and reviewed briefly when Trouble visited.

Certificate Ceremony

As Geoffrey continued to fill his chart of resistance to Trouble and was able to perform his preferred story of himself with fewer constraints, we decided to have a celebration. When he accumulated ten acts of resistance against Trouble (a goal that he decided for himself), his mother, the principal, and his teachers were invited to a certificate ceremony. By that time, Geoffrey was starting to make friends in his classroom and therefore also invited a peer, which happened to be another student who was just starting to work with Marie-Nathalie. The ceremony took place and consisted of Geoffrey explaining all of his ten acts of resistance and his strategies to the audience. He was then offered an official certificate titled "Anti-Trouble Certificate" and read "granted to Geoffrey for his success at resisting Trouble ten times." This ceremony was then followed by a lunch in Geoffrey's honor.

Three considerations were taken into account when crafting the certificate. First, it was written in such a way that it underscored the number of successes which could not be taken away from him, whatever happened; it was concrete and implied that the work was in progress. This choice of language was important—a "Victory Over Trouble Certificate," for instance, would have set the stage for performance expectations. Second, in addition to the number of behavioral successes, the certificate emphasized internally owned characteristics as indicators of progress (e.g., "Geoffrey has demonstrated great courage and determination in choosing to take these actions."). These statements publicly established that Geoffrey was truly making efforts and had good intentions, which school staff members had not necessarily noticed, given the recurrence of problems. Third, it also included a reference to others' new perceptions of Geoffrey to emphasize the validity of these changes and involve the community in the celebration (e.g., "His peers have noticed that Geoffrey is a better sportsman."). This statement was particularly important since people often perceive themselves through others' eyes, especially when caught in a problem-dominated identity that robs them of their own sense of competence.

The certificate ceremony was very affirming for Geoffrey, who had never been honored for anything related to school. It had the effect of a ritual that acknowledged turning points in his life and publicly marked a new beginning. It also provided Geoffrey, his mother, the teacher, and the principal with an opportunity to interact in a relaxed context of celebration and fun that made visible their preferred side. Specifically, Geoffrey and his mother could experience the teacher and principal as smiling and caring human beings opposed to the usual experience of them as harsh disciplinarians; conversely, the teacher and the principal could experience Geoffrey and his mother at their best, proud of and happy about their accomplishments. This reversal of context of knowing each other further opened possibilities in preferred directions as it allowed each participant to connect in more positive and genuine ways. Such shared positive experiences could now partially act as a buffer to problem-saturated stories and foster further collaboration.

Finally, this event inspired Geoffrey's mother to create a home file titled "Geoffrey's Achievements," in which she placed the success chart. She also framed the certificate and displayed it in their living room for everyone to see. These documents became symbols of the preferred story and they would support all involved in the pursuit of its cocreation.

Success Spies

Geoffrey felt progressively more comfortable performing his preferred story of himself and was now making friends. It was decided that John, who was invited to the ceremony and who was simultaneously starting to work with Marie-Nathalie against shyness, would be part of the team. They decided to create a small group that they chose to call success spies. Although they both had a sense of each other's struggles, Geoffrey and John reviewed what their successes looked like (they both stated they didn't need this discussion because they both felt they had noticed the problems sufficiently to spy on them). They were then each invited to make a chart to document the successes they would notice of one another. If Geoffrey felt that John had not noticed a success at resisting Trouble, it was agreed that he could tell him and vice versa. They agreed to meet weekly and review the observations.

This collaboration proved to be highly effective. They were both extremely thrilled by this project and very vigilant at their task. After three days, Geoffrey worried that John had not noticed events that he considered major successes and on his own decided to discuss the situation with John. They thus both ended up having a consultation in Marie-Nathalie's absence, which resulted in the satisfaction of seeing documentation of four accomplishments each and adding two additional successes on their charts. By the time everyone met, they had both noticed fourteen moments of success. Meetings were now mostly spent discussing what was charted, what each spy thought was significant in the other's achievement, and what the child himself felt most challenging. Meanings and strategies around each incident were explored. Spies reported that the team was extremely helpful in three main ways: First, it allowed them to feel less isolated and stigmatized by knowing that someone else was fighting a problem (i.e., it challenged individualism); second, it allowed them to get constant support from each other whenever a challenging situation occurred (i.e., provided a nonpunitive, inclusive resource when problems arose); and, third, a powerful positive surveillance was now created around their preferred way of being (i.e., it challenged evaluation and problem gaze). After four weeks, as the number of successes became overwhelming and the excitement of charting was diminishing, it was agreed to have a spy party once twenty successes (their decision) were documented.

The Spy Party

The spy party became a very exciting project for the students. They agreed on a hand code (a dragon) that would represent their belonging to the group, agreed on the color of the group's clothing for the event (black), and crafted invitation cards to each of the special guests. Because of the size of Marie-Nathalie's office, guests had to be limited to a friend each, their parents, their teacher, and the principal. At the last minute, another student from the same class and his mother were invited as this student had just been referred following a series of panic attacks and worries about coming to school. The spies felt that this other student might be a good candidate for the group and that perhaps they could help him fight his problem too. Cakes, cookies, and soda were brought by each member, and the room was decorated with balloons. The spies first read a speech that they had prepared in honor of the other, mentioning some of the major accomplishments on the chart. Guests were then invited to share what they had noticed about the spies' success. Geoffrey and John were surprised to hear how much their parents and all the other guests noticed their performance of the preferred story. Geoffrey's mother had been so impressed and touched by her son's kindness and sense of responsibility (now more visible since he had defeated Trouble) that she had been inspired to be a success spy at work and enjoyed it. She also shared that neighbors noticed how Geoffrey was different, and she was proud that he now even helped other students avoid Trouble. Guests were finally invited to take an oath to focus on students' successes against their problems, and a picture of the group was taken. Geoffrey's mother proposed to have a spy reunion at the same time the following year, an idea that pleased everyone.

The party was also going to be videotaped so that participants could review it as well as circulate this new story of themselves with other family members, but technical problems interfered. Instead, a summary letter was written and distributed with copies of the photographs.

Interestingly, when spies were interviewed afterward as to the most meaningful comments made during the party, they both reported parents' observations made about the other spy's progress. When invited to discuss the comment about them that was most meaningful, they shared that they were impressed that the other's parent noticed—as well as their friends—their progress. Unexpectedly, the spy party had a significant effect on the student who had been newly referred for worries and panic attacks. This student reported that it had been reassuring for him to know that other students had problems, too; that he could now talk to his fellow spies when the worries would attack; and that if they had succeeded in fighting their problems, then he could do it, too.

It is important here to note that the party had a powerful effect on the students because of how they made sense of it. It represented an acknowledgment of their steps in a preferred direction and allowed them to publicly share the meanings of these accomplishments. This process is thus very different than simply bargaining with a young person for a certain amount of behaviors (e.g., doing homework, doing chores) in exchange for a party. This later situation has no relevance whatsoever to the construction of their personal stories, as the goals and intentions guiding the behavior changes are to have a party, not to live a preferred life. The changes are thus not owned in the same way.

As Geoffrey increasingly felt that his preferred identity was recognized at school, it made it easier for him to perform it more readily—more experiences of appreciation led to less frustration; fewer Trouble outbursts; less blaming, punishing, excluding, and rejecting; and less isolation. It connected him further with others and brought forth more care and thoughtfulness. In other words, it reversed the initial problem cycle to an appreciative cycle where the more preferred events were noticed, the easier it was to replicate their performance. In this situation, Geoffrey could start thinking, "Maybe I can be successful since so many adults seem to think so," and this hopeful experience would renew his commitment to his preferred way of being.

A PAST TO THE PREFERRED
STORY AT SCHOOL

The audience to the preferred story was now more developed. School staff members, in their attempt to understand the changes, were increasingly transitioning from a story of Geoffrey as unwilling and uncaring to that of a student who was willing to make efforts and who cared about others. For the preferred story to survive, it was important to thicken it, deepen it, and extend it both in the past and the future. Another narrative therapist who had worked with Geoffrey three years prior to this intervention was thus invited to visit Geoffrey. Geoffrey was very touched and flattered that this therapist, who lived relatively far, would come to see him and be intrigued by his accomplishments. Geoffrey proudly related to his visitor his accomplishments, showed him his certificate, and explained to him all his strategies. Memories of past work and past successes were then connected to this developing preferred story. Meaningful events that were long forgotten because they hadn't fit in the problem-saturated story were recalled and shared. Discussing them invited Geoffrey to review his past from another's perspective, enrich his preferred story, and fill in some time gaps.

This visit was rendered even more meaningful when a few weeks later, the therapist wrote a letter to Geoffrey sharing that he had recommended Geoffrey's strategies to another person, who had found them very helpful. Geoffrey was delighted. The discussion of the letter opened a whole new area as Geoffrey shared that he had been increasingly helping other students stay out of Trouble.

A PAST TO THE PREFERRED STORIES AT HOME

When asked who in his family could have predicted that he would one day escape the Trouble lifestyle, Geoffrey spontaneously mentioned an adoptive aunt, whom he hadn't seen for a long time. Geoffrey shared that this aunt had always believed in him and supported him, and it was decided that we'd invite her to a meeting. The goal of this meeting was to explore what the aunt had always known about Geoffrey's abilities to succeed and continue to enrich Geoffrey's preferred story of himself. This meeting proved to be highly rewarding. This aunt was able to share how Geoffrey had always been an extremely affectionate child and related examples of how he used to write lovely notes and cards to her and his mother. She shared how he was responsible, loving, compassionate, and caring with his little brother, whom he often protected from Trouble. Memories of how Geoffrey used to be one of the best and most appreciated players on a soccer team were brought forth with numerous examples of moments of courage, teamwork, and gentleness. Geoffrey was glowing with happiness to hear these anecdotes shared about him. It provided him again with the opportunity to enrich his preferred story from the perspective of another, whom he loved, trusted, and respected dearly. It is with great pride that he then proceeded to tell her his most recent successes at resisting Trouble.

In this meeting, his aunt connected the past to the emerging preferred story and Geoffrey provided her with an account of the present. The retelling of these events supported the very existence of the preferred self and tied his lived experience into an extensive long-standing narrative of courage and kindness. This exchange further ensured the future survival of the preferred story because it provided it with complex details, a time frame, a real past, and an additional meaningful witness. All of these elements were necessary to counterbalance the powerful, well-established, and four-year-old story of Geoffrey the bully. The meeting was concluded with a discussion of the aunt's ability to discern and support Geoffrey's special talents as well as what he now needed from her to continue his journey on that preferred path.

EXTENDING THE AUDIENCE TO THE PREFERRED STORY

The final step was to extend the preferred story's audience further into the community. As many people as possible needed to be recruited into the restorying to accomplish the following:

- Compensate for the huge number of witnesses to the problem-saturated story.
- Strengthen the valid existence of the preferred story by telling and retelling it.
- Increase the number of members on Geoffrey's virtual team.
- Create more opportunities for Geoffrey to experience himself in a preferred way.
- Deepen Geoffrey's own understanding of his anti-trouble strategies by explaining them to others.

Because the staff at Bay Area Family Therapy Training Associates was interested in the process of restorying in schools, the success spies and their parents were thus invited to a meeting facilitated by Dr. Jeff Zimmerman. At the meeting, each spy's struggles and successes were explored in addition to their experiences of being success spies. The meeting, conducted for the first time by another therapist, allowed for new questions, perspectives, and ideas to be explored around the developments as well as a new way of enriching their preferred stories. Moreover, an outsider witness group, previously called a reflecting team, watched the discussion behind a one-way mirror and was given the opportunity to comment on the interview.

Later, the spies reported that they very much enjoyed listening to the reflecting team. They were very excited about this process not only because of the unusual aspect of the one-way mirror but also because of the process of hearing strangers comment and question their stories. It was very reaffirming for them to experience adults being interested, impressed, and respectfully curious about their achievements. The spies recalled several of the comments made about their strategies and about team members' own life experiences.

The outsider witness group was useful in the restorying of the students' lives for several overlapping reasons (White, 1995; Zimmerman & Dickerson, 1996):

- It allowed students to take a reflective position; that is, it provided them with an opportunity to be asked questions and be presented with new associations without needing to answer immediately, thus allowing space for unstructured reflection and exploration.
- It exposed students to the multiple possibilities, outside of their usual views, from which their preferred developments could be understood.
- It allowed students to thicken (enrich) their preferred stories in the past, present, or future with the team members' speculations and fantasies.
- It tied students' preferred stories to the lives of the team members, who by situating their comments in their personal experience demarginalized the spies' struggles and increased the feeling of belonging to a community of resistance to problems.
- It challenged adultist structures, since in this context students were the knowledgeable experts teaching adults. This was very empowering and affirming of their beliefs in their own agency and their abilities to contribute to others' lives (a sharp contrast with Geoffrey's earlier experience of feeling worthless and wanting to die when he felt powerless to change adults' negative view of him).

Finally, because this interview was videotaped, it also provided the spies with additional documentation of the preferred developments and an opportunity to show the video to others, extend the audience beyond the therapy room, and reflect further on the experience of the interview.

A Comment on Parent Involvement

It is interesting to note that in this particular case example, the parent's involvement was occasional due to work requirements, time, and contextual constraints. Geoffrey's mother was involved in the initial work to externalize the problem in the family setting and encourage the cocreation of a preferred story, but later her participation was mostly as a witness to celebrations and successes. Specifically, Geoffrey's mother and Marie-Nathalie had a phone conversation—or Marie-Nathalie left phone messages (inviting her to question Geoffrey around new and preferred developments)—about every two or three weeks on average, with a family meeting every six weeks. One may speculate that this provides evidence of how different versions of the self are expressed depending on the context and the audience. Geoffrey and his mother were very close and experienced Trouble less than what occurred at school perhaps because his mother always acknowledged Geoffrey's performance of his preferred self, while the school inadvertently supported the problem-dominated version of himself.

CONCLUSION

This work highlighted the importance of addressing the context in which clients perform the stories of their lives. Interventions omitting such issues are not only likely to fail at the restorying process but are also accountable for the harm they may cause by involving clients in a process that may be further discouraging and distressing. This is particularly the case for individuals presenting with long-standing problem-dominated identities that have recruited extensive audiences, such as school settings. We believe it is also important for counselors who try to do narrative work to be clear about the theory behind externalizing and reauthoring the identity before they try to use some of these ideas. Otherwise, these practices could be used in a way that inadvertently replicates, not challenges, the problem or the structure of power that supports it. This different perspective and the resulting practices were successfully used with several other students from all grade levels and covered a variety of problems, such as academic underachievement, hyperactivity, anger, boredom, and worries.

Finally, it is worth mentioning that this series of intervention also affected the school staff's attitude toward problems. These ideas made it possible for teachers to reconnect with their initial attraction to their profession: the reward of helping and caring for young people, as opposed to punishing them. A few teachers now acknowledge that students' behaviors did not necessarily represent who they actually were and preferred to be but were rather often the result of expectations, specifications, and restraints, which had shaped their actions into problem habits. As for the student population, the visible success parties and certificate ceremonies publicly moved the referred students from the status of problem students to the ranks of privileged and successful students in the eyes of their peers. They were thus becoming more popular, appreciated, envied, and even admired by everyone.

11

Brain and Behaviors

*How Young People Change
and How Educators Can Help*

S o far, we have examined the psychological, relational, and contextual contributors to bullying and disrespect with young people as well as the ingredients of a culture of respect. You may be wondering how this material fits with the current and cutting edge brain research. It does, in multiple and complex ways. Let us take you through the life of Steven to illustrate the scientific overlap of these ideas.

THE VISIBLE STORY

Steven (age doesn't matter) doesn't like school. He often struggles with boredom, daydreaming, disrespect, disconnection, shouting, under-performing, conflicts with peers, bullying, and making choices that displease educators. Currently, his class is focusing on individually solving math problems. His teacher notices that, as usual, he is not focusing on the task and calls on him with a voice of authority and a threat to get his work done. Steven responds with an annoyed "I don't want to do this." The teacher, accustomed to this scenario, snaps back with an angry "Well you have no choice, so just get it done." Steven, now visibly frustrated, ups the ante as well and shouts, "This is stupid and I won't do it." The teacher strikes back with, "Do you want me to send you to detention again instead of having a lunch break?" While the elementary school version of Steven would just cry, withdraw or fume, the high school version of Steven snaps back defiantly and hatefully, "Sure, go right ahead." Steven does not want to be totally humiliated in front of his peers and uses the only option he can think of to save his pride.

THE INVISIBLE STORY

Steven's brain is not connected to the task. Many young people's brains can only tolerate a limited amount of passive listening time that is often just about equivalent to their age (that is, a fifteen-year-old will passively listen for fifteen minutes) (Tileston, 2004). This listening time is shorter for youth who are preoccupied and struggling with unhappiness. Steven knows that he doesn't understand math very well, which triggers a feeling of incompetence when faced with the material. A significant portion of his brain power (easily over 75 percent) becomes preoccupied with feeling inadequate with what that means about his identity, and with fear of engaging in an activity which may confirm his inadequacy. His brain being a comfort-seeking device, it automatically disconnects with unpleasant tasks (Damasio, 1994). Steven is stuck between not being able to do the task and being uncomfortable with the vulnerability of acknowledging he can't do it, especially for a teacher perceived as unsafe. His limbic system is further activated by the teacher's threat. The threat releases the stress hormone cortisol, which impacts his brain's ability to remember and organize information (Bluestein, 2008).

With the increased blood flow to his limbic system, amygdala, and hippocampus—and the blockage of activation of higher functions (Siegel, 1999)—his social intelligence becomes comparable to that of a squirrel. It triggers a familiar pattern of neuronal sequence in his brain and reinforces it at the same time. Teachers have threatened and punished before. The neuronal pathway of responding with disrespect is becoming faster and stronger with every single one of these unpleasant interactions. At this point, recircuiting the pattern once the initial trigger occurs is unlikely as alternative options have been less and less "patterned." There may even have been some pruning of neurons (LeDoux, 1996), which before may have supported respectful interactions, care, and a commitment to learn. The brain is a pattern-seeking device and this pattern of interaction with the teacher is now well established and quickly recognized. The punishment of being sent to detention is powerful. It significantly increases Steven's growing hatred of school. By removing the possibility of playing and having enjoyment, the teacher also prevents him from getting perspective and letting go of the earlier unpleasant interactions (Tate, 2007). The detention also prevents movement, which would oxygenate his brain and release potent neurotransmitters, essential in learning, such as dopamine and norepinephrine (Tileston, 2004). Transitioning to motivation and commitment to improve after recess is therefore impossible for Steven.

For Steven's brain, being in school is like learning the complex footwork of Argentine Tango when the music does not resonate in your body and you can't connect with the rhythm. It would be very difficult, if not impossible, to remember the steps and perform correctly. Your memory would simply be at a loss as how to encode and retrieve this information in your brain. The experience would be even more intolerable if, on top of this, you didn't like the teacher or your dance partners. The experience would bring hatred if you were forced to do this, were constantly criticized for your mistakes, and never acknowledged for your effort.

THE CONTEXTUAL STORY

Steven's mother and stepfather have a new baby and are considering sending Steven to live in Mexico with his grandparents. They are struggling financially as the stepfather has recently lost his janitorial job. As a result, they offer only one decent meal per day to Steven, in the evening, as a full tummy increases the likelihood of him sleeping. They have not shared this with the school because they are embarrassed and ashamed of the situation and do not expect help since so far, the school has only been critical of their son and their parenting. Since the brain needs glucose and various nutrients to function at its best (Schmitz, 2007), Steven's brain starts the school day in a less than optimal state with both unpleasant emotions and lack of nutrients.

THE HISTORICAL STORY

When young children experience an unpleasant emotion, such as fear or anger, they seek to be comforted by a parent or caring adult. In the safety of that process, their brains learn to manage the arousal and they eventually internalize ways to sooth themselves (Siegel & Hartzell, 2003). If a child experiences an intense negative emotion and there are no trustworthy adults available or the caregivers react with anger, then the child is faced with a double injury: his negative emotions increase and his ability to handle the neurological arousal decrease (for both the present and future situations) (Siegel, 1999). This is the case with many children entering kindergarten and being forced to say goodbye to their parent right there and then with little or no transition time to feel safe. For some young people, like Steven, this can set the tone for a challenging school journey if handled inappropriately. In such a situation, the child's limbic system is triggered and his mind becomes dominated with a powerful fight or flight mechanism. When this is repeated day after day, school becomes associated with negative emotions right from the start. Similarly to many young children, his attempts at dealing with his intense feelings then involved hiding under a classroom table and creating for himself a safe space from which to examine the new environment. Unfortunately for Steven, his teacher found this behavior unacceptable and repeatedly called the counselor or principal to get him out of there.

While many children may eventually recover from such a difficult beginning, especially if they eventually develop a meaningful connection with peers and teachers, some do not. For Steven, the troubles insidiously progressed from there on. As he grew older, he switched from fear, to a sense of not belonging, to disconnection and resentment at being forced to go to school. His brewing of unhappiness made it difficult for him to listen and tolerate the long periods of sitting. Steven was often disliked by his teachers, and he disliked them in turn, becoming progressively known as "uncooperative." Since a young person's brain is very present oriented, altercations with his teachers led Steven to focus mainly on the threats of punishments and his "survival." Rarely was he compelled to calmly and safely examine his actions before the conflicts. As a result, Steven's understanding of these situations essentially became that teachers were "mean." This understanding coupled with a lurking and frightening sense of being inadequate led him to increasingly hate school.

DEAD-END OR FUTURE POSSIBILITIES?

Think carefully. What would you say is the teacher's need at this point?

In our experience it is usually either to get Steven on task or, sadly, to "get rid of him."

What would you say is Steven's need at this point?

In our experience with young people, the need is to avoid suffering, which in Steven's case is avoiding math, avoiding punishment, and perhaps avoiding interactions with his teacher. Most educators understand that a student will want to avoid suffering which is why, sadly, suffering is used to such an extent. What they don't realize is that a young person's way of avoiding suffering will not necessarily be what teachers want it to be. In other words, they don't realize that a student's way of responding to suffering is not an increased motivation to do what the teacher wants, but rather a decreased desire to please the teacher, a decreased interest in the subject, and a decreased sense of being able to succeed. This is called learned helplessness, and it has been researched, demonstrated, and explained in multiple fields since the 1960s (Bandura, 1969; Jensen, 2000a; Seligman, 1975, 1990; Seligman & Maier, 1967; Sprenger, 2002).

Why, then, learned helplessness is still so poorly understood by a large number of educators is mind-boggling and, if anything, is probably the result of their own personal experiences of powerlessness as young people. If Steven was punished several times for the same behavior and it didn't change, it is completely illogical to think that another punishment, or a harsher one, will "finally get through" to him. What Steven needs the most is a relationship with a caring and proactive educator who will express compassion, invite collaboration, have a contextualized perspective of his struggles, and understand the complex factors that mediate his neurological and emotional reactions.

THE POSSIBLE FUTURE

Steven is transferred to a new school. The new teacher, Katie, is committed to proactive, respectful interactions that minimize the use of power. Katie knows that at least 75 percent of her interactions with Steven need to be satisfying for a relationship to build. She goes out of her way to get to know Steven, his favorite activities, preferred peers, most productive times of the day, and his general life. She gives him attention when things are going well or neutral. She also knows that when there is a problem, frustration will get Steven to most likely behave in quite inappropriate ways. She understands that his brain has developed a pretty powerful and intense program of reacting in angry ways. Katie's task, then, is to (1) develop a safe, respectful, and collaborative relationship; (2) avoid triggering the destructive emotion program as much as possible; (3) deal with the program in a deescalating way when it is triggered; and (4) contribute to the development of an alternative, stronger, and more appropriate neuronal network. This may seem like a daunting task to busy educators. However, with practice, commitment to proactive and compassionate ways of being, and a little knowledge in brain research, it is feasible. Progress will occur in small increments with regular steps backwards that can be used to consolidate a stronger progress. The following concepts are helpful for Katie to remember:

1. Respectful and Safe Relationship

Relationships profoundly shape the brain and the activity of its neurons. Interpersonal relationships not only determine which information is noticed and encoded in the brain, but also how experience is processed (Siegel, 1999). Because of the way the brain is structured, young people can integrate learning respect only if *experiences* of respect have formed a canvas for encoding a future imprint of the idea. The brain's scaffold is essentially experiential at first, as other forms of material attach to experiential encoding.

Relationships also provide a forum whereby enjoyable emotions are amplified through shared experiences, and uncomfortable emotions are diminished by the process of feeling understood (Siegel, 1999). All intimate connections between individuals involve a compelling resonance between the right hemisphere (nonverbal expressions) as well as the left hemisphere (logical verbal interpretations) of both speaker and listener (Siegel, 1999). From this state of cooperative activation, the mind is able to heal, performing at its maximum complexity and developing a stable sense of preferred self, functioning across time and emotional states.

Safety in the relationship is particularly crucial as it allows for the engagement of higher cortical functions (Belvel & Jordan, 2003). Steven can learn that the teacher appreciates and respects him regardless of his poor performance and mistakes. No genuine growth or effort will take place as long as the relationship doesn't feel safe.

For Katie then, focusing on being the best possible person she can be, anchored in compassion, contextualized perspective, externalizations, respect, and genuine interest in Steven can, in and of itself, trigger change. Interactions are shaped by all parties involved and especially by the bearer of power. If one important party of the pattern of interaction changes, then there is a greater likelihood that the other party will change too. This, of course, is mediated by the length of time the problem has been experienced and the other influences on the student's life. The longer the active history of the problem, the longer it will take to repattern the brain with progress not necessarily being visible at first.

2. Avoiding Triggers of the Destructive Emotions Program

Emotions actually direct the flow of activation in the brain to one area or another. Emotions are the "central organizer" of all incoming information (Ciompi, 1991). They shape what is perceived, remembered (state dependent memories), believed, interpreted, ascribed meaning, and form the subsequent response (Damasio, 1994). When a young person such as Steven becomes angry, there is a specific program, a pattern of neuronal firing that is triggered and that initiates certain behaviors without him necessarily having an awareness or sense of control over it. A high degree of arousal in his amygdala becomes expressed through him shouting. Rational thinking is suspended and perception of nuances may be clouded (Goleman, 1995). The brain of young people who may have had little support in processing experiences may not be very skilled at noticing the situational nuances, their unique meaning, and in expressing varied emotions. They may interpret all events through narrow categories such as frustrating, frightening, and fun (Siegel, 1999). Katie can minimize the triggering of the anger neuronal network by paying attention to three characteristics of the brain: (1) sensitivity, (2) specificity, and (3) window of tolerance.

Sensitivity

Each individual has a different threshold at which point something becomes a source of stress or triggers emotional reactions (Siegel, 1999). Sensitivity refers to how a little thing can trigger, at times, a big response. This sensitivity is affected by recent experiences. As such, Steven had a lower tolerance to stress on Mondays because he had spent the weekend feeling rejected by his family. Coming out of this context, his brain was primed to react more quickly to protect him from feeling increasingly inadequate. In other words, having spent a weekend at home feeling intensely inadequate, Steven's brain would engage more rapidly than at other times into a physiological fight or flight reaction to any perceived threat to his feeling of adequacy. A difficult math problem or the teacher's comment would be sufficient to trigger the pattern. This process in and of itself would block the possibility that information be processed in higher cortical areas of his brain, making math simply impossible neurologically.

Katie, having observed the problem pattern and having experience with students who struggle more after weekends, purposely gives Steven assignments she knows will reconnect him with his sense of competency and worthiness on Monday mornings. On individual assignments such as homework, she asks Steven to do what he can for thirty minutes, which reduces the likelihood he will get overwhelmed by the seemingly endless amount of work to do. Steven experiences success if he is able to do his best for thirty minutes, as opposed to only if he completes an assignment. Katie also goes out of her way to reconnect personally with him to reduce his sensitivity, make visible his success at facing certain tasks, and call home regularly to report meaningful efforts.

Specificity

Emotions trigger the activity of certain specific parts of the brain. As mentioned above, uncomfortable emotions typically trigger the amygdala and limbic parts of the brain, shutting down all higher cognitive functions of self-reflection and problem solving (Damasio, 1994). They mobilize the body for a fight or flight response and focus strictly on the dangerous aspects of the object/subject perceived as a threat, with practically no self-awareness. Pleasant and comfortable emotions enhance the brain's functioning on a more complex level, making new connections to old knowledge and expanding the neuronal network to integrate learning.

Katie uses experiential learning in her class with all students. She attempts to attach positive emotions and personal meaning to all lectures to ensure her students' brains can maximize the encoding of the information. She also uses stories, gives regular breaks for exercise, and makes learning fun to keep her class happy and engaged. Her teaching style minimizes all students' experiences of frustration.

Window of Tolerance

Each person has a unique range of emotions that they can tolerate neurologically while maintaining some form of self-control. Depending on life experience, this window can include or not include a wide range of emotions. When a young person's negative emotions are escalated by punitive dialogue or harsh threats, the youth's brain can simply fall out of the window of tolerance. The same can occur just in facing a task that is perceived as too challenging and feeling overly pressured to do it. Outside of this window, there is at one end an excessive sympathetic activity associated with an increased heart rate, faster breathing, and pounding in the head, while at the other end of the window there is numbness, mental paralysis, and shutting down of mental ability (Siegel, 1999). In either case, the person is unable to function and may feel like being in a car with both the accelerator and brakes fully on at the same time (Siegel, 1999).

Windows of tolerance can be widened in contexts that are safe and where one feels supported and valued. Teachers who know their students' struggles can invite students to perform more challenging tasks after having established a firm foundation for safety, trust, and a sense of self-worth. Students are more willing to explore novel situations when they feel appreciated. This also implies that the teacher has communicated that mistakes are okay and are part of learning, which makes risks much smaller and less threatening to students' self-worth.

3. Deescalating the Program When it Does Occur

The intensity of an emotional experience is determined by the number of neurons that fire together and the amount of neurotransmittors released in the synaptic connections (Damasio, 1994). The more intense the emotion, the greater the need to be understood at that very moment in time, in part because of the heightened vulnerability embedded in the experience. A failure to be understood results in a sense of isolation and sometimes shame (Siegel, 1999), which can worsen the original problem and increase the negative emotion loop firing in the neuronal circuit of the brain.

Katie avoids cornering Steven into intense emotions and instead, prioritizes listening to him, giving him an experience of being understood, and allowing him to go to a pre-agreed upon and collaboratively chosen safe place to calm down. This may simply mean Steven's choice of sitting in a peaceful corner or walking alone to another classroom and back, to kinesthetically calm down his brain with the production of endorphins, serotonin, noradrenalin, and dopamine secreted during movement (Jensen, 2000b; Tate, 2007). When Katie sees him become agitated, she responds in a quick, gentle, and calm manner that was discussed previously with Steven as being helpful. This allows Steven to reach peaks of intense emotions less often and develop instead the ability to calm himself down. Every time he does this, it affects the wiring of his brain, making a calm ending become a more probable neurological response and the intense destructive emotion a less probable response. Neurologically, this means activating the orbitofrontal cortex to inhibit the program involving the destructive response and redirect its energy to the metacognitive cortical activities such as abstract thinking and self-reflection. In doing this, she empowers Steven to self-regulate his own emotions as opposed to always being sent to talk to the principal or the counselor. If the state (emotion) of the brain is changed, the behavior is automatically changed as well (Jensen, 2003).

4. Contributing to the Development of More Appropriate Neuronal Networks

Katie contributes to the development of new neuronal networks by:

- creating new meaningful experiences
- making visible positive experiences that are already there but not noticed

New experiences of both connecting with the teacher, as discussed above, and learning can definitely be triggered in most students. Much has been written in the last decade on efficient ways to engage young people's brains (Begley, 2007). For example, many authors emphasize the importance of asking interesting questions since whatever the individual perceives as novelty will wake up the brain and cause it to produce norepinephrine (Sprenger, 2005). Others recommend the use of music to reduce stress and engage other regions of the brain (Sousa, 2001). Others still recommend paying attention to brain "hooks" (Tate, 2007) such as needs, novelty, meaning, emotions, and humor to enhance experiences of learning. Humor, in particular, has been examined since laughter causes the body to release endorphins (natural painkillers) and has been shown to enhance attention, recall of information (Shammin & Stuss, 1999), creativity, and productivity (Feigelson, 1998). The chances that new material will be remembered are also increased if it is connected to information that is older and relevant to the person (Sprenger, 2005) and if students are allowed to talk about it with each other (Tate, 2007). It is therefore possible for an educator to trigger interest and motivation in Steven. The ability to be motivated to learn and connect still exists in his brain but is buried under many layers of distrust, frustration, feelings of inadequacy, and desire to avoid failure. These layers can be peeled through for the motivation to emerge. Students who feel motivated and successful at school engage in much less disrespect and problem behaviors.

Noticing the absence of problems has significant impacts on individuals' sense of ability to change (White, 2007; White & Epston, 1990; Zimmerman & Beaudoin, 2002). Unfortunately, educators tend to give 99 percent of the positive feedback to the students who are performing well and practically none to the students who are struggling and would be most affected by appreciation (Koenig, 2000). Such noticing empowers young people to realize that they can make conscious choices that better fit the person they wish to be (Seligman, 1990). Noticing successes also allows the teacher to comment on the fact that many successes are simply dependent on practice. Students' commitment to learning can be significantly enhanced when they start seeing their mistakes as representing a need for practice rather than as inadequacies (Dweck, 2007). Also, with some young people, noticing successes and small steps is the only way into self-awareness and self-reflection. This is particularly the case if they have a habit of avoiding self-examination because in the past adults' focus on them was mostly experienced as criticism. The noticing of efforts, intentions, and successes triggers a new neuronal network that, coupled with the excitement and positive feelings about self, can, with repetition over time, override the old destructive state of mind.

CONCLUSION

Knowledge of the neurological basis for behaviors helps Steven's new teacher maintain contextualized perspective and compassion in the face of unpleasant interactions. It helps her maintain an externalized view of the problem, an understanding that given an experience of choice, Steven would not act this way. It allows her to use her power as an educator in proactive ways. She knows to listen to the suffering, notice the intentions, efforts, and successes; and create space for learning to occur. Over time and through repeated experiences, Katie will notice that Steven's explosive anger habit will reduce in frequency and intensity and will recover faster given his increasing trust in the relationship and the development of new skills. The brain has an incredible plasticity, and caring adults have the incredible privilege and responsibility of shaping its complex web.

Part III
Prevention

*Scaffolding a Complex
and Sound Culture of Respect*

12

Creating a Partnership
With Response-Able
Youth

Be the change you wish to see in the world.

—Gandhi

So far, we have discussed how to understand and respond to actual incidents of bullying and disrespect. We have offered ideas on how to respond to problems one-on-one with a young person, on the playground, and in classroom contexts. This section will discuss ways to influence the school culture to minimize the likelihood that disrespect and bullying can occur in the first place.

While many districts spend enormous amounts of money on various preventative schoolwide programs teaching students this and that, there is ample evidence that the resulting progresses are, most of the time, small and short lived. The main reason for this limited result is that many of these programs not only target just the students, but they also do that in ways that are incongruent with students' experience. Brain research has overwhelmingly demonstrated that learning is encoded through lived *experience* (Damasio, 1994; Siegel, 1999) and not rote memorization of "I statements" and role plays. The lived experience of respect that students gain by being in the school culture in itself can be far more powerful than any intellectual lesson.

Moreover, the adults in the school can have a far greater impact on the culture than the students. Educators are the foundation that remains year after year in the school. They set the tone for much of what happens intellectually, emotionally, and relationally with students. If adults are resentful, stressed, impatient, and intolerant, young people will be unhappy, resentful, and more likely to engage in problem behaviors. Every single adult's response to students' various behaviors contributes in fantastic ways to the school culture. Even students who never engage in any disrespectful gesture will be affected vicariously by witnessing their teacher or principal yell or punish a student who was disrespectful or simply bored with a task. They learn how to treat that peer, how to respond if the teacher becomes annoyed, and they learn to not trust the educator should they too have the misfortune of making a mistake one day.

Interviewed, students know exactly whom they would seek out for advice when they make a mistake and unfortunately, in many schools, they cannot trust any of the adults. The middle and high schoolers, in particular, fear that the situation will be taken out of their hands, that adults will not listen and will take actions without listening to them. They fear adults will make things worse and they are often right. Over and over, we have heard stories of students taking the risk of telling an adult about their victimization by other students and how the adults' well-meaning interventions just made the harassment more intense, insidious, and worse.

The only way to effectively prevent disrespect and bullying is to create a *culture* that is *incongruent* with the development of such problems.

By definition, *cultures* are set by the attitudes, shared values, and actions of its members. In a school, this means that the culture is determined by: (1) common beliefs, (2) individual people (students and adults), and (3) the relationship between them.

By definition, *incongruent* means a difficulty for two ways of being to coexist. For example, it is generally incongruent to be violent to others if you experience great compassion for them. It would be incongruent to unfairly treat students of color if you understand the politics of racism. It would be incongruent to marinate into consumerism if you value the environment.

A culture incongruent with disrespect and bullying focuses on both reducing the occurrence of emotions associated with bullying and disrespect (resentment, anger, powerlessness, isolation) and increasing the opposite experiences of appreciation, compassion, agency, and connectedness. In other words, the culture becomes one of care and respect in the face of all types of struggles at all times.

Do adults and students contribute equally to the culture? No. A teacher who is impatient will have a greater impact (intensity) on a larger number of people (quantity) than a student who is impatient. Culture is significantly shaped by the people who hold the power to speak, set rules, and determine what is acceptable, what will be noticed, what values are applied, and what matters. Teachers and principals model ways of being; they are in the spotlight all day and even at lunch, with other teachers in the staff room.

They will have an impact on whether the rest of the staff is energized, and think positively or negatively about students. In that sense, educators can be assumed to have on average 60–70 percent of the responsibility in shaping the culture and young people about 30–40 percent.

This is not to say that educators *feel powerful*. In fact, we might even say that many educators feel quite powerless in addressing chronic problems of disrespect and bullying in their school culture even though technically they have more physical, emotional, and intellectual power over their students than the reverse. The question then becomes why do so many educators feel powerless to change even just their classroom's subculture if they have more power? The answer has to do with being pressured to teach in ways that do not fit their better judgment (standards and district pressure), and most importantly, *misusing* the power that they could have on students. There is, indeed, much that can be done with the power that educators do have. With a story, allow us to plunge deeper into an exploration of the beliefs, the people, and the relationships that create a school culture that is incongruent with bullying and disrespect—a culture of tolerance, respect, and collaboration.

BUBBLE TROUBLE

Long ago, Africa was ruled by powerful warrior kings. King Akbari was the most powerful king of them all. It is said that if you stood on the highest point in Akbari's kingdom and looked in all four directions as far as you could see, until the earth curved, you could still not see King Akbari's entire kingdom. King Akbari lived in a small village in North West Africa called Uzama. Early each morning, Akbari and his warriors rode through the Village of Uzama to make sure that all was safe, secure, and free from intrusion.

On one particular morning, when Akbari and the warriors were coming back from their morning ride, as they approached the village, they saw something on the riverbank sparkling, shining, and shimmering in a rainbow of colors. It was a big, no it was a huge, no it was a . . . a . . . gigantic bubble! When Akbari and his warriors saw this bubble, they stopped! King Akbari looked at the bubble and he looked at his warriors. Akbari's warriors looked at their king and they looked at the bubble. Then they all turned back and looked at their king. Akbari jumped down from his horse and ran toward the bubble, stopping a royal distance from the bubble. Pointing his sword toward the bubble, Akbari shouted,

"This is Big Trouble!"

King Akbari turned and looked at his warriors and declared, "I am going to get rid of this big trouble right now." Mounting his horse and holding his sword high, Akbari rode down the riverbank. Riding swiftly like the winter's north wind Akbari charged the bubble. His sword hit the bubble and bounced off. He lost his balance and tumbled headfirst into the bubble, landing smack dab right in the middle! The angry king beat on the inside wall of the bubble with his fists. Using his head, his shoulders, and his feet, Akbari tried to break the bubble, but the bubble would not break.

King Akbari called for his red warrior. The red warrior, dressed entirely in red from the top of his head to the tip of his toes, stepped forward, bowing low before his king, and asked, "My king, how may I serve you?" Akbari shouted, "Get me out of this trouble!" The red warrior stepped back, looked at the bubble, and looked at his king. He said, "My king, I am afraid that I will hurt you." Akbari shouted, "I will be okay! Just get me out of this big trouble." "As you wish," replied the red warrior, mounting his red horse, with his red machete in hand. It was as pointed and as powerful as a bolt of lighting. With his red hair blowing in the wind, he charged the bubble. His machete hit the bubble and bounced off. King Akbari was still in the middle of the bubble.

From inside the bubble, King Akbari called for his blue warrior. The blue warrior, dressed entirely in blue from the top of his head to the tip of his toes, stepped forward, bowing low before his king, and asked, "My king, how may I serve you?" Pressing his nose against the inside wall of the bubble until it was flat, King Akbari screamed between his clenched teeth, "Get me out of this trouble!" The blue warrior jogged down the riverbank, with his long knife in hand and like an arrow shot from a bow. The blue warrior ran toward the bubble. At high speed, his knife hit the bubble and bounced off. Akbari was still locked inside the gigantic bubble.

The sun was high in the sky. The bubble was surrounded by knives, spears, machetes, and swords. Akbari's warriors sat on the ground around the bubble scratching their heads. King Akbari sat in the middle of the bubble with his head in his hands. At that moment, from the direction of the village, children's voices could be heard. It was the children coming to the river for their noonday bath. As the children rounded the bend they stopped. Their mouths dropped open, and their eyes grew big. They could be heard saying, "What a big bubble! It's beautiful! I've never seen a bubble that big! Look at the colors! From the very back, a small voice said, "That's my daddy in the middle of the bubble." She was Princess Akimi, King Akbari's youngest daughter.

When King Akbari heard the children's voices, he stood and called to his warriors. "Warriors, stop the children; keep them away from this big trouble." Following their king's command, the warriors ran toward the children. The children, thinking it was a game, began to laugh and to run from the king's men. Well, little African girls are very smart and quick on their feet; they can outrun, outskip, and outdance around any old warrior, any day. King Akbari's daughter ran, skipped, and danced around all the warriors, until she stood before the bubble and her father. The king's daughter looked at the bubble and she looked at her father. She looked at her father and she looked at the bubble. Standing before the bubble, Akimi leaned forward and with just two of her little fingers, she pinched the bubble.

The bubble went "poof" and it was gone.

Looking at her father, Akimi said, "Daddy, if you treat it like trouble, it will act like trouble; if you treat it like a bubble, it will act like a bubble."

SOURCE: (Adapted from Deborah Simon)

Reflection Questions

- If you can use power, does that mean that you should?
- What percentage of what we see as problems with young people are really problems?
- Can you think of an example of a problem-related interaction with a student that, upon reflection, didn't need to be a problem?
- How do you determine when to involve young people in solving problems?

LESSONS FROM THIS STORY: THE BELIEFS

Broadening What We See

Young people engage in a much greater variety of behaviors than adults. They are creative, impulsive, explore different ways of being, and replicate much of what they see in the various contexts of their lives. Most adults want to see order, productivity, and tasks accomplished in a linear way. Adults like the comfort of things unfolding as planned or expected. When a situation doesn't fit with the plan, adults often feel destabilized, surprised, and many may feel threatened as did King Akbari. Depending on your own life experience with the unexpected, there may be a temptation to see any student deviation from the plan as "bad," "disrespectful," or as "trouble." When educators see students' unexpected behaviors as trouble, they automatically greatly reduce their ability to respond. Schools where students' meandering ways of thinking and behaving is met with constant negative and controlling educator response create a context of distrust, stress, and resentment. Schools with the highest sense of respect, as measured both by students' and educators' perceptions, are often schools where educators are more "mellow," "relaxed," and expect young people to make mistakes or forget. They assume students will occasionally run in the no running zone, that they'll forget their homework, that they'll have days where they will be less able to pay attention, and that they'll probably say something they would rather not have said at one point or another. These behaviors are not seen as problems but rather as a common part of childhood/adolescence.

When issues are seen as part of childhood/adolescence and development, students can focus on learning to deal with the issues in their simplest form. This is in sharp contrast with having to deal not only with the issue but also with an angry adult and a threat. In the Bubble Trouble story, King Akbari's reaction escalated the problem; he became part of the problem and no longer a powerful observer able to make decisions with perspective. Educators reacting with their own frustration to students' behaviors become part of the problem too. Their frustration contributes not only to the worsening of the current problem but also to the increased likelihood of the problem reoccurring simply by preventing deep learning to occur and damaging their relationship with students.

Broadening How We Respond:
Big Versus Small Interventions

Once a situation is determined to be a problem—and some truly are—there can still be many options. Unfortunately, in the highly stressed world of schools, educators often feel like they have very little time to think about or address problems. There is often a temptation to "nip in the bud" any out of line, unusual student behavior to "make sure that it doesn't get out of hand" or to ensure "the student will never think of doing that again." In such context, it is easy to fall into the habit of big adversarial interventions even when something could be treated simply as a bubble. We have seen a police officer being summoned because a first grader bit another, a third grader being suspended for having picked up an empty lighter on the ground on his way to school, and middle school students sent to detention because they argued about needing to drink water at the wrong time on a hot summer day. Some educators and their students live in a constant battle zone where adult authority rules and strikes at the slightest slip and where students rebel and become hateful. While these adults are often desperate to contain the disrespect rampant in their school, their constant threats and punishments mainly aggravate students' resentment and inability to experience kindness. It is the ultimate irony: the more educators feel pressured in time and upset by disrespect, the harder they threaten and punish and the more likely it is to happen. This has a lot to do with the relational patterns of interactions discussed in Chapter 5, as well as how our brains are wired (Chapter 11). When adults overthreaten and punish frequently, they are no longer helping young people learn and broaden the scope of their knowledge. They have fallen out of their roles as educators.

A tremendous amount of research in multiple domains (social, developmental, psychological, neurological) exists to support the evidence that young people learn when they feel appreciated and safe (Belvel & Jordan, 2003; Bluestein, 2008; Kohn, 1999; Siegel & Hartzell, 2003; White, 2007). Average public schools with the least amount of bullying have a principal suspension rate of 5 percent or less and no detention rooms. Teachers, yard duties, and student-patrols help students discuss their conflicts and find resolutions. Reminders replace threats, compassionate questions about each party's perspective replace truth-seeking judgments, processing feelings replaces punishment. Students who are occasionally sent to the principal's office trust that they will be given an opportunity to tell their stories and do not have to distort them since there will most likely not be any consequence. If there needs to be a consequence, and that definitely does happen, then students generally feel that the consequence makes sense and is fair. For example, if a student graffitis the play structure, the student has to clean it up (a detention would be irrelevant). Problems can be treated as opportunities for students to learn and as opportunities for adults to truly be educators who help young people think differently. Problems require the inquisitive mind of the adult attempting to solve the mystery of why a young person got stuck in a behavior and what can help. In such context, low profile interventions address problems without damaging the student's sense of worth or the educator-student relationship. Low profile interventions address problems with the least possible amount of interference with instruction (Tate, 2007).

Broadening the Responsibility

When all of the responsibility for solving a problem falls onto one party, pressure is intense and poor decisions are more likely to happen. As was the case with King Akbari, it becomes tempting to use power and give orders which may be the poorest choice of them all. In school, young people may have lots of ideas on what contributed to problems, what could solve them, and how to prevent their reoccurrence. While adults can maintain the final authority to decide, it is well worth it to create a partnership with young people and support them in becoming response-able.

THE PEOPLE

The Response-Able Youth

If I am I because I am I
And you are you because you are you
Then I am, and you are
But if I am I because you are you,
And you are you because I am I,
Than I am not and you are not

—Rabbi Mendel of Kotzk, (as cited in Carroll et al., 1995)

The concept of being "response-able" has been discussed by Steven Covey (2004) as being able to experience both emotions and rational thinking at the same time leaving the individual able to make better choices. Applied to youth, this means that young people would experience problems as constructively solvable and themselves as having manageable emotions that they are competent to handle. Youth can only become response-able when they are encouraged to process, think solutions through, and empowered to see themselves as capable, worthy individuals. Being response-able is an experience of oneself that grows over time and over multiple interactions with others. In that sense, the school culture has a huge impact on the development of this experience of self. One single adult may contribute to this experience but it becomes more deeply engrained when the culture and most of its members are on board with supporting youth's thinking and problem solving time after time. Since young people are also influenced by what happens at home, there will always be some students who will import poor communication habits and leftover frustration to school. These can be buffered to a certain extent by the culture and the deescalating attitude of the others, providing fertile ground for enriched learning.

The response-able youth takes into consideration the following three areas when problem solving:

1. Oneself
   - Response-able youth are aware of their own *feelings*. This allows them to choose to comment on their emotional experiences or the perceived feeling of the other.
   - Response-able youth trust that they can be heard and have the ability to handle the situation. They know arguments can end in a constructive manner because they have witnessed the unfolding of

problem solving a number of times and they have specific *tools* to respond. They don't need an adult to solve every misunderstanding.

- Response-able youth are *confident* about their worthiness and their rights as a member of the school.

2. Others
   - Response-able youth take notice of the others' feelings.
   - Response-able youth understand that some unknown contextual, historical, or personal factor is probably contributing to the interaction. This allows them to have greater compassion and feel less personally attacked.

3. A range of actions
   - Response-able youth choose actions that are deescalating in conflict, preserving of self and other's sense of worth, and mostly congruent with their personal values as well as those of the community in which they evolve.
   - Response-able youth are encouraged to be the best person they can possibly be regardless of what others do.

For example:

Kari stealing Tyler's lunch box and taunting him with it!

Tyler, not moving:	Did something happen to you and make you frustrated today, Kari? Are you trying to share the frustration with me?
Billy sarcastically shouts at Malia:	I can't believe you did that. You're totally stupid or what.
Malia responds calmly:	I did this for a reason, Billy. If you don't understand, it doesn't mean that I'm stupid. You could ask a question instead of hurting my feelings.
Frank:	We won. We won. We beat your team ten to nothing.
Andres:	Stop saying that. It makes me upset. You wouldn't want me to do that if I won next time, would you? Plus, didn't we agree earlier that having fun was more important than winning?

Again, for youth to respond in a calm manner, they need to have been exposed to others responding in a calm and respectful manner. Youth are in school six and half hours per day on average and more than 80 percent of this time is spent paying attention to an educator's demands. Witnessing an authority figure responding to situations over and over again has a powerful influence on social learning. Time-wise, educators can have more influence than anyone else on the experiences that are shaping whom the young person is becoming, often more than parents.

Proactive Educators

> *I have come to a frightening conclusion. I am the decisive element in the classroom. It is my personal approach that creates the climate. It is my daily mood that makes the weather. As a teacher I possess tremendous power to make a child's life miserable or joyous. I can be a tool of torture or an instrument of inspiration. I can humiliate or humor, hurt or heal. In all situations, it is my response that decides whether a crisis will be escalated or deescalated, and a child humanized or dehumanized.*

> —Haim Ginott (1995)

Proactive educators' moods do not so much depend on what students do, but rather on how they—educators—choose to be as people. Their moods and responses to incidents do not fluctuate up and down based on what happens in their classrooms, but rather is grounded in their values and beliefs. For example, if students raise their voices, educators can choose to lower or keep theirs even toned. They do not match or escalate the external imbalance. As stated by S. Covey (2004), "Proactive people can carry their own weather with them. Whether it rains or shines makes no difference to them" (p. 71).

Proactive educators take the time to think and appraise carefully the multiple perspectives that may be contributing to a situation. It is often what educators tell themselves in their own minds that hurts them the most, not what actually happens to them (Byron, 2007). The hurt arises from seeing events and people in a narrow and reactive lens. One may intensely repeat to oneself that the situation is dangerous, as with King Akbari, or that the other is responsible for the problem, as in many adult-youth relationships. Since thinking shapes actions, narrow reactive views lead to ineffective and inappropriate actions.

Proactive educators are able to simultaneously hold an awareness of themselves (emotions, thoughts, actions), their students, and the context. Such big perspective maximizes their experiences of power as they can see more options and make better choices. Power comes from knowing that a variety of surprising and upsetting incidents are to be expected with young people and in schools. Accepting the unknown allows educators to respond with curiosity and a focus on where they always have a tremendous power— the possibility of controlling their own mind and fostering learning in the minds of youth. People experience a lot more power when they focus on what they can influence rather than on what seems annoying and out of control. They accept what happens and respond to it in the best possible way.

Proactive educator's power comes from:

1. Consideration of oneself
   - focusing on their own congruency with their values and preferences
   - cultivating compassion
2. Consideration of others
   - creating emotional and physical safety for their students by remaining calm regardless of what happens

- listening with a respectful intention to understand the unique experience of their students, without judging
- nurturing the relationship at all costs
- cultivating contextualized perspectives

3. Consideration of actions
   - focusing on what they can do to improve the situation
   - taking actions that will have a positive effect on students' experiences of themselves and their relationships with others

A good example of this was shared with Marie-Nathalie by a middle school teacher, Todd Phoenix. Todd was struggling with the STAR testing pressure that was placed upon him and his students, many of whom were underprivileged and performing poorly academically. On the day of the test, he brought in a big bouquet of flowers, irises, into his class and placed them in a visible place. He then took a few minutes to discuss with students the fact that some of the flowers were blooming today and some were still in buds and would bloom later. "You are a worthy person regardless of how you do on this test," he said. "Some of you will just bloom later, in your own time." This discussion brought peace in the classroom, changed the meaning of the test, and allowed for a more relaxed and peaceful atmosphere. Todd did what he could to affect the culture of his class that day in spite of the tense atmosphere of his school. He used his power where he could; he reduced the meaning of the test he didn't believe in and eliminated the pressure and stress that was placed upon him and his students. He was true to his own values and beliefs, even in the face of something he had no visible control over.

Schools can spend an enormous amount of money training their staff month after month on how to deal with bullying, then social anxiety, then . . . In the end, the most powerful and greatest overarching training a staff can receive is how to remain proactive, patient, and hold perspective in the face of whatever hardship occurs during class.

Be the best possible person you can be regardless of students' behavior.

THE RELATIONSHIP

The fundamental law of human beings is interdependence. A person is a person through other persons.

—Archbishop Desmond Tutu

A Partnership

Educators' relationships with their students are everything. Students will go the extra miles, make the unthinkable efforts, pay attention, try hard to change themselves to please adults whom they like, respect, and feel appreciated by. Young people who bully and disrespect often have not had that much of this experience, if any at all, with a significant adult.

Many have given up hope that adults can be trusted and respected. A partnership implies minimizing power and hierarchy between the partners and favoring collaboration, as was discussed in Chapter 4. It also implies conveying that the other has worthy opinions and the right to speak about what matters to them. A partnership means accepting that young people can often solve problems because they offer a different perspective on situations, just as in the Bubble Trouble story.

In our story, King Akbari was caught in his own view of the bubble as a danger and wanted to shelter children from it. While safety is important, how often does our extreme preoccupation for the safety of young people result in unnecessary exclusions, loss of solutions, and deprivation of meaningful explorations? How skewed is our balance between *living life* versus *avoiding death or injury*. Our position regarding this philosophical matter has a great impact on the quality of life we allow for ourselves, as well as the richness of life experience we offer to youth.

A partnership also means that the young person is never perceived as "the problem." If you treat a youth as problem, one thing is certain, he or she will act as a problem, which may simply double the complexity of the initial issue. In a partnership, each individual brings baggage into the relationship and it is addressed in a respectful way that focuses on the best that each partner can bring to the collaboration. In a partnership, everyone pays attention to their potential contribution to a problem, as opposed to a hierarchical blaming of the other. For instance, how do you decide if a youth is underperforming versus the adult overexpecting, or if the youth is annoying versus the adult being impatient?

Power Has a Price and Partnership Pays Off

Commitment to partnership is visible on many levels and, in particular, in the way people speak. If you are in a park and you hear someone call a name, you know just by the tone of the voice if this person is calling an adult or a child. The tone of voice is often soaking with authority and not collaborative. Similarly, the words you will use to talk to a young person may transpire power. A good example of this is in the use of "I want" versus "I wish." As shared by a father Norvin Powell, wanting something invites an experience of will and using power (personal communication). In contrast, wishing something invites an attitude of wondering how we can make it happen. It allows for reflection, time, patience, and understanding.

Educators as Partners

Most educators enter the profession with enthusiasm, a love of young people, and a determination to make learning interesting and captivating for students. Some spend their evenings, weekends, and summers concocting fascinating projects and plotting interesting ways to teach the rather boring curriculum. After an average of four years, research (Merrow, 2001) shows that many are burned out or resentful. The profession and its narrow requirements didn't yield the satisfaction anticipated. Many leave, some put in their hours, and then some, somehow, manage to retain their enthusiasm and patience for young people. How do they do that? Our conversations with many skilled educators revealed a profound ability to see beyond the visible problem and a commitment to help. More than anything, these educators see their role as facilitating learning that starts where the student is rather than where the adult wants the student to be. If the student is afflicted with anger, the educator will attempt to help with the anger; if the student has a chaotic home environment, the educator attempts to provide safe and comforting interactions at school; if the student struggles with poor attention, the educator tries to notice what captures attention. The educator becomes a chameleon based on the student's needs. This contributes to a caring environment where students feel respected and seen as people. This is in sharp contrast with teachers who see their goal as teaching the curriculum and who experience students' issues as obstacles preventing them from reaching their goals. Assistant Superintendant Honey Berg uses a helpful metaphor to teach this concept to her staff: "If I organize a meeting in Chicago for all educators in the USA but give directions only from San Francisco because that's where I am, many people will get lost along the way! Instruction, education, needs to be tailored to the needs and point of view of the recipients!" Proactive educators' starting places are the students' experiences.

Students' issues are part of life; they are unavoidable. Schools with a "trouble mindset" see students as things to be controlled, tamed, and taught. In schools encouraging partnership, educators see students as young people with minds buzzing with both ideas and emotions. That is unchangeable. What we do have power over is our attitude when we encounter them, our ways of addressing them, and our willingness to consider the young person's perspective.

A Partnership Exploration Exercise

This exercise allows you to apply the ideas of this book to a real situation you are experiencing.

Step 1: In one sentence, name a problem that you are experiencing with a student.

Step 2: Externalize the problem in the space below and restate the sentence above.

Step 3: If you haven't included yourself in the problem and made the statement strictly about the student, try to restate the issue by writing how it affects both you and the student in nonpreferred ways.

Step 4: Make sure you write how you might inadvertently contribute to the problem, and add a sentence that completes the pattern of interaction.

Step 5: Consider the effects of *your* contribution to the problem on the student's problem. Does it make it bigger or smaller?

Step 6: Once your contribution is visible, think of an alternative way you sometimes have to handle the situation and which also leads to a more constructive outcome.

Step 7: Write what usually allows you to respond in such preferred way and what is helpful for you to remember.

Step 8: How do you feel about yourself and your role when you respond in your preferred way?

Step 9: How does being able to respond in preferred ways affect the student, the problem, and your relationship?

Step 10. How does responding in ways that are congruent with your preferences and values affect you in general?

Your resulting presentation of the problem may look something like this:

Nick drives me crazy (Step 1). His *impulsivity* makes him do random, annoying and disrespectful things to all of us (Step 2). When *Impulsivity* gets Nick to blurt inappropriate things, I feel myself getting impatient (Step 3). When *Impatience* gets to me, I feel like snapping at him and threatening him with a consequence of some sort (Step 4). I know that when I succumb to that he just gets more agitated, resentful, and even less able to contain his *Impulsivity* (Step 5). At my best, I have in the past taken a deep breath. I then gently remind him that I know he can be more caring of his peers. I ask him to think about what he's doing and its effects (Step 6). I can do that when I remember that Nick is adopted and has been through many unhappy foster homes (Step 7). When I respond with patience, I feel much better about myself as a person and educator. I feel caring, responsible, and helpful in contributing to his learning of social skills (Step 8). I noticed that it may not always work, but it often does bring his attention back without damaging our relationship or his self-worth, and it seems to little by little increase his ability to contain the *Impulsivity* (Step 9). I realize that when I make that effort, I have to extend less energy and time to deal with the escalating conflict and feel better about the situation just for having handled it in ways that I prefer (Step 10).

This exercise provides you with an experience of the minds of proactive educators who take responsibility for their inadvertent contributions to problems, focus their efforts on where they have power, and notice possibilities patiently bringing out better experiences for their students. This pattern of interaction is summarized in Figure 12.1. Proactive educators create a learning environment for learning to occur in the midst of unpleasant situations, allowing young people to become response-able. Other examples of questions to ask oneself are given in Resource E: Educators' Problem-Solving Questions.

Figure 12.1 Partnership Between Proactive Educators and Response-Able Youths

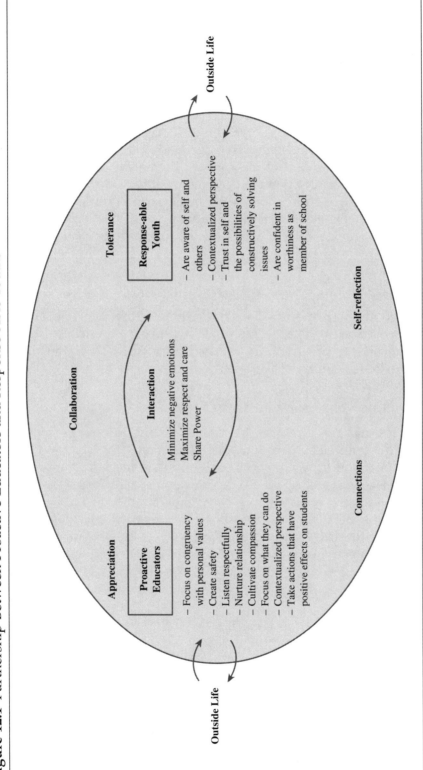

Example of Proactive Strategies

The following ideas are a short list of some strategies proactive educators and adults can consider in responding to challenging interactions with young people.

Your Brain Can Slow Down and Think!

Since humans speak at a rate of 125 words per minute while the brain can process over 800 per minute (Carroll et al., 1995), proactive educators use their remaining processing ability to understand, consider peace promoting options, and respond in a deescalating way. If emotions are too strong and your 800-word capacity is dominated by anger, it is worth it to wait. Given the powerful impact a single decision can have on youth, sometimes not responding immediately and taking the time to consider alternatives over a few hours is worth it. Isn't that what we want to encourage young people to do, to slow down and take the time to think before responding?

Be Upset in a Caring and Respectful Way

To be kind and respectful does not require liking someone, agreeing with the behavior, or disregarding your own upset experience. It simply means choosing to act in a way that is congruent with your values as opposed to being congruent with your emotional upset.

If You Can't Experience the Care, Pretend It!

Brain research has demonstrated that our mind uses our perception of our body to determine how we actually feel (Ekman, 1992; Ledoux, 1996). In other words, if you truly pretend to care about an incident, the body will seek internal congruency by modifying how you actually feel, reconnecting you with a genuine experience of care. Now, granted it is far better to actually feel the care in the first place, but if that experience seems buried too deeply under the frustration, pretending may assist you in responding initially to events in a way that may be more congruent with your values. With time and a genuine commitment to experiencing yourself in such a way, caring and respectful ways of being will flood in without effort.

Remember the Intention Equation

There are four variables in the "conflict math problem" that are quickly appraised when there is a conflict. Two on your end and two on the student's end: your intentions, your actions and the student's intentions, the student's action. Unfortunately, you only know of your intentions, which you generally perceive as good and you only know of the student's behavior which you generally perceive as a problem. That can lead to an experience of justified anger at the student where you feel you come from a place of "goodness" and the other from a place of "badness." The trick is that students have this perception as well, especially the younger students.

They often don't plot to do something problematic and can be startled by the adult's upset, leading them to think the adult is mean. We must all learn to assume that the other's preferred and overarching intentions are good, even when older students' anger may get the better of them and lead them to sometimes plan poor choices.

Practice Receiving and Constructing on Anything

Practice flexibility and open mindedness by learning to value whatever comes your way. The "yes and" exercise, included in Resource D, provides an opportunity to practice accepting whatever is offered by a partner and adding an idea that is constructive and expands possibilities. This exercise encourages the development of creativity, playfulness, and flexibility. It is a popular and life-changing exercise in many of Marie-Nathalie's university classes and in-services for schools.

Notice the Words You Tend to Repeat in Your Head When You Are Upset

The intense upset is almost never about what you see per se. Most of your upset comes from what you tell yourself in your mind about the incident. Even the relationship you have with a student is shaped by a series of selective memories, interpretations, and stories you hold onto. Can you tell yourself something else that creates less upset? It's not necessarily about giving up your story but about dwelling less on it *and* being willing to see other possibilities.

Give Up the Right and Wrong Notion

This narrow interpretation will almost always favor your perspective and what you like, while diminishing the student's. It is guaranteed to lead to an escalation of disrespect. Try in your mind to find a logical reason for the student to behave that way; try to find one or two good explanations to totally justify the student's action.

Remember That There Is a Lot of Unknown in Your View of What's Happening

There is always something unknown that happened before the incident. It never just starts there. If you don't have compassion for a student, it means that you don't understand the complexity of his or her experience. As eloquently stated by Andrews (1991), try to "see the student in relation to their lives as opposed to yours" (p. 142).

The "Invisibles" are More Important Than the "Visibles"

Intention, effort, context, and history are much more important to attend to than the visible actions. The big picture of your relationship with students and students' sense of worth are always more important than the situational problem.

TEACHER QUESTIONS

"Okay, This All Sounds Really Nice, but Sometimes I'm Burned Out and I Can't Take It Anymore."

Most teachers have experienced the student who just can't follow directions without making annoying comments. Even if it's the only thing the teacher asks, the student doesn't do it. It is easy to wonder whether we are allowed to have and express some frustration at this student.

In these instances, it is important to remember that sometimes students behave day after day in ways that are very upsetting because of nonschool related issues. This can progressively eat away our precious ability to have compassion, perspective, and patience. Although avoiding frustration completely is nearly impossible (except for seasoned Buddhist monks!), you can limit and contain it by what you choose to focus on in your mind. If there are three main active elements in an interaction (self, other, relationship), you can switch your focus from one to another at any time to boost your ability to be congruent with your values. If focusing on the other with compassion and perspective doesn't work, then you can switch to considering the critical long-term importance of a student-teacher relationship, or you can switch to saving yourself, not by reacting but rather by being congruent with your choices. In other words, when you are simply ready to explode and are at your wit's end, it may be helpful to hold on to being constructive as a gift to *yourself*. There are tremendous advantages to you in avoiding the escalation of conflicts on several fronts:

1. Your health. There is much evidence that within seconds, anger and frustration have a dramatic impact on reducing your number of T4 cells in your immune system on top of affecting your heart, blood pressure, and digestion (Kiecolt-Glaser, McGuire, Robles, & Glaser, 2002; Smith, Glazer, Ruiz, & Gallo, 2004).

2. The shaping of your brain. Because of the plasticity of the brain, every reaction, especially intensely emotional, reinforces a pattern of neuronal firing in your brain. This means that each time you get really angry, you increase both the intensity and likelihood of getting really angry again. If you make an effort to redirect your anger into perspective and patience, it will be easier to do it the next time. In this sense, you have the power to shape who you are increasingly becoming (Begley, 2007).

3. Future interactions with other students. As many students likely witness your response, they develop appreciation, respect, or distrust towards you. If it's difficult to remain constructive with one student, remember that doing so will facilitate your future relationships not only with this particular student but with many others who may be silent but very attentive.

4. Your personal and professional performance. When you lose it, you lose it on both fronts, as a person and as someone who has a

professional responsibility in the face of "unpleasant customers." Think of your values as a person, the kind of person you are proud to be, and your commitment to your job. Do it for your own satisfaction of being congruent with yourself, doing the best possible teaching work you can, and giving yourself permission to learn.

Finally, as discussed above, you can also pretend to be patient even if inside you are ready to explode. It is amazing how pretending to be confident or calm can grow on you especially when the results are positive. On many occasions, you will even find yourself experiencing it because physiologically, simply putting your face, body, and mind in the appearance of patience will act as a trigger for the emotional component of the experience. You will probably need to process what happened later on, but for now, at least, you will have kept the damage to a minimum.

Remember that reacting with anger hurts *you* and multiple students. In the end, constructive problem solving will save you much more time and energy than chronic conflicts.

"I Think That I Am Respectful and Considerate of Students' Perspectives Most of the Time. There's Just This One Student . . . "

Every now and then, teachers run up against the one student whom they just "can't stand and who is just plain mean." Often, with this type of student, we just don't try anymore.

Being respectful and collaborative with the students who do what we want is fairly easy. It is with the students who struggle that these values are truly tested. It is the actual conflicts that make visible how committed an educator is to these values.

"Every Day I Enter the Class and I Have to Take a Deep Breath Knowing That I Will Have to Deal With a Particular Student."

Usually, with these students, as we anticipate, problems happen even if we try our best to be nice.

What percentage of your reactions to the student are colored by the accumulation of past frustration and what percentage is associated strictly with what the student may have done just now? When asked this question, many educators realize how intensely colored by past resentment their reaction is. The relationship is stuck in mud where the starting place is always sticky and clouded by past negative experiences. Another student would engage in the exact same behavior and the teacher might just let it go. Just being able to realize the extent to which our reaction doesn't come from the present situation with the student may allow us to respond in a more fair way.

13

Spotlight on Stories of Successful Prevention

S tories of success are always inspiring. They provide food for thought, hope, and companionship as we try on different ideas. In this final chapter, we invite you first into the minds of proactive educators from a variety of schools and later, into a specific school that has cultivated and nurtured a culture of partnership with response-able youth.

For the first section, we have interviewed educators who were committed to creating a respectful partnership with young people. We asked them to share the details of what unfolded through their minds as they faced challenging situations. Their thinking and responses are outlined below. We would like to encourage you to imagine how you would handle each of these events. How would you respond? How would you use some of the ideas discussed above? What would you pay attention to? What would be your goal? Where possible, we have purposely not specified the ages so that you can apply these stories to the age group most relevant to your work.

STORY 1: "YOU'RE UGLY"

Sylvia came to get Kyle from the classroom. Kyle reluctantly came with her. As they were sitting down in her room, Kyle blurted out, "You're ugly, you know."

Temptation: Reply to the little brat with an equivalent or more hurtful comment.

What the educator saw: A student who has probably endured the same experience.

What she thought: This probably has nothing to do with my actual appearance.

How she saw her role: I need to use the opportunity to talk about a habit or an experience that probably creates problems in the student's social life.

How she responded: "That is a hurtful thing to say, Kyle. I wonder what's happening for you right now. Did something frustrating happen? Are upset feelings getting you to say things?"

The effects on the child: He lowered his eyes and replied, "We were just about to get to see a movie that I really wanted to see. The teacher had promised us all week that we would see it if we got our work done and I had worked for that."

Effects on the relationship: Since the educator kindly brought the student back to class the relationship was greatly enriched. She thanked him for explaining the situation to her and they made an agreement that next time, they would talk about "the effects of frustration on how we communicate."

Effects on the culture: Kyle shared the story with his friends who all thought that Sylvia was a cool person to talk to when you have a problem. Kyle felt understood, respected, and experientially learned a great deal about sharing his feelings rather than insulting. His happiness that afternoon allowed his classmates and his teacher to see the best of him. His social relationships improved in the subsequent months.

STORY 2: THE CLIPBOARD

It was early afternoon when a second-grade teacher in a small public elementary school (with diverse socioeconomic population) heard angry and threatening shouting in the class next to hers. She paused her own class for a moment to checked out what was happening next door. She was startled to see a student shouting at and threatening his classmates huddled by their substitute in the back of the room. The student had a clipboard, which he violently shook in the air. The principal was immediately called for help.

Temptation: Call the police.

What the principal saw: A young child.

What she thought: This student has a reason to be so upset; something must have happened to him. I wonder what that might be.

(Continued)

(Continued)

How she saw her role: I need to take care of him by calming him down, deescalating his anger and giving him a safe place to process his frustration. I need to take him with me so the students and the teacher can continue working on their project.

How she responded: She calmly walked to the student, picked him up, as a hurting child, and carried him to her office. She had to restrain him because he was so upset so she asked her office staff to call the student's mother.

Effects on the child: He eventually calmed down.

Effects on the relationship: The student respected her more. The student came back to school with less hatred.

Effects on the culture: The students know they can trust the principal to be calm, effective, and have their best interest in mind. They were not further traumatized by: (1) seeing police officers take away one of their peers and (2) seeing their peer panic and be pushed even further into extreme emotions at the sight of the officers.

STORY 3: SIGN LANGUAGE

During morning writing lessons, a lower-grade student screeching at random intervals kept interrupting a first-grade teacher. He was also regularly being prompted to keep his arms and legs to himself.

Temptation: Isolate him in the far corner of the class.

What the teacher saw: A young boy who is not aware of how he impacts the community.

What she thought: I remember from a training that teachers should see a behavior seven times to understand it (where it comes from, what it needs, almost as if I can make friends with it and take care of it).

How she saw her role: I need to calmly help him practice better judgment.

How she responded: Each morning, she would greet him with a handshake and a hearty, "Good morning! Are you ready for a great day?" He agreed. She and the student would then rehearse their agreed-upon hand signals and simple guidelines (one finger raised meant "no hitting," two fingers raised meant "no kicking," and three fingers raised meant "no loud voices in class"). Quite often throughout the days, he would need a reminder and she would flash him a sign. He would quietly and quickly recorrect his behavior.

Effects on the child: He calmed down and improved his sense of what is appropriate behavior.

Effects on the relationship: Having this collaboration opened up trust and helped build a special relationship between them.

Effects on the culture: Students and teachers realized that there are more ways to communicate than just verbally.

STORY 4: THE VIOLENT DRAWING

A teacher was alarmed and frightened by one of her student's drawings of a character with a gun, a sword, and some bloody carnage. She sent the student to the principal's office, who called the parents, who called a psychiatrist for an evaluation. In the meantime, suspension was considered since the student was seen as a potential danger to the school. The student was sent to the Bay Area Family Therapy and Training Associates (BAFTTA) advocate.

Temptation: Be afraid of the student, imagine him as "one of those" dangerous ones.

What the advocate saw: A frightened and withdrawn student.

What she thought: I wonder what was the child's intention.

How she saw her role: I need to comfort the student and create a safe space to talk.

How she responded: She gently asked the student where he got the idea to draw this.

The effects on the child: The child felt safe enough to share his story. He had been preoccupied by the Star Wars scene where a snow camel is cut open by Harrison Ford to keep him warm for the night. The student had been exposed to the movie during a sleepover at a friend's house and was uncomfortable telling his parents because they were not supposed to watch movies. The student loved animals and had been horrified by the scene. His preoccupation led him to draw what was stuck in his mind.

Effects on the relationship: The child developed trust and discovered that talking about preoccupations really helped.

Effects on the culture: The student went back to class relieved, more able to pay attention, and free from the frightened gaze of his teacher. Everyone could relax.

STORY 5: GIRLS' MEANNESS

Two girls who had previously been good friends were constantly saying mean comments to each other. At some points, as these comments were escalating in meanness, the teacher overheard one of the girls say, "All your relatives are going to die and you will be all alone."

Temptation: See them as mean-spirited, separate them, or send them to the principal's office.

What the teacher saw: Two people at a stage in their lives.

What she thought: Becoming friends is a long process with ups and downs, peaks and valleys; they need to learn that and how to disagree without hurting each other.

How she saw her role: I need to facilitate growth and listening. In this situation, I can help them learn to solve this issue so that their friendship can grow.

How she responded: She asked them to sit apart for the rest of the day, then had them involved in a group discussion about friendship. Later on, she pointed out the times when they solved their problems respectfully.

The effects on the students: They both learned how to be better friends and how to handle disagreement with anyone.

Effects on the relationship: They learned that they could trust the teacher to help them. They also learned that they can come to her with a problem or a success and expect that she'll work with them.

Effects on the culture: The verbal meanness was actually resolved. If the educator had punished the girls or simply separated them physically in the class, the problem would have continued secretly and probably escalated without any adults knowing about it.

STORY 6: THE BRAND NEW ATLAS

Throughout the year, Matt always argued about everything, didn't pay attention, and made frustrating little sarcastic comments here and there. One day Todd brought to class an expensive and beautiful atlas he had finally bought after many months of consideration. After only a few hours in class, Todd found it soaking in water by the sink. He was just furious knowing exactly who was the last student to have handled it…Matt.

Temptation: Wonder if Matt did it on purpose, raise his voice, and send him to the principal's office.

What the teacher saw: A student who really had something going on.

What he thought: This can't go on. We need to get to the bottom of what's behind this.

How he saw his role: I need to have an important conversation with this young person.

How he responded: With sadness, he asked the student why he did that?

The effects on the student: The student, with sadness also, replied "because you don't like me."

Effects on the relationship: Todd was able to very sincerely, with some sadness still, clarify and state that this was absolutely not true. They had a "heart-to-heart" conversation where both were emotionally vulnerable in sharing how they perceived and interpreted each other's statements. They both agreed to make an effort with regard to the other's concern.

Effects on the culture: Students witnessed the toughest student in the class constructively resolve interpersonal conflicts with the teacher and learned they could trust their teacher. It created a more genuinely peaceful and bonded classroom.

SPOTLIGHT ON A SCHOOL WITH A SUCCESSFUL PREVENTION MODEL

Washington Open, Santa Clara, California

Type of school: public magnet elementary school

Rate of suspension: an average of three students per year

Average number of referrals to the principal's office: three per week

Total number of students: 360

Demographics: varied

Test scores: significantly above average in all areas for all grades

Principal and staff's main philosophy: The child is more important than the task.

School Description

Washington Open skillfully embodies all of the characteristics of cutting-edge research on education and child development. While parent involvement may be the most visible aspect of such an effort, anyone who has the privilege of spending some time there will quickly be impressed by the staff's philosophy and attitude toward young people.

This is exemplified by teachers' comfort with being called by their first names and by their trust in and support of students' ability to solve many problems, including relational issues, mostly on their own. At Washington Open, students are allowed to be learners; they are encouraged to think, to delight in learning through science and art and experiments. They are encouraged to own their school as a community. Students know that their opinions matter and they feel valued and respected in numerous contexts. Teachers make a deliberate effort to connect with each and every student in a personal way; this, thereafter, withstands difficulties, if any, and provides a rich context for learning. Teachers know students well enough to make a more accurate estimate of their learning potential (i.e., Washington Open teachers expect academic performance within reach of each individual child). This ensures experiences of success, self-esteem, and the development of a positive attitude towards learning. The deemphasis on competition, comparison, and evaluation allows students to feel safe to try challenging tasks without being afraid of failure and/or social stigma. Such adult-student connection is well-documented as the foundation for a school culture of respect, tolerance, care, trust, and appreciation.

Let us now summarize how this group of staff generally provides a living example of many of the ideas that was discussed throughout this book.

Reducing the Negative Emotions Contributing to a Culture Of Problems and Disrespect

Competition: Minimized. Students are rarely set against each other as individuals or as classes. They seek to do the best that they can, which is different for each individual.

Comparison: Minimized. Students are not compared to one another or to other classes, as the comparison implies that one is better than the other which is both simplifying of the reality, hurtful to the ones being negatively appraised, and encouraging of put-downs socially.

Evaluation: Minimized. Students are not graded per se. They are encouraged to progress at their own pace, to engage in their best writing or work towards the "next step." They do not experience a negative gaze judging their work but rather acknowledgment of their efforts, appreciation of their personal performances, and encouragement to improve in areas that have been discussed collaboratively as being an interesting next step.

Rules: Minimized. The term "rules" is used for a limited number of safety issues, which makes sense to students and the staff tries to use the term "agreements" for other guidelines. The student council participates in setting and updating agreements with the principal. When an agreement or a rule is broken, it can simply lead to reminders (the no running zone, for example) or conversation (hurtful words, for example) where students are invited to think and articulate why this is important for the community.

Achievement: Diversified. Performance improvement is achieved through different methods. It has a different meaning, is less emphasized at all costs, and is not numerically evaluated. The staff uses the curriculum as a goal and performs well on standardized testing but privilege child development and actual learning over rote memorization. As a result, no homework is given in the lower grades except for an occasional practice packet and the teachers emphasize that the packet should not be forced on students. In other words, it is better to have an incomplete homework than to have a child hateful of learning. Starting in third grade, students are given about one hour of homework per week, which they organize on their own. Homework slowly increases as the student reaches fourth and fifth grade.

Power and hierarchy: Minimized. Students call teachers by their first names and as many decisions as logistically possible are discussed with the students. Students' opinions are sought and respected even if the teacher would at times have preferred otherwise.

Right and wrong terminology: Minimized. These words represent a narrow and simplified view of problems and are seldom used since the staff is genuinely interested in understanding young people's perspectives. When adults truly see situations from young people's eyes, their ideas can always make sense some way or another.

Truth seeking: Minimized. The W.O. staff is drawn to the multiple perspectives and subjective stories of students. These are often very different from one person to the next. Since the intention is to understand and not to punish, young people do not need to submerge themselves under the weight of complex lies to avoid punishment and educators do not need to turn into judges wondering how to use their authority.

Rewards/punishment: Avoided. The staff is more interested in creating a culture of students with intrinsic motivation rather than a group of young people who will make efforts only for a carrot and only under surveillance. Students here have generally developed strong internal values of respect, collaboration, and appreciation in the lower grades which allows them to focus more on academia in the upper grades without being bogged down by constant socioemotional stressors.

Increasing the Experiences That Promote a Culture of Care

Connection: Maximized. The staff gets to know students really well, especially in small group activities, field trips, occasional overnight trips, and through meaningful class discussions. Experiencing students in many different capacities allows educators to have a much richer view of the whole child and the possibility to nurture the relationship from many different perspectives. A student may seem irresponsible with schoolwork and be completely overzealous in setting camp in a field trip or in helping a struggling classmate. Educators get to see the multiple, and at times contradictory, ways of being of students which allows them to build on each students' unique talents. Efforts are also made to connect students with each other from within-classroom team projects, to a variety of across-grade buddies. In the morning, for example, students may be invited to share with their neighbor exciting news of the day or something that is on their minds. They may also be involved in taking care of younger grades such as reading to a younger buddy. The result is a tightly knit community where students know many other teachers and students throughout the school.

Appreciation and tolerance: Maximized. Educators look for opportunities to appreciate students. There is very little pressure on students to fit a narrow mold and consequently, relatively few students are steered toward psychological testing and mental health diagnostics. When teachers appreciate students and are tolerant of their differences, other students too are more likely to appreciate them and put up with some otherwise annoying little habits.

Compassion and respectful curiosity: Maximized. Every effort is made to understand what it is like to be a young person from their intense desire to play, to move around a little too much, to have a hard time paying attention, and the insecurities provoked by novelty. For example, students get to meet their new teacher for the following year before the end of the school year. They visit what will be their new classroom and get a chance to introduce themselves and their interests to their new classmates. This reduces the beginning of the school year anxiety and students can even get excited ahead of time thinking of some of the projects that they will get to do. This simple process reduces negative emotions and increases a sense of safety, care, and community.

Contextualized perspective: Maximized. Since educators know the parents more and seek to appreciate students, it becomes easier to assume that some contextual factor is contributing to issues. By nature of their philosophy, educators are more prone to see a problem as resulting from patterns of interaction with the environment rather than as internal deficiency.

Collaboration: Maximized with both adults and other students. On a daily basis, individual students are asked for an opinion about something, which may range from the next class activity to stating the name of two students whom they would like to have in their class the following year (as the teacher is making placement recommendations). Students feel involved in the shaping of their own school lives and more committed to the decisions that they thought through for themselves. In that sense, adult power is minimized and students' involvement is maximized, allowing for the growth of response-able youth. Students are regularly encouraged to help each other in class and learn that each one of them has talents and struggles. This also becomes visible on the playground, where any issue will attract the caring and resourceful attention of many other students putting their heads together to solve it and recruit the help of supportive yard duties if necessary.

Self-reflection: Maximized. Students are encouraged to think about their personal goals and how they might achieve them. Student-led conferences in October are not so much a time when parents are given information, but rather a time when teachers invite students to set goals for themselves, think about how they might achieve them, and how adults might help them. Self-reflection is also encouraged when there is a success or a problem given that there is no behavioral modification and that experiences are processed. In addition to self-reflection in the social and academic areas, music, art, meditation, and yoga are incorporated into the weekly schedule of some classes.

The People

We invite you to meet the people of the Washington Open community, namely the principal, a veteran teacher, a parent and some students. We also describe some of their activities.

Interview With Principal Lori King

MN: Lori, what is your goal as a principal?

Lori: My goal is for students to learn, develop their own values as people, and have problem-solving skills. In many schools, principals want immediate changes and are encouraged to come down hard on students. In this school, we don't do that. I don't want students to do things to please me or out of fear, but rather because of their own personal choices. Fear-based motivation doesn't last.

MN: I imagine that this view greatly affects how you handle problem behaviors such as bullying and disrespect?

(Continued)

Lori: Yes, I think being a principal is about figuring things out, not about punishing. Being sent to the principal's office means more one-on-one time for the *student to try to solve a problem*. It means that I can help *the student* with my skills and it does up the ante because I am the principal. I tell new staff that they have to be able to tolerate emotional messiness because kids are emotionally messy. What becomes uncomfortable is if it triggers your own stuff—this is where most of us get into a reactive mode, which does nothing to help solve the problem.

MN: What do you do to remain congruent with your values when a student-related problem triggers your own feeling?

Lori: If I find myself reacting, I have the child sit down and I do other things while we both cool down or shift into a nonreactive mode. I remind myself of my values and what I am trying to do as a principal, which is to teach and facilitate learning. I know that if I respond with anger, it will escalate the situation and then my work will be increased sixfold. It's not beneficial for me or for the student who will go into a primitive stage mentally and emotionally and shut down.

MN: So what does an interaction with a student who has been sent to you look like?

Lori: Well, with the K–third grade, I mostly have conversations with them. Students' emotions bubble up and they don't understand why they're reacting. Their behavior is almost always about a misunderstanding, feeling thwarted or hurt. Generally, students are so good about moving on quickly once they understand the story and the other students' reasons for doing what they did. Older students generally seek me out when there is a problem that they have not been able to solve through other means; they have learned how to talk it out with their peers—they use their words—but somehow they are stuck and need support and another perspective. The teachers do an outstanding job of having students take responsibility for solving conflicts, by allowing them time to talk, through conflict managers and through conferencing with the teacher.

MN: So would you say that you rarely intervene with big disciplinary measures such as calling the police or suspending?

Lori: The only times I might suspend are if it becomes a real safety issue and I need the student to think about this in a more serious way. I never do it in anger or even with a punitive intention. I also avoid engaging in harsh punishments like calling the police, especially with the lower grade kids . . . they've only been on Earth for five–six years, what could they have possibly done so wrong to warrant police action?

MN: Yes, I think principals sometimes feel like they have to do something and they are not sure what to do, so what comes to their minds are these harsher consequences. Can you give me an example of a situation you could have addressed with a high intervention punishment but chose not to?

Lori: Yes, there was this unusual situation where two students were encouraged to physically fight over an argument. They didn't want to fight. But one of their peers was really pushing for it and he created such a momentum around it that a group of kids did gather in the field to watch the event. The students still didn't want to fight and were pushed onto each other. As soon as that happened, many quickly got scared and ran to get help. They had never seen this in this school. It would have been easy to suspend them or take away an upcoming end-of-the-year field trip.

MN: What did you do instead?

Lori: I didn't want to punish. I didn't want to label those kids. I didn't want to make it about them as "bad people" but rather about having to learn something and about how a community agreement was broken (the community agreement being: use appropriate words to solve problems or conflicts). When we judge and label kids then they don't feel heard; they believe what is said about them especially if it is by a teacher or principal and they act the way they are told to think they are. I told the students that there would be a consequence and that I would think about it and gave myself some time before making a decision. I also interviewed some staff members to get their counsel; we have a lot of wise people here on staff. In the end, I decided to have them do community service so that it would be meaningful. I had them move boxes and equipment that needed to be transferred from one place to another, clean rooms, and pick up trash. They worked hard. I think physical labor is often empowering to children; they see what they can do and there is immediate success with their actions. The students and I had a conversation before where we processed why we did this. We all did the work, and I too had to stay extra time on a Friday afternoon but that was okay. Then we processed afterwards again.

MN: What effects do you think it had on them?

Lori: Well, when I asked them what they had gotten out of the community service, one of them said, "We have to make a wrong right and undo what we did to our community." I wanted them to understand that as a community we had agreements to use our words to solve problems, that we would not physically harm others. They broke those agreements and now had to make amends, in other words, they needed to "mend" what was broken (agreements). The parents and teachers were pleased with the outcome. I see discipline as moving up a spiral where positive learning occurs. You move higher and higher—evolve so to speak—as opposed to punishment where people move downward in their sense of self-worth and development.

(Continued)

(Continued)

MN: What inspires you to engage in these collaborative and respectful practices?

Lori (showing a small board): I look at this quote often: "See everything, overlook a great deal, correct a little." I really believe in it and sometimes it's hard because you don't necessarily see immediate results; sometimes you're not sure you're having an impact when "correcting a little." But it does happen. I see the growth in students from the beginning of the year to the end. It's pretty amazing.

> "See everything, overlook a great deal, correct a little."

MN: Yes, I guess when principals punish, they see students cry and regret their actions, which may provide an impression of having had an impact. In reality, the regrets are often only a short-term impact with potentially many other negative implications rather than long-term learning.

Lori: That's true.

MN: Aside from community service and conversational processing, I wonder how you might respond to students who simply struggle over and over again with problem behaviors and bullying. Do you have respectful and proactive ways of responding to these situations as well?

Lori: Yes, we have a cohort of students in one grade level who struggle with many social issues. We looked to see what their needs were, where they could benefit most and many of them were placed with the same teacher to help support their social growth—the classes may appear imbalanced based on the visual behavior that is mostly seen. We will hire a specialized educational consultant, Patricia Belvel (see Belvel & Jordan, 2003), who has worked with us before, to support the teacher and this spicy class. All our classes have both similar and different setups based on whatever is needed for their particular students' growth.

MN: This is very interesting. Is the educational consultant in the class all the time?

Lori: No, but she spends time with the students during the first two weeks and helps coach the teacher. She will also help out in a few other classes.

MN: Are the students engaged in some special activities?

Lori: The first two weeks of the school year are focusing strictly on curriculum that they already know which creates a context where they generally feel academically competent. Teaching per se becomes out of the equation and the teacher can then focus on social skills in a supportive manner.

MN: Can you give an example of how their time might be used?

Lori: During these first two weeks of school, all fourth graders have lunch only with their classes to encourage "class team-building." This time becomes an opportunity for this grade and their teachers to develop collaborative ways of being together, get to know each other's talents, have fun, and problem-solve spicy ways of being as a group. They learn appropriate skills for the playground, which mirror the skills and expectations that the teacher has for them in the classroom. They practice collaborative and community-oriented behaviors until they are cemented—the teacher provides consistency for students inside and outside the classroom.

MN: What happens after the two weeks? Does the consultant come back for weekly visits?

Lori: Yes, she will visit and follow up on any issues or concerns that the teachers may have and see that the skills and expectations are applied and consistent.

MN: Was this done before?

Lori: Yes, this was done before at this school and had yielded tremendous success where the students really learned to work collaboratively with each other and bonded beyond what was expected. In one particular class, the students became the most connected group of their grade level and were able to really develop into responsible leaders.

MN: That seems like a very interesting, experiential, and out of the box way of handling social problems. I'll look forward to hearing more about the unfolding of this process. On a final note, given the commitment to collaboration and mutual growth in this school, what would you say is the most important thing that you are learning from children?

Lori: I have discovered that each student interaction yields a different problem-solving effort. Although there is a structure that I adhere to when dealing with disciplinary situations, I have learned the tremendous healing power of listening and asking questions, not telling, but asking students for clarification of what they were feeling, why they think they acted the way they did. Students who are given this opportunity appear to be able to better regulate their future behavior because they have processed it out loud to another. The true meaning of discipline is to teach. I keep this meaning in mind whenever I meet with a student.

Schoolwide Practices Fostering
Care, Respect, and Response-Ability

Schoolwide events are time consuming and their effects must be carefully evaluated before deciding to schedule them. Too often, assemblies become a time when students who struggle are expected to engage in problems and they do. In many schools, students are bored and require more containment than they would otherwise. Washington Open's assemblies are designed so that the majority of students enjoy them. They do not, for example, engage in weekly award giving assemblies, which leave a few students feeling good and many others feeling bored, resentful, unnoticed in their efforts, and frustrated at the superficial meaning of the event. While the intention is to express appreciation, and foster a more positive climate, the result can often be the opposite on a greater number of students. Here are examples of schoolwide events organized at Washington Open that produce positive feelings for the majority of students:

- Assemblies are held presenting skilled professional storytellers or exciting performances (often the parent community offers a wide range of free talents).
- "Open sing" invites adult and student volunteers (about 20 to 30) to colead peaceful, playful, and educational songs.
- Game days, silly hair days, and spirit days are designated throughout the school year, determined by the student council.
- Halloween game day features an entire day of a fair with each class organizing a game booth.
- On their birthdays, all children receive a pencil with ribbons and a little card from the administrators, allowing for students to know the administrators outside of needing help or of having a problem.
- School plays involve everyone who wishes to be in the plays with auditions held only to determine roles.

Interview With Veteran Teacher Linda Boucher

MN: In your experience, what is it about this school that makes it a community of care and respect?

Linda: I think everyone in this community is included in growth—parents, students, teachers, and principal. Parents get to know different ways of doing things, they broaden their horizons and it gives them a sense of the possible range of students' behaviors. The key is also that teachers have a commitment to find what's good in each child and build on that. Adults and students react to situations. Adults need to get behind reactions and find out whom the student really is.

MN: Do educators at Washington Open have ways of finding out whom the students "really are," or in other words, to find out the many different ways that they can be?

Linda: I think we all respect children. We value them as individuals and we listen to what they have to say. If there's an issue, we try to figure out what's behind it for *them* rather than us adults making judgments and deciding what *we* think the issue is.

MN: Would you say that it takes a lot of respectful curiosity and trust in children?

Linda: Yes, it does, and a commitment to figuring things out. We get to know each student, and we spend time working with them as individuals; we don't facilitate a one size fits all classroom. I see a real difference in students after the October conference because they set goals for themselves. We can then start building on positives and get started in really knowing the students.

MN: If students focus on achieving their own goals, how do you deal with report cards?

Linda: Many years ago, the Open teachers created our own narrative progress report to reflect our philosophy. We are now using the district standards-based report card that evaluates children with respect to standards. We are still committed to the narrative report, however, where the focus is on positive developments and next steps and we see this as the heart of the evaluation process. This letter for each student makes visible their contributions to the class community and their journey towards their own goal.

MN: That seems very different than in many schools.

Linda: Yes, a lot of teachers feel like they need to control and they navigate through issues where they think that right and wrong is important. I tell kids that they're never in trouble and that making mistakes is part of growing up. Sometimes new teachers or unsupported teachers have a hard time to let things go wrong in the class and they want to fix it; the only people who can really fix it for good are the students themselves.

MN: What is it that allowed you to develop this way of thinking?

Linda: I had a fabulous mentor at Christa McAuliffe and I used to watch her let kids talk. She would just listen to them. To an observer, it seemed like nothing was getting done but in the end those conversations had powerful long-term impact. When we take the time to deal with issues in the lower grades, then students can work much better in the upper grades.

MN: So your mentor really helped you develop alternative ways of responding to students early on?

Linda: Actually, my early teaching days were several years before. As a beginning teacher, I too wanted to stop students from being hurt and was more likely to solve issues for them. . . I reentered teaching after being at home for eleven years with my children. Watching my mentor Angela work with

(Continued)

(Continued)

> students helped me develop alternate ways of working with students. It was a process for me that felt more appropriate the more I practiced it. So now I take a deep breath and ask them to cool down. I ask them to say what they think is going on, what they need. With young kids it's almost always an inability to get what they want in appropriate ways. I accept that they're just learning to do this. After we talk, I usually ask them if this happened again, what would you do?

MN: Can you share an example of a situation where you could have been punitive but chose instead to handle it by facilitating a conversation?

Linda: Yes, what comes to my mind is this one time on a field trip. A driving parent arrived with his group of students and was furious with a child because the child had thrown a library book outside the window on the highway. She wanted the child suspended. I took the student aside and asked him to tell me his story. It turned out that the children were playing the "I spy" game. When it was his turn, he really wanted to do the library book. Since they had agreed to pick only things that were outside of the car, he had tried to hold the book outside the window. Little did he know that the wind was way too strong for him to do this.

MN: What is it that you kept in mind when you initially approached the student for his story?

Linda: I kept in mind that there was something that we didn't know and I wondered what motivated him to do that.

MN: How did you see your role?

Linda: I really saw my role as helping the student learn to make better choices.

MN: How did you deal with the parent? Some parents are pretty invested in punishments. That must be an issue sometimes given the parent involvement here.

Linda: At Open, we are all growing and learning. This was an opportunity to include the parent in the process. I simply shared the process I had gone through with the child with the parent who had been involved. In the end, the child did chores at home to earn the money to pay for the lost library book.

MN: What effects do these collaborative ways of handling things have on your relationship with students?

Linda: The students learn that they can be understood by their teacher and forgiven for their mistakes.

MN: What effects do you see these ways of responding having on the general school culture?

Linda: I think that the students can in turn be forgiving to other students when these others do something that seems careless.

MN: I know that you are retiring but if you were to change your plans and become a principal, what would you do to recreate such a school culture from scratch?

Linda: If I was a principal I'd make sure all the staff has respect for children. I would do lots of staff development to build community, search for common beliefs, and share things that are going well with our students so that we grow with each other. I would encourage people to trust the intentions of the other, to assume that everyone is trying to do their best. I would want the staff to really support each other in bringing the best out of kids.

MN: May I ask how your personal life was enriched from your many years of teaching experience at Washington Open?

Linda: I have been involved at Open for twenty-four years: nine as a parent and fifteen as a teacher. Prior to teaching here I taught at a traditional school with a few teachers who viewed children with the same sense of respect they do here, and I also taught at another parent participation alternative school. I have loved being a part of a learning community where the emphasis is on success for all and where everyone grows and learns.

> "I have loved being part of a community where everyone grows."

MN: What kept you going so successfully all these years?

Linda: I valued that Open is not only a school but also a community. We try to stay positive, to support each other, and celebrate successes.

MN: Now that you are retiring, what would you most like students and fellow staff members to remember about you?

Linda: I'd like to be remembered as someone who valued them as people and encouraged students to do their personal best.

Teachers' Community Building Activities

At Washington Open, students are given an opportunity to get to know each other across grade levels, to help each other, and contribute in significant ways to their school climate. The following are grade level activities that create a structure for these connections to unfold.

• *Gingerbread cookie escape.* Kindergartners read stories about gingerbread cookies and how they might run away. The day after baking their cookies, they come to school and their cookies have run away, going through first grade classrooms and leaving havoc and clues everywhere they went.

Effect of the activity on the kindergartners: fun, playfulness, opportunity to visit and familiarize themselves with the school.

Effect of the activity on the first graders: playful distraction from the denser curriculum, sense of care and amusement at contributing to the little ones, recognition that they were one of them not too long ago.

- *Buddies.* All classes have buddies. For example, second graders read to kindergartners. Some students take this responsibility seriously and work even harder at mastering the reading of a book so they can read it to their younger buddies.

Effects: Support knowing one another across age, learning to relate, appreciate, and accept the different levels of growth; encouragement of a culture of care and helpfulness in spite of the age differences.

- *Business day.* Fourth graders create their own business as a math and social skills project. They learn to assess their "market," plan the responses of the younger community, invest, ensure profit, and calculate their financial losses. They create their own money and distribute it to all the students in the school who come as a class and "buy" items from their booth. These items range from homemade cookies, to juices, to cards, magazines, toys, etc.

Effects: Fun, excitement, community building, lived experience of math in a meaningful and engaging way.

- *Student leaders.* Fourth and fifth graders volunteer to patrol the playground and help out with conflicts or play with lonely children. They go through a thorough training on social skills and problem solving and then get to practice these skills. In the morning, some of them also act as safety patrol helping students cross the parking lot and get out of cars in the drop-off zone.

Effects: Practice of important social skills empowers students before middle school; involvement in taking care of younger students and keeping their school a caring and safe community.

- *Student council.* A student from each class, even kindergarteners, participate once per month in meetings to determine spirit days and what might need improvement in the school culture.

Effects: Development of an empowering ability to observe the community, and reflect on possible ways of improving their school culture; practice articulating their thoughts and an increased sense of worth, agency, and self-confidence.

Challenges Still Occur: A Parent's Story

Creating a partnership with response-able youth does not mean the absence of problems. It only means that problems are less likely to happen in frequency, tend to be less intense, and are resolved in a different way that encourages deeper learning, problem solving, and collaboration. Schools do not have control over the baggage that students bring from home and their various other life contexts. In our experience, schools that focus tremendously on partnerships with students who disrespect also have to be very careful with the recipients of disrespect and bullying. Sometimes so much attention can be given to the student who struggles—in an attempt to gently shift the behavior—that the recipient of bullying can feel unheard or actions taken may not appear drastic enough. Washington Open staff seem to generally try hard to validate the experiences of all parties. We have invited the mother of a student who was mistreated to recount her experience.

Our eight-year-old son came out of a warm and friendly first- and second-grade class that looped for two years together. The bond amongst the children and the teacher was genuine and created a safe environment for the kids to grow. Our son could be described as a kind and a safe, inclusive playmate for all. Many children were drawn to my son in his first- and second-grade classes.

In the third grade, our son encountered a competitive and socially sophisticated classmate who repeatedly excluded him from the main group of boys with whom our son tried to associate. The subject classmate (a strong athlete, a leader among the boys and extremely competitive), would belittle and exclude our son from activities and conversations he had with other boys—sometimes right in front of our eyes. While our son was not the only target of exclusion, he was ostracized to the point that he stopped trying to join in the group and ended up playing alone or with a few, inconsistent, stray friends.

In our house, we described kids who have behavior problems as "kids who are still learning." This catch-all phrase is applied liberally to kids who do not focus on their work at school, kids who act out inappropriate behavior, and kids who lack manners. We quickly categorized our son's classmate as a kid who was competitive and who was "still learning." Yet, we progressively saw our son's presence in the classroom shrink. We encouraged our son to verbally address the situation himself by confronting the classmate in a polite but stern manner. We practiced phrases with him and spied on him from afar at school to see how he was doing. Given our son's nonconfrontational demeanor, he was not successful in this endeavor and we finally decided to seek a private conference with the teacher to discuss how we could help our son. We were confident she could lend us some of the wisdom, which her thirty-eight years as a teacher endowed her. When discussing the matter, the teacher helped us gain perspective on the situation as follows:

(1) She offered positive insights about our son and his performance at school so that we knew she understood who he was. She indicated he was academically successful, focused, and a safe friend for kids in the class.

(2) She confirmed the existence of the problem. That helped a lot. To hear a professional acknowledge the truth of what we were experiencing was a beginning. She told us that she had seen the subject student acting as our son had reported. She had noticed our son's isolation and had first tried to seat him at a table with the student hoping they would bond, but later separated the two so our son might make new connections. She also told us that our son was not this child's only target.

(Continued)

(Continued)

(3) She proposed a plan whereby our son could seek immediate attention if he needed assistance discussing matters with the subject student both in class and after recess. The teacher became an available "sounding board" for our son's recess troubles. The few times our son reported direct problems, she handled each matter by discussing the problems with both involved promptly.

(4) She brought in the school counselor to lead "friendship" centers during classtime so that all students could learn social etiquette and ways to relate better.

(5) She referred us to the same school counselor who conducted "friendship" lessons in our son's class so we could get her perspective as parents.

(6) She conducted class meetings among the students wherein each student could discuss a problem without giving names, and the group would problem solve together.

(7) She occasionally checked in with us to report on our son's social successes in the class and at recess.

The teacher supported my son, and honestly, I think she understood his gentle demeanor. They had a friendly and trusting relationship. The teacher gave my son vehicles to participate in class like science show and tell. She ended most school days with an offer of a hug to her students, in which my son always gladly partook.

The teacher sat down with my son and the subject student on a few occasions (two or three times) when she witnessed a transgression. She facilitated a discussion between them. She also tried to rearrange seats in the classroom in an effort to encourage new bonds between various kids. At a follow-up conference, the teacher reported that in her presence our son had no problem articulating his problems to the other child. She also reported the subject student repeatedly attempted to explain the problem as a "misunderstanding."

Our son and the subject classmate spent the remainder of the school year avoiding each other. Our son eventually began to engage in the group (encompassed by a much larger group) at recess, but continued to avoid the group in the confines of the class.

> "He knows he handled a difficult, but common, problem without breaking down and falling apart."

While the teacher was able to help our son find his voice and to help legitimize his complaints, she was not able to change the personality of the other child and was only minimally able to help our child step out of his shell to bridge the gap that had been established early. At Washington Open, parents are permitted to write requests for placement in a class the following year. Though we had never before written a request, we quickly wrote to request that he be separated from the other student in the fourth grade. We not only got our wish, but we were relieved to know that he was placed with many of his old friends from his first and second grade looping class. Upon learning this information, we set our sights on fourth grade.

Our son now looks at his third grade year as a hard one. He knows he handled a difficult, but common, problem without breaking down and falling apart. He became more guarded toward his classmates and learned some hard lessons in friendship. He *discovered some loyal friends that he didn't know he had. He found that some of his "good" friends weren't so good to him. He also found new, unlikely friends. He learned that the problem wasn't about him and practiced important life tools on how to handle others who may not treat you well. Thank goodness he is resilient and we are now looking forward to fourth grade.*

Being the target of bullying and disrespect is intensely painful for the recipients and their families. As adults, we usually want to see these problems go away and be resolved quickly. Unfortunately, human beings take time to learn. Just as we wouldn't expect punishment to improve a child's poor reading skills, harsh and quick fix measures do not help students learn better social skills. This mother's wisdom in helping her son think of the child as "a learning kid" helped her son keep a broad perspective in the face of the struggles. This language avoided the pitfalls of hating, which would only increase the hurt for her son and escalate the conflict with the student needing to learn. In the difficult journey that he endured, perhaps this boy learned to become a mountain, that is, one who is able to maintain his integrity and internal sense of self in spite of the harsh storms around him (Kabat-Zinn, 1994). Also, while progress is not always immediately visible with collaborative methods, it usually prevents the bullying issue from going underground and becoming more intense, insidious, and hurtful.

This escalation of insidious bullying is particularly common in schools where educators' response is to come down hard and punish to send a message. If a student didn't like another in the first place, he certainly won't like the student more after being punished. Such punishments may give an impression to parents that something is done, but in reality, it usually increases the hatred of the bullying student, prevents learning, and leads to more hurtful and long lasting forms of bullying. In the situation described above, the teacher both empowered the recipient of the mistreatment and created a space for the mistreating student to think about his behaviors. Since the mistreating student changed minimally, he will be participating in the class supported by a consultant that the principal scheduled for next year. This setup will up the ante in both requiring and encouraging behavioral change in ways that will promote a collaborative and deep learning.

Students' Perspectives and Experiences at Washington Open

We asked a few students from different grade levels what they thought Washington Open teachers did well, how they treated students, and how they solved problems. Here are some of their answers.

MN:	What do you like about the way teachers treat kids at W.O.?
Meika (second grade):	I've really liked my teachers at W.O. because they don't yell very often. My teacher this year yelled only three times and my kindergarten teacher never ever yelled.
J. Henri (third grade):	The teachers here help kids feel good. They actually tell you "good job" when you do something and do really fun activities in the centers. They make learning not hard.
Lainey (kindergarten):	I like to go to school and see my teachers because they plan fun activities for us like cutting strawberries!
Megan (sixth grade alumni):	Washington Open teachers treat their students with respect and kindness. In other schools, teachers aren't always as nice, and might use force with words rather than kindness to solve problems. They also aren't always as willing to talk through a hard problem in class, so students would get frustrated easier. Other adults sometimes don't listen to what each kid wants to say, but the teachers at Washington Open almost always have time to listen.
MN:	Do teachers have helpful ways of solving problems?
Meika (second grade):	Yes, teachers do class meetings and all the class has ideas to help the two kids solve their problems. Sometimes they solve their problems alone where one kid might say what the other kid did and the other says what the other one did. One never gets in trouble. Our teacher never sends kids to the principal's office. She said she did it once in twenty-two years! It's much better that way because if you do it in class then you have friends to vote for you and you have more people giving ideas while at the principal's office you would be alone, and that would be rough.

"Teachers do class meetings and all the class has ideas to help the two kids solve their problems."

| Megan B. (sixth grade alumni): | When solving conflicts, the W.O. teachers let each child have a little "cool-off" time if they need it, then work out the problem by talking through it. Then, at the end, both kids are happy. After a child listens and participates in one of these conversations, they know how to solve conflicts when they see them at recess or lunch. That is part of the reason that Washington Open has a happy climate. |

When everyone can speak their minds, think, function in a safe and supportive environment, and not grapple with resentment, learning in its more profound sense can unfold in a truly magical way.

Conclusion

We hope that the practices in this book have inspired you to travel into student–educator relationships with a fresh outlook and to look at your school's community with new vision. We would like to acknowledge that examining cultural and educational pressures, both positive and negative, on the self and others can be difficult and uncomfortable at times. We salute your patience and dedication to explore new ideas, despite the limited amount of time available in your demanding and stimulating vocation.

You are encouraged to follow a curious and compassionate role, listening and more closely understanding the perspectives of young people who call out to you from your schools and communities. Bullying and disrespect tend to disappear in a climate of caring, connected people. Students have even told us that the Bugging Bug (a symbol of disrespect) is allergic to kindness.

As we conclude this book, you may still have one question: What, in the end, happened with John?

John, whose personal story welcomed you into this book, was quickly relieved by externalizing conversations. While mapping the effect of Anger and Depression on his life, it became very clear to him and his family that John wished to reclaim his life and actually did want to live, despite his feelings of shame and humiliation. After sharing his experience with compassionate and respectful others, exploring his small successes at freeing himself from the problem, and having his teachers' and his parents' support against the problem, John was progressively able to reconnect with his preferred self. We then proceeded to explore what it meant about him and his values that, despite all of his violent fantasies, he had actually never harmed anyone. Peace, respect, and nonviolence were clearly articulated as preferences. Marie-Nathalie invited John to ponder the difficulty involved in controlling anger to uphold one's values. In the end, Marie-Nathalie said, "Who is really the strongest—the one who just engages in the mean gesture that comes through his mind or the one who holds on to his values of respect even in the most challenging situations?" John lifted his head, stared at Marie-Nathalie, and with a slow voice filled with calm and assurance he responded, "The one who holds on to his values of peace is really the most courageous." We had just broken the cycle of bullying and disrespect in John's life.

Resource A

Glossary

Audience. A group of people who witness a protagonist in a certain way. Since we see ourselves through others' eyes, audiences can be very important in supporting our preferred view of ourselves. In other words, if people see us as clever, it will be easier to experience ourselves as clever. Groups of people, such as families, classrooms, and communities, who witness our different ways of being are audiences.

Bullying. Repeated aggressive behavior or harm doing directed toward one student by another or a group of students. It is often associated with an imbalance of power. Bullying is distinguishable from childhood teasing, which occurs occasionally and does not involve an imbalance of power. (Olweus, 1993)

Collaboration. A process in which people work together toward common goals by sharing knowledge and ideas. Intellectual, creative, emotional, and social goals can be met using collaboration. Collaboration does not require leadership.

Compassion. An experience of sensitivity and understanding in the face of other's suffering. Having kindness and showing it to those that suffer in an attempt to increase their freedom from pain.

Contextual blocks. Invisible pressures that limit people's sense of possible ways of being. Originally connected to a culture's set of discourses and specifications, these pressures intersect in complex and unique ways for each individual. Contextual blocks work in such a way as to prevent individuals from conceiving of certain options. For example, the option of a boy hugging another boy affectionately is often blocked in patriarchal and homophobic cultures.

Culture. The conventional pattern of values, beliefs, symbols (including language), norms, and behaviors that have been transmitted to and are shared by an identifiable group of individuals year after year. Cultures teach informally and formally how to perceive the world, think, communicate, and behave (socialization process). The process is assumed to involve learning rather than specific genetic programming. It happens in a gradual and systematic way that renders it invisible to individuals unless they are exposed to a process of questioning or a culture shock. Cultures shape individuals and are shaped by them, especially by the holders of the power. Cultures can also be said to define possibilities and conditions for action.

Deconstruction. The continuous process of taking apart concepts to reveal and recognize the underlying ideas and assumptions that form that concept's belief.

Discourse. A pervasive and insidious cultural system of beliefs and customs, which shape people's lives at all levels (i.e., language, thoughts, feelings, behaviors, dreams, values, expectations, roles, relationships, understandings, lifestyle, politics). Discourses provide guidelines and assumptions that direct the manner in which people experience their lives. Discourses structure so much of individuals' lives that it is rare to question them and impossible to completely escape them. One can only learn to become aware of their effects and make choices as to which prescriptions may be more congruent with preferred ways of being. Discourses include, for example, individualism and capitalism.

Externalization. The process of acknowledging that people's identities are separate from unwanted problems. Problems are treated as external entities to one's sense of self because they are believed to develop as a result of complex and unique experiences of contextual blocks (originating from discourses). For example, Shyness might get in the way of having friends.

Habit. Pattern of behaving, feeling, or thinking that tends to be recurrent and that may not necessarily reflect the individual's preferences and values. Although the word habit is incongruent with the poststructuralist conceptualization of the narrative ideas inspiring this book, it can still be useful in actual conversations with young people as long as adults remain connected with the more accurate theoretical concepts.

Perspective. A point of view based on an awareness of the big picture of time, history, context, and relationships. Individuals having perspective are usually able to consider more than their own experiences such as others' experiences and the multiple factors shaping an event. This point of view may be affected by an individual's attitude and value system.

Problem. An unhelpful way of being that can be named, circumvented, explored, and clearly distinguished from an individual's preferred identity. Problems usually develop when people are unable to successfully fulfill the pressures in the contexts of their lives (specifications of a particular discourse), or when they attempt to fulfill them and feel unhappy with the results. Problems include Bullying habits, Self-Doubt, Worries, and so on. Chronic problems are those that are recurring and persistent.

Preferred story. A series of experiences that become articulated as representing one's preferred way of being. For a story to become salient in one's life, it must be connected to relationships, witnessed by an audience, and explored in time. For example, people thinking of another as a Helpful person is a preferred story.

Problem story. A problematic way of being that, over time, has come to be taken as a representation of an individual's identity. Problem stories can often take over people's lives in such a way that their actual values, special talents, and successes at avoiding the problem become discounted or unnoticed. In many ways, problem stories offer a very simplistic and reductionist view of an individual that excludes, in particular, this individual's preferences and values. For example, one might think, "Everyone thinks I'm a Troublemaker, and I really hate that reputation."

Respect. An acknowledgment of the value of others, including their thoughts, feelings, bodies, and presence. Being considerate of others includes those who have differing values, thoughts, and opinions.

Specification. A cultural pressure that prescribes very specific ways of being and that originates from cultural discourses. It is usually identifiable by its implication that an individual should or shouldn't engage in a certain behavior. For example, the belief that boys should not be sensitive is a specification.

Tolerance. Acceptance and open-mindedness of other people's struggles and mistakes. It entails a nonjudgmental attitude that does not discriminate against another person or group.

Unique outcome. An action or event that illustrates a person's preferred identity and that could not have been predicted given a problem story. For example, a student with a problem reputation for being mean who engages in devoted care for his younger sister is an example of a unique outcome.

Resource B

Summary Table of Strategies

The following is a table that lists practices that help educators connect further with students and enrich everyone's school day with appreciative, respectful interactions.

Contextual Blocks Existing in Schools	Antiblock Values	Examples of Practices That Encourage Antiblock Values
Rewards and punishments	Respect Shedding adultism Appreciation Connection	Have limited (or no) award assemblies. Have limited meaningless or manipulative public praise for individual kids. Express appreciation often. Support internal motivation. Be aware that punishment may support problem stories. Develop alternative ways to express acknowledgment. Invite students into the determination of their own consequences for behavior. Remember that students are often punished in many situations and that it can be overwhelmingly discouraging.
Ever-existing rules	Respect Shedding adultism Diversity Connection Self-reflection	Have an absence of posted rules. Follow the spirit of the law rather than the word of the law. Develop a broader contextual perspective of right and wrong. Understand the unique needs of each student. Have students write the class codes, rules, or agreements.

Contextual Blocks Existing in Schools	Antiblock Values	Examples of Practices That Encourage Antiblock Values
		Clarify for yourself and the staff the intentions behind a rule and whether or not the intentions should take precedence. Be aware of when rules cause problems instead of easing the situation.
Performance at all costs	Self-reflection Connection Collaboration	Make time for self-reflection. Facilitate conversations to clarify priorities as a group. Discuss what the pressures to perform place on the unique community. Reevaluate your vision of self as an educator as well as the nature of the relationship you want to have with students. Connect with values and philosophies instead of engaging in a succession of exercises. Provide time for reflection on teacher's personal position on issues. Keep learning fun and curiosity alive (in the end, it is more important than performance).
Evaluation	Collaboration Connection Respect Shedding adultism Self-reflection	Set performance goals for class instead of individual. Put students in charge of evaluating their own classroom climate. Minimize the quantity of unnecessary evaluative comments. Be self-aware of the habit of evaluating everything about students. Develop relationships that go beyond the standard roles. Have individuals set their own goals for performance, be self-reflective, and report on their own review of performance.
Cultural differences and misunderstandings	Community Diversity Connection Appreciation	Have role models of different racial and ethnic backgrounds. Encourage teachers to attend cultural awareness workshops. Incorporate the valuing of diversity throughout the curriculum, including female role models and those of different races. Show great interest for cultural customs and day-to-day experiences.

Contextual Blocks Existing in Schools	Antiblock Values	Examples of Practices That Encourage Antiblock Values
Hierarchy	Collaboration Leadership Respect Shedding adultism Connection Community Diversity Self-reflection Appreciation	Introduce cross-age buddies, who meet weekly, between classes. Facilitate groups of administrators, teachers, parents, and students to meet, study, and debate issues. Ask students' opinions on topics. Involve students in curriculum planning. Use cooperative learning strategies and peer tutoring programs. Have community service projects. Create a context where everyone can be at his or her best. Create arrangements to receive feedback from students. Connect with people as people. Enjoy a more democratic environment. Be accessible, visible, open, and inclusive. Implement student-led conferences. Have students teach their specialties. Honor student opinions and voice on ideas. Provide skilled student mediators. Call adults by their first name. Experience a true student government.
Adultism	Community Diversity Respect Shedding adultism Connection Collaboration	Give students opportunities to interact and be enriched by a greater number of positive role models. Provide a context for peer group helpers and conferences. Provide meaningful, engaging academics. Implement cross-age activities. Give a voice to students (i.e., have students decide the context and décor of the room, among other tasks). Let students make announcements on the intercom, in several languages. Create cross-age student groups that meet weekly to discuss academic and personal issues. Be genuinely interested in listening to students about experiences. Have a school environment that represents the students, including open spaces for gathering, student work, murals created by students, and so on.

Resource C

Discourses

All cultures carry their own set of discourses. Discourses are the underlying beliefs that structure and guide people's thoughts, feelings, and actions in a given culture. Some discourses have more harmful effects (e.g., racism, homophobia, adultism) than others, which become harmful only when taken to an extreme level (capitalism, individualism, patriarchy).

Specifically discourses become problematic and invite problems when they privilege the following:

- A narrow set of normative ways of being that may not fit with everyone's disposition or preference
- Certain outcomes over others to such an extent that the loss of other values is costly to the culture or the individual in question

Discourses have broad effects that contribute to many more issues than disrespect. We now discuss their potential implications on families and young people.

ADULTISM

Most adults are very committed to the well-being of children and spend enormous amounts of time pondering ways to foster growth. Despite these intentions, these same adults may at times and inadvertently engage in disrespectful practices toward children, which can have negative effects. These disrespectful practices are referred to as adultism (Zimmerman, 2001). Adultism is adults' misuse of their power in relation to children. It is an unnecessary level of disrespect, disqualification, and disregard that is very distinct from adults' responsibility to protect and support young people's development. Adultism occurs in Western cultures because of three major underlying beliefs about children: Children need to be contained, children are less experienced in life and therefore have less-worthy opinions, and children have less power, so they should be the ones to make the effort to adapt to adults' mood and decisions. All three of these beliefs are questionable.

First the need to be contained as a developmental explanation does not stand because it doesn't apply to the majority of children in most situations. If young people intrinsically needed to be contained, we would not find them working at a young age in other countries often with heavy responsibilities usually granted here to adults only. Even within our culture, many young people are very autonomous and articulate when raised in an environment that supports their voice. Some are even more responsible and autonomous than certain adults.

Ironically, educators often place expectations on students that they themselves do not meet. Think back to those staff meetings. Consider those staff members who whisper their opinions to their neighbors, giggle in the back of the room, correct papers while the meeting is going on, allow their cell phones to interrupt, and say unmannerly comments during discussions. Somehow these actions are tolerated with adults but not with children. Perhaps it is the belief that educators will disrupt to a limited extent and exert some self-monitoring, whereas students' disruptions may escalate so seriously to cause a state of utter destruction of the classroom. Is this fear realistic?

Second, the belief that life experience grants worth to someone's opinion is used only when it suits individuals in power. Indeed, this myth is used often with young people until they are in their twenties; then, around age thirty or forty years, their opinion reaches a status of worth. Around age sixty years, their opinion begins to suffer again from a disqualification. Really, then, a broader look at this belief makes clear that status is granted only in middle age and therefore not because of accrued life experience; otherwise it would simply continue to accrue. This is perhaps because the group in power in a capitalistic society consists of working-age individuals capable of contributing financially to the community and governmental institutions.

Third, in our culture power and status are associated with a right to speak. Therefore, if you have little power, you must adapt, adjust, and swallow the demands of those with more power, even if they are unfair or unrealistic. Accountability to change, then, is not based on a reciprocal and fair assessment of the situation but rather simply placed on the shoulders of the subjugated individual. This is visible in many institutions in America, where a moody boss, for example, expects secretaries to be patient. In schools it is seen in constant seemingly innocent comments:

There was an experienced teacher who was fond of saying, "I keep telling the kids 'one of us has to change and I'm too old to change.'" At the time I thought it was funny. Now I see it kept her from evaluating her own behavior and its effects on her students.

—Mindy (retired school teacher)

The only difference with children is that they are sometimes treated like this everywhere and do not have other contexts of life where they may experience more respect.

Part of facing adultism is to recognize once again the value of diversity and not place individuals' worth on a hierarchy based on narrow criteria. It is recognizing that although young people may have less experience on a quantitative level (which is not necessarily true, as many underprivileged youth have seen much more of life than certain adults), on a qualitative level their views are simply different, creative, fresh, and inspiring. When young people are treated with respect and spoken to as other worthy human beings, they develop a sense of autonomy, responsibility, critical judgment, and articulate opinions. Respect becomes a lived experience that is easy to replicate. When they grow up in an adultist environment, they become resentful, fearful, or sneaky, or they simply lose their own sense of self and opinion to such an extent that their answer to most questions becomes "I don't know."

Reflection Questions

How, then, can adults balance mentoring young people and at the same time honoring youth's right to speak? As discussed earlier in this book, for adults to fully commit to such a process they must realize that adultism also has a great cost on their own personal lives.

What do you think adults lose when they consider themselves superior to youth?

Can you list ten things that young people may teach you or contribute to your life? How about creativity, mindfulness, spontaneity, openness, curiosity, enthusiasm, flexibility, self-care, ingenuousness, and directness, to name only a few?

INDIVIDUALISM

Individualism is a belief system that centers on the individual as the unit of focus. Certainly, most of the mental health issues in individualistic societies are interpreted, understood, and classified as located within the individual or the individuals around them (family therapy). How *healthy* is defined and by whom is questionable as historical reviews reveal that people with the authority to determine these criteria never portray themselves as inadequate. Certain aspects of individuals are privileged initially and progressively become the norm. Over the last fifty years, the field of mental health (still dominated by White men) has literally doubled the number of diagnoses possible to label a person's functioning. This can offer the advantage of helping people who suffer from disorders previously misunderstood, but it can also reduce normality to a very strict and narrow set of agreed-on criteria. It is frightening to see how narrow standards have become for children, in particular: Too much energy is attention deficit hyperactivity disorder, and not enough is depression; too much protest (oftentimes very justified given certain abusive situations) is oppositional defiant disorder, and not enough verbalization is passive-aggressive disorder or lack of assertiveness; too much attention to detail and pleasing others is obsessive behavior, and lack of care toward accomplishments or people is antisocial behavior. The current culture is simply moving toward a sanitization of mental health, where any slight difference is medicated or treated as an imperfection as opposed to a valuable difference that can contribute in meaningful ways to society. This is particularly of concern with children who are often medicated with drugs that are heavily publicized yet poorly researched.

An interesting alternative would be to classify problems as occurring when individuals function in contexts that shape and limit their experience of themselves in problematic ways. For example, passive aggressive personality disorder could certainly be an effect of a context where individuals have limited possibilities of expressing their frustration directly and can only do so in a more insidious way; depression can certainly be classified in a context often associated with some form of oppression, whether by other individuals (domestic violence, abuse) or a system (racism, heterosexism, patriarchy); anxiety is a problem that develops in disempowering contexts, where the individual may feel that the demands are greater than his or her abilities. This would elicit very different forms of treatment and conversations that would be inclusive of a greater number of factors.

RACISM AND INTOLERANCE OF DIFFERENCES

In the United States, the race of educators versus that of students is outrageously disproportionate. Indeed, White teachers constitute nearly 90% of all educators, while young people of color are approaching 40% of the student population (Kivel, 2002). Although most teachers want to think of themselves as culturally sensitive, few have attended any cultural sensitivity training. By cultural sensitivity training, we do not mean a process of learning stereotypes about different cultures but rather a process of becoming aware of internalized discriminatory messages and noticing its implication in our work. Some teachers are keenly aware of this lack within their community, stating the following:

> I remember bringing up the issue of [social] class and how the teachers were mostly middle class and the students were from working-class families and how that affected parent-teacher communication and how teachers had certain expectations. So I said there might be some class issues, and it wasn't like people shot me down or weren't interested—they had no comprehension of what I was trying to get at: that our middle-class values could possibly be different from the values of the kids or the parents. It was a nonissue for them. It was something they didn't think was relevant. At the second school I was at, which was poorer, the staff would talk about that a lot. We were aware of how we were educated and that, while it was somewhat diverse, teachers were mostly White, parents were recent immigrants, many of whom didn't speak English, education levels were much lower, and we were aware of how that affects the dynamic, how it affects the way you deal with them, your homework policy, and how you try to make them comfortable at the school.

The current educational system in the United States is extremely unfair to minority students by virtue of the distribution of resources: In the 1990s, White, suburban schools had twice the funds per student than urban schools usually populated by racial minorities (Kozol, 1991). Kivel (2002) also addressed this issue:

> Students are given a direct measure of their social worth and future chances by the amount of money they see spent on their education. When we look at the differences in educational expenditure, we have to acknowledge that most white students have tremendous educational advantages over students of color . . . it is hypocritical for us to contend that everyone has an equal chance to succeed when white children systematically have better educational opportunities than children of color. (p. 203)

A principal of color eloquently shared with us the impact of racism on his experience as a privileged middle-class administrator and asked to ponder the implications of these social limitations on students:

> I am a person of privilege. I have a college degree. I own my own home. I'm an administrator. I make good money. Yet if you ask me to line myself up with others in the community as to how I feel I have access to resources, I will be down at the end. Even though I have these privileges, I see myself as different and having less opportunity. Now think of the children who are from ethnic backgrounds. If I feel this way, think how do they feel?

Reflection Questions

How do you support students from underprivileged families with little time, support, and resources to perform academically?

What do you do in your day-to-day activities in school to promote an appreciation of diversity?

How have you modified the curriculum to present a richer perspective of other countries in the world?

TO WHICH EXTENT ARE YOU CULTURALLY SENSITIVE? A SELF-TEST

Most likely, as an educator you are in this field because you like children and want to promote the best in them, regardless of their gender or race. You may even think that you treat all children equally, despite differences in color. Those are your intentions. Like everyone else you are likely to be biased by the messages that permeate your culture, whether you want to or not. Do this short exercise as honestly as you can to get a glimpse at some unwanted beliefs that may inadvertently affect your behaviors. Only three categories of social groups were chosen for simplicity, but many more could have been included.

Self-Test 1

Visualize someone from this group. What does the person look like?	Gender	Race	Sexual Orientation
Doctor			
Successful lawyer			
President of the United States			
Construction worker			
Gardener			
Drug dealer			
Criminal			
CEO of a company			

Did you find any particular bias in the images that come to your mind? Especially polarizing White men into privileged positions and men of color into underprivileged status?

Self-Test 2

Mark the groups for which you may have a negative feeling. This may include groups about which you are willing to tell jokes or groups from whom you

(Continued)

(Continued)

may be uncomfortable hiring an individual should you be an employer. It could also be a group at whom you would swear if a member of that group were to cut you off abruptly in traffic.

Group	Check only groups for whom you have or could have a negative feeling	Self-Test 3 (see instructions for Self-Test 3 to be completed later)	
		a. Child	b. Self
Black			
Hispanic			
Vietnamese			
Arabic			
Muslim			
Japanese			
Indian			
Turquish			
Pakistani			
Israeli			

Self-Test 3

Go back to the previous table and fill out the last column, this time writing a checkmark if you would be even slightly uncomfortable in the following situations:

1. Your child wants to marry a member of this group. Imagine having this person at all your family dinners and having grandchildren who are of mixed racial heritage.

2. You are to marry someone from that group. What feelings would you have exactly? List those feelings:

_____

_____

_____

_____

Self-Test 4

1. You have to find a gynecologist for yourself or your daughter. Your insurance lists the following names as covered under your benefits. Whom will you choose?

   Dr. Yin Yang Yen

   Dr. Asad Aboudaram

   Dr. Antonia Orozca

   Dr. John Campbell

2. The brakes of your car have broken in a frightening incident; you absolutely need them to be repaired as soon as possible by a reliable person. The first opening at your local car repair shop is with a woman. Do you trust her ability to fix your car? What if she is a person of color? How does her race or gender affect your response?

_____

_____

_____

_____

3. Someone is suing you professionally. Although you haven't done anything wrong, this situation has the potential of becoming ugly. From which groups would you prefer to hire a lawyer? Circle all that apply.

    Man Woman

    White Black Hispanic Asian Arabic

    Young Middle-Aged Older

At this point most people are surprised to discover some discomfort with one or two groups. Again, this does not reflect your character but the cultural training that has shaped your life. In fact, your mere willingness at taking these tests and reading this section is a reflection in itself of your intentions to behave in a just way. Unfortunately, one's beliefs and biases are stronger predictors of behaviors than intentions. It is difficult to be exposed all your life to pejorative images of certain groups without this process having an effect on the behaviors of the most well-intentioned person. What is important is to become aware of these unwanted beliefs and how they may subtly color our actions and attitudes. The beliefs you have uncovered do not accurately represent people from these groups but rather some stereotypes. In addition, many of these groups are in underprivileged positions because of low socioeconomic status and not because they are lazy or unwilling. If you were a parent and your child were starving, you may very well steal or sell drugs—especially if you had repeatedly tried to get a proper job and were rejected.

As an educator, depending on your school's community, you will come across children from all groups and must be keenly aware of your unwanted bias as well as how it inadvertently affects your behaviors.

CAPITALISM

How does this capitalism affect schools and bullying? The more-is-better model certainly applies. In education there is a belief that you can always learn more. The emphasis is also placed on the subjects that will earn more money in the capitalistic culture. Children are rarely pressured, for instance, to do more in the arts. In recent history, the curriculum has increased, and there seems to be a belief that more can always be stuffed into a child's mind. As described by the famous writer Paulo Freire (1970/2000), we use a banking model of education, where adults can always deposit more knowledge in the passive recipient of a child's brain. With the recent trend in categorizing schools based on test scores, an additional emphasis has been placed on teaching an ever-broading curriculum. This is not without serious cost to children, teachers, and the next generation of workers in terms of accumulation of frustration, stress, and feelings of inadequacy.

Capitalism also influences what is produced in the media. Extensive research is conducted on how to produce the maximum entertainment at the lowest possible cost. People often believe that violence, for instance, has increased in film productions because it is sought by a large audience. Although some of this may be true, what is largely unknown is that violence is the cheapest way to create suspense in a program (Gerbner, 1994). Violence is easy to export abroad, with no translation being needed; violence does not require intricate dialogue, plot, or even scenery. The number of violent films, and violent visual graphics in general, has almost doubled in the last thirty years, with young people in particular being targeted. Whereas evening family shows are estimated to present six to seven acts of aggression per hour, cartoons for children usually contain approximately twenty to thirty acts of aggression per hour (Fox, 1996; Gerbner, 2002). The average child in the United States has viewed 200,000 acts of violence and 16,000 murders on TV by the age of 18 (Media Education Foundation, 2002). Capitalism and the desire for wealth has created a media industry so greedy for financial gain that ethical values are much less considered in most productions.

PATRIARCHY: A COMMENT ON BOYS AND MASCULINITY

Patriarchy is a system of beliefs in which males typically have more institutional power than females. It implies, among many other things, that emotions, activities, and colors are generally divided into two groups and assigned to each gender. In this process, both genders lose access to a wide range of multiple, helpful ways of being. It is beyond the scope of this book to discuss the extensive effects of patriarchy at length as there are countless publications on its implications (Ashton-Jones et al., 2000; Katz, 1999; Kilbourne, 2000; Kimmel & Messner, 1998; Kivel, 1999; Pollack, 1999; Tannen, 1990). We do, however, want to discuss why boys are almost always the main perpetrators of physical aggression in schools. Some experts have proposed a biological perspective, that males are genetically programmed to be aggressive. But many anthropological studies across the world disproved this theory, given that some cultures have very low rates of male aggression (review by Kimmel & Messner, 1998). Others have proposed a transgenerational pattern transmitted from grandparents to parents to child, where the abusive behavioral patterns are learned in childhood and re-acted as young adults; but this has been disproved as well, given that many girls are subjected to abuse and never re-act it as young people or adults (Jenkins, 1990). Others, starting with the classic study of Bandura (1969), demonstrated that television and the media encourage youth to engage in aggressive behavior through social learning. Yet, given that most boys witness aggressive media and not all commit acts of aggression, this factor alone is not sufficient either. As discussed earlier, in the last decade, with the social constructionist movement, it has become clearer that the overlap of many sociocultural characteristics of one's life context (discourses) influences people's choices and behaviors. The following list describes some of the characteristics promoted in Western cultures about boyhood and aggression:

- In much of the media for young people, the masculinity of heroes has become represented by a single amplified and exaggerated characteristic: physical power (e.g., Sylvester Stallone, Arnold Schwarzenegger). Research on popular toys for boys clearly shows that since the 1970s the size of the biceps of toy figures such as Luke Skywalker or GI Joe has increased from sixteen inches to twenty-five inches (Katz, 1999). The current physiology of these male heroes is barely realistic and certainly unlikely to be attained by most young males. In a culture where being a boy is tied to being tough and powerful, it only makes sense that this inner quality be expressed through aggression. In other words, if being tough and powerful are desirable inner determinants of masculinity, a natural outlet to publicly demonstrate this characteristic is aggression. How else can one prove to another that he is indeed powerful (especially since boys don't actually feel powerful in their lives).

- Aggression is also portrayed as the solution to problems. If asked about their opinions on aggression, almost everyone would say that they are opposed to such behaviors. What are many parents tempted to do when a boy gets in trouble for fighting at school? Spank. Marie-Nathalie recently listened to a father talk about his twenty-five-year-old daughter, whom he felt was very irresponsible. He stated, "If she were a boy, man (smacking his fist in his other hand) I'd put some sense into her." He was definitely not the first well-intentioned parent to say that he wanted to teach a lesson or toughen his child through physical aggression. Studies demonstrate that parents and teachers may tolerate a lot of mischief from boys, but when adults decide to discipline, they punish them very harshly. Some scientists have speculated that this practice not only presents aggression as a solution to upsetting interactions but may also model insensitivity and intolerance.

- After puberty, and certainly in middle and high school, boys feel they cannot safely relate to friends or family members by being openly affectionate and caring without risking being called a sissy. Again, because masculinity exists mainly as distinguished from femininity and because femininity implies caring, young men may get trapped in patterns where they believe that the only acceptable physical contact is aggression. A friend recalls this story:

> I was biking with my best friend, and as we were crossing a bridge over the highway, he suddenly smacked me. After managing to avoid falling off the bridge and onto the highway, I asked him why he did that. His reply was, "I'm only joking man. What's wrong with you? Are you a homo or something?" Hitting me was the only way he could express affection to me in such a homophobic culture; I learned that guys could do pretty much anything to you and then say I was just joking, and you had to take it.

In addition to underscoring aggression as a way of relating between teenage boys, this story is also very revealing in that the individual who is considered inadequate is not the aggressor but rather the victim. Through aggression, the perpetrator has shown his superiority over a supposedly weaker other. In a world of masculinity, the victim is often the one who has a fault, who is suspected, analyzed, questioned—not the aggressor, who is being a real man. In schools, young men who are victims are more likely to be referred to therapy than are their perpetrators (unless the aggression is serious).

Another father recalled the following:

> As a child, I always bullied my one-year-younger sister. The more family members got upset and asked that I stop, the more I did it. I bullied her pretty much throughout our childhood, but at the same time when we went out to the park or to dances, I always had an eye on her. I really, really cared a lot about her and wanted to make sure that nothing would happen to her.

In this story, aggression is clearly exemplified as the only possible way of relating affectionately with a loved one: Aggression is used to express care and to protect.

Aside from those cultural messages of masculinity and aggression, it is important to also remember that boys, especially after age seven or eight years, are often socialized to refrain from expressing a multiplicity of emotions. Anger for some young men can thus easily become the only acceptable way to express many experiences. Aggression can thus be seen as the outcome of the clash of gender specifications and social discourses involving masculinity, which is further emphasized or deemphasized by one's belonging to different subgroups defined by age, socioeconomic status, race, ethnicity, religion, and so on.

Resource D

"Yes and" Exercise

This exercise[1] promotes equality in a relationship and requires partners to cooperate around the coconstruction of a plan. It emphasizes how two individuals can be connected while respecting each other's contributions and preferences.

GOALS: To practice valuing and respecting differences
To practice being open-minded and receptive
To listen to and then acknowledge a partner's ideas
To appreciate individuality and still create connectedness

GROUP SIZE: unlimited pairs of two

TIME: 15–30 minutes

MATERIALS: chairs, optional

PROCESS:

1. Invite the participants to sit in chairs or on the floor facing a partner, with the pairs scattered around the room.

2. Introduce the exercise, presenting some of the following information and offering your own examples where appropriate:
   - This exercise will give us practice in valuing and respecting other people's ideas, taking the time to acknowledge and find some value in each suggestion; it will also open our receptivity to other ideas and perspectives.
   - We have all been well-trained to look for what doesn't work; therefore, we typically respond to novel ideas with "yes, but"—not even considering what may be of value in another's idea.

- In the long run, this has the effect of narrowing our world down to only our own ideas and ways of doing things.
- "Yes and . . ." is a process that requires participants to listen to what their partners say and acknowledge the value and the richness of each contribution.

3. Instruct participants to plan a vacation where each partner adds one idea at a time. Each partner must always respond to the other's idea by appreciating what was offered.

4. Have the participants use this sentence (you may want to write it on a flip chart or chalk board): "What I like about your idea is . . ." and they must name something they can honestly say they like about the idea. Instruct them to keep searching until they can find something they like—if they only give lip service, their partner will know and feel judged.

5. After the appreciation (which is the "Yes" step), he/she can say: "And . . ." adding his/her own idea.

6. Reminder: In this exercises there are no restrictions whatsoever to limit the vacation, so budget, practicality, plausibility, possibility, and laws of physics do not exist!

7. Conclude the exercise by asking participants to discuss some of the following questions:
- What was your experience of this exercise?
- How did it feel when your partner appreciated your ideas?
- Was it hard to find something positive about your partner's contribution?
- What effect did this attitude have on your participation?
- What effect did this attitude have on your vacation plan?
- What effect might the "Yes, and . . ." attitude have on your relationship/s?
- How would it be if everyone could hold on to this attitude in day-to-day interactions?

NOTE

1. This exercise was previously published in "Working with Groups to Enhance Relationships" by M. N. Beaudoin and S. Walden, Whole Persons Associates (1998).

Resource E

Educators' Problem-Solving Questions

1. Do you have a connection with this young person? Is it reciprocal? Is it safe?

2. Do you have an understanding of the big picture or complexity of his/her life?

3. Do you have compassion?

4. Can you externalize the problem?

5. Have authority/power and consequences reduced the problem or made it chronic?

6. Can you exert your authority/power elsewhere than on the child?

7. What is your goal for this young person (an experience not a behavior)?

8. What is this young person's goal for him/herself? Preferences?

9. What does this young person need: control, attention, support, confidence?

10. What may be obstacles or pressures that get in the way of improvement?

11. How can we address these obstacles?

12. What gives this young person experiences of success? What's empowering?

13. How can we create more positive learning experiences?

14. Do I need to change my expectations? (i.e., maybe child can't go from hitting to not hitting but to some fist clenching, holding a supportive reminder paper in his/her pocket . . . consider creative options)

References

Andersen, T. (1987). The reflecting team: Dialogue and metadialogue in clinical work. *Family Process, 26*, 415–428.

Andrews, F. (1991). *The art and practice of loving*. Los Angeles: Tarcher.

Ashton-Jones, E., Olson, G. A., & Perry, M. G. (2000). *The gender reader*. Needham Heights, MA: Pearson.

Bandura, A. (1969). *Principles of behavior modification*. New York: Henry Holt.

Baumeister, R., Bushman, B., & Campbell, W. (2000). Self-esteem, narcissism, and aggression: Does violence result from low self-esteem or from threatened egotism? *Current Directions in Psychological Science, 9*(1), 26–29.

Beaudoin, M.-N., & Taylor, M. (2004). *Creating a positive school culture: How principals and teachers can solve problems together*. Thousand Oaks, CA: Corwin.

Beaudoin, M.-N., & Walden, S. (1998). *Working with groups to enhance relationships*. Duluth, MN: Whole Person Associates.

Begley, S. (2007). *Train your mind, change your brain*. New York: Ballantine Books.

Belvel, P. S., & Jordan, M. M. (2003). *Rethinking classroom management: Strategies for prevention, intervention, and problem solving*. Thousand Oaks, CA: Corwin.

Benson, B., & Barnett, S. (1998). *Student-led conferencing using showcase portfolios*. Thousand Oaks, CA: Corwin.

Bernal, M. (1987). *Black athena: The Afroasiatic roots of classical civilization*. New Brunswick, NJ: Rutgers University Press.

Bird, J. (2000). *The heart's narrative*. Auckland, New Zealand: Edge Press.

Bluestein, J. (2008). *The win-win classroom: A fresh and positive look at classroom management*. Thousand Oaks, CA: Corwin

Bruner, J. (1996). *The culture of education*. Cambridge, MA: Harvard University Press.

Byron, K. (2007). *A thousand names for joy*. New York: Harmonie Books.

Carroll, R., Faieta, D., Florence, G., Joesting, L., Martin, B., Ostach, J., Van Hook, D., & Warnemuende, M. (1995). *Communicate!* New York: Kendall/Hunt Publishing.

Cheshire, A., & Lewis, D. (2000). *Reducing bullying in schools*. Auckland, New Zealand: Selwyn College.

Christa McAuliffe Elementary School. (2003). *Orientation manual*. Retrieved September 24, 2003, from http://www.cupertino.k12.ca.us/McAuliffe.

Ciompi, L. (1991). Affects as central organizing and integrating factors: A new psychosocial/biological model of the psyche. *British Journal of Psychiatry, 159*, 97–105.

Covey, S. (2004). *The 7 habits of highly effective people*. New York: Free Press.

Damasio, A. (1994). *Descartes' error: Emotion, reason, and the human brain*. New York: Penguin Books.

Dewey, J. (1989). *Freedom and culture*. Amherst, NY: Prometheus Books.

Dewey, J. (1999). *Individualism old and new*. Amherst, NY: Prometheus Books.

Dickerson, V. (1998). Silencing critical voices: An interview with M.-N. Beaudoin. *Gecko, 2*, 29–45.

Dobson, T. (1985). A kind word turneth away wrath. In R. S. Heckler (Ed.), *Aikido and the new warrior*. Berkeley, CA: North Atlantic Books.

Dreikurs, R., & Grey, L. (1970). *Parent's guide to child discipline*. New York: Hawthorn Books Inc.

Dweck, C. S. (2007). The secret to raising smart kids. *Scientific American Mind, December*, 365–375.

Eisler, R. (2001). *Tomorrow's children* [Videotape]. Northampton, MA: Media Education Foundation.

Ekman, P. (1992). An argument for basic emotions. *Cognition and Emotion, 6*, 169–200.

Feigelson, S. (1998). *Energize your meetings with laughter*. Alexandria, VA: Association for Supervision and Curriculum Development.

Fleming, M., Lyon, G., Oei, T.-Y., Sheets, R. H., Valentine, G., & Williams, E. (1997). *Starting small*. Montgomery, AL: Southern Poverty Law Center.

Fox, R. (1996). *Harvesting minds: How TV commercials control kids*. Westport, CT: Greenwood.

Freedman, J., & Combs, G. (1996). *Narrative therapy*. New York: W. W. Norton.

Freeman, J., Epston, D., & Lobovits, D. (1997). *Playful approaches to serious problems*. New York: W. W. Norton.

Freire, P. (2000). *Pedagogy of the oppressed*. New York: Continuum. (Original work published 1970).

Friedman, S. (1995). *The reflecting team in action*. New York: Guilford Press.

Garrett, A. (2003). *Bullying in American schools*. Jefferson, North Carolina: McFarland & Co. Inc.

Gerbner, G. (1994). *The killing screens*. Northampton, MA: Media Education Foundation.

Gerbner, G. (2002). *Against the mainstream: The selected work of George Gerbner* (M. Morgan, Ed.). New York: Peter Lang.

Gergen, K. (1985). The social constructionist movement in modern psychology. *American Psychologist, 40*, 266–275.

Gergen, K. (1991). *The saturated self: Dilemmas of identity in contemporary life*. New York: Basic Books.

Ginott, Haim G. (1995). *Teacher and child: A book for parents and teachers*. New York, NY: Collier.

Goleman, D. (1995). *Emotional intelligence*. New York: Bantam.

Gootman, M. (2001). *The caring teacher's guide to discipline*. Thousand Oaks, CA: Corwin.

Gougaud, H. (2000). *Contes du Pacifique*. Paris, France: Seuil.

Grant, J. M., Heffler, B., & Mereweather, K. (1995). *Student-led conferences: Using portfolios to share learning with parents*. Ontario, Canada: Pembroke Publishers.

Hall, S. (1997). *Race: The floating signifier*. Northampton, MA: Media Education Foundation.

Hill, L. D. (2001). *Connecting kids*. British Columbia, Canada: New Society Publishers.

Hoffman, L. (1990). Constructing realities: An art of lenses. *Family Process, 29*, 1–12.

Hooks, B. (1996). *Cultural criticism and transformation*. Northampton, MA: Media Education Foundation.

Huntemann, N. (2000). *Game over*. Northampton, MA: Media Education Foundation.

Jenkins, A. (1990). *Invitations to responsibility*. Adelaide, Australia: Dulwich Centre Publications.

Jensen, E. (2000a). *Different learners, different brains: How to reach the hard to teach*. Thousand Oaks, CA: Corwin.

Jensen, E. (2000b). Moving with the brain in mind. *Educational Leadership, 58*(3), 34–37.

Jensen, E. (2003). *Tools for engagement: Managing emotional states for learner success*. Thousand Oaks, CA: Corwin.

Jhally, S. (1998). *Advertising and the end of the world*. Northampton, MA: Media Education Foundation.

Kabat-Zinn, J. (1994). *Wherever you go there you are*. Boston: Hyperion.

Kagan, L., & Spencer, D. (1994). *Cooperative learning*. San Clemente, CA: Kagan Publishing.

Katz, J. (1999). *Tough guise*. Northampton, MA: Media Education Foundation.

Kiecolt-Glaser, J. K., McGuire, L., Robles, T. F., & Glaser, R. (2002). Emotions, morbidity and mortality: New perspectives on psychoneuroimmunology. *Annual Review of Psychology, 53*(1), 83–105.

Kilbourne, J. (2000). *Killing us softly 3*. Northampton, MA: Media Education Foundation.

Kimmel, M. S., & Messner, M. A. (1998). *Men's lives*. Needham Heights, MA: Viacom.

Kivel, P. (1999). *Boys will be men*. British Columbia, Canada: New Society Publishers.

Kivel, P. (2002). *Uprooting racism*. British Columbia, Canada: New Society Publishers.

Koenig, L. (2000). *Smart discipline for the classroom: Respect and cooperation restored* (3rd ed.). Thousand Oaks, CA: Corwin.

Kohn, A. (1996). *Beyond discipline: From compliance to community*. Alexandria, VA: Association for Supervision and Curriculum Development.

Kohn, A. (1999). *Punished by rewards: The trouble with gold stars, incentive plans, A's, praise, and other bribes*. New York: Houghton Mifflin.

Kozol, J. (1991). *Savage inequalities: Children of America's schools*. New York: HarperCollins.

LeDoux, J. E. (1996). *The emotional brain*. New York: Simon & Schuster.

Luvmour, J., & Luvmour, B. (2002). *Win-win games for all ages: Cooperative activities for building social skills*. British Columbia, Canada: New Society Publishers.

Madsen, W. C. (1999). *Collaborative therapy with multi-stressed families*. New York: Guilford Press.

Media Education Foundation. (2002). *Behind the screens*. Northampton, MA: Author.

Merrow, J. (2001). *Choosing excellence*. Lanham, MD: Scarecrow Press.

Nylund, D. (2000). *Treating Huckleberry Finn*. San Francisco: Jossey-Bass.

Olweus, D. (1993). *Bullying at school*. Malden, MA: Blackwell Publishing.

Perez, M., Vohs, K., Joiner, T. (2005). Discrepancies between self- and other-esteem as correlates of aggression. *Journal of Social and Clinical Psychology, 24*(5), 607–620.

Pierce-Picciotto, L. (1996). *Student-led parent conferences*. New York: Scholastic.

Pollack, W. (1999). *Real boys*. New York: Henry Holt.

Reiman, J. (1998). *Thinking for a living*. Marietta, GA: Longstreet.

Riesler, E. (2001). *Tomorrow's children*. Northampton, MA: Media Education Foundation.

Robins, K. N., Lindsey, R. B., Lindsey, D. B., & Terrell, R. D. (2002). *Culturally proficient instruction*. Thousand Oaks, CA: Corwin.

Schmitz, M. (2007). *Brain-building nutrition*. Berkeley, CA: North Atlantic Books.

Seligman, M. E. P. (1975). *Helplessness: On depression, development, and death*. San Francisco: W. H. Freeman.

Seligman, M. E. P. (1990). *Learned optimism*. New York: Knopf.

Seligman, M. E. P., & Maier, S. F. (1967). Failure to escape traumatic shock. *Journal of Experimental Psychology, 74*, 1–9.

Shammin, P., & Stuss, D. T. (1999). Humor appreciation: A role of the right frontal lobe. *Brain, 123*(4).

Siegel, D. J. (1999). *The developing mind*. New York: Guilford Press.

Siegel, D. J., & Hartzell, M. (2003). *Parenting from the inside out*. New York: Penguin Books.

Smith, R. (2004). *Conscious classroom management: Unlocking the secrets of great teachings*. San Rafael, CA: Conscious Teachings Publications.

Smith, T. W., Glazer, K., Ruiz, J. M., & Gallo, L. C. (2004). Hostility, anger, aggressiveness, and coronary heart disease: An interpersonal perspective on personality, emotion, and health. *Journal of Personality, 72*(6), 1217–1270.

Sousa, D. (2001). *How the brain learns* (2nd ed.). Thousand Oaks, CA: Corwin.

Sprenger, M. (2002). *Becoming a wiz at brain-based teaching: How to make every year a best year*. Thousand Oaks, CA: Corwin.

Sprenger, M. (2005). *How to teach so that students remember*. Thousand Oaks, CA: Corwin.

Tannen, D. (1990). *You just don't understand*. New York: Ballantine Books.

Tate, M. (2007). *Shouting won't grow dendrites*. Thousand Oaks, CA: Corwin.

Thompson, M., Cohen, L., & O'Neill Grace, C. (2002). *Mom, they're teasing me*. New York: Ballantine Books.

Tileston, D. W. (2004). *What every teacher should know about classroom management and discipline*. Thousand Oaks, CA: Corwin.

Vitto, J. (2003). *Relationship-driven classroom management*. Thousand Oaks, CA: Corwin.

Weatherford, J., (1988). *Indian givers: How the Indians of the Americas transformed the world*. New York: Fawcett.

White, M. (1995). *Re-authoring lives: Interviews and essays*. Adelaide, Australia: Dulwich Centre Publications.

White, M. (1997). *Narratives of therapists' lives*. Adelaide, Australia: Dulwich Centre Publications.

White, M. (2000). *Reflections on narrative practice*. Adelaid, Australia: Dulwich Centre Publications.

White, M. (2007). *Narrative maps*. New York: W. W. Norton.

White, M., & Epston, D. (1990). *Narrative means to therapeutic ends*. New York: W. W. Norton.

White, M., & Morgan, A. (2006). *Narrative therapy with children and their families*. Adelaide, Australia: Dulwich Centre Publications.

Winslade, J., & Monk, G. (1999). *Narrative counseling in schools*. Thousand Oaks, CA: Corwin.

Winslade, J., & Monk, G. (2000). *Narrative mediation*. San Francisco: Jossey-Bass.

Zimmerman, J. (2001). The discourses of our lives. *Journal of Systemic Therapies, 20*(3), 1–10.

Zimmerman, J., & Beaudoin, M.-N. (2002). Cats under the stars: A narrative story. *Child and Adolescent Mental Health, 7*(1), 31–41.

Zimmerman, J., & Dickerson, V. (1996). *If problems talked*. New York: Guilford Press.

Zinn, H. (2001). *A people's history of the United States*. New York: Harper Perennial.

Index

CORWIN

A SAGE Company

The Corwin logo—a raven striding across an open book—represents the union of courage and learning. Corwin is committed to improving education for all learners by publishing books and other professional development resources for those serving the field of PreK–12 education. By providing practical, hands-on materials, Corwin continues to carry out the promise of its motto: **"Helping Educators Do Their Work Better."**